Six Capitals

SIX CAPITALS

The revolution capitalism has to have
—or can accountants save the planet?

JANE GLEESON-WHITE

ALLEN&UNWIN

SYDNEY•MELBOURNE•AUCKLAND•LONDON

Published by Allen & Unwin in 2014

  This project has been assisted by the Australian Government through the Australia Council, its arts funding and advisory board.

Allen & Unwin
Sydney, Melbourne, Auckland, London

83 Alexander Street
Crows Nest NSW 2065
Australia
Phone: (61 2) 8425 0100
Fax: (61 2) 9906 2218
Email: info@allenandunwin.com
Web: www.allenandunwin.com

Cataloguing-in-Publication details are available from the National Library of Australia
trove.nla.gov.au

ISBN 978 1 74331 916 1

Set in 11.5/16 pt Minion by Bookhouse, Sydney
Printed in Australia by McPherson's Printing Group

10 9 8 7 6 5 4 3 2 1

For Jackson and Scarlet Hill

In memory of my aunts
Janet Fischer and Nancy Tomlinson

CONTENTS

Accountants as agents of revolution? Now
there's a thought.

JONATHAN WATTS, 2010

How do you get economists and business people
to take the environment and its relationship with
the economy seriously? Change its name to one
that resonates with commercial values. What's a
word that denotes great value, preciousness to a
capitalist? I know—'capital'.

ROSS GITTINS, 2012

Without a focus on a range of capitals, providers
of financial capital simply do not have the information needed to allocate resources most effectively.

PAUL DRUCKMAN, 2013

. . . everything will be fungible, nothing will
be valued for its own sake, place and past and
love and enchantment will have no meaning.
The natural world will be reduced to a
column of figures.

GEORGE MONBIOT, 2014

Preface

CAN ACCOUNTANTS SAVE THE PLANET?

I N OCTOBER 2010, JOURNALIST JONATHAN WATTS reported from the United Nations Biodiversity Conference in Nagoya, Japan, an apparently anomalous phenomenon: the arrival of 'money men' at a forum previously reserved for nature lovers. Where flora and fauna once prevailed, now 'natural capital', 'biological resources' and 'eco-financing' predominated. What were accountants doing at a conference on nature?

At the time I was completing *Double Entry*, a book which began as a desire to celebrate the material origins of the Renaissance with the emergence of double-entry bookkeeping in fourteenth-century Italy—and ended as a history of accounting. It traced the story of accounting from the beginning of recorded time in Mesopotamia to the Renaissance, when monk and mathematician Luca Pacioli first codified Venetian bookkeeping, which influenced the rise of capitalism and was implicated in the financial scandals of the new millennium, including the collapse of Enron and the global financial crisis.

Double Entry demonstrated that accounting has played
a central if rarely remarked upon role in the epoch-
shifting moments of our history, from the invention of
writing to the wealth and cultural efflorescence of the
Renaissance, from the industrial revolution to the rise
of the global economy following the Second World War.
So when accountants suddenly started appearing in
places they had never been before, such as biodiversity
conferences, I took note. Early in this new millennium,
in the wake of the biggest financial breakdown since
1929 and amid crises in food, water, energy, weather,
employment, population and wealth distribution, when
we all sense that life as we have known it is changing
in profound and unpredictable ways, I wanted to know
what the accountants were up to.

Especially as Watts had opened his story with a rather
extraordinary claim on their behalf:

> So it has come to this. The global biodiversity
> crisis is so severe that brilliant scientists,
> political leaders, eco-warriors, and religious
> gurus can no longer save us from ourselves.
> The military are powerless. But there may be
> one last hope for life on earth: accountants.

Now someone was figuring accountants as superheroes
and suggesting they might be able to save the planet. This
astonishing claim informed *Double Entry*'s concluding
chapter on the failure of our national Gross Domestic

Product (GDP) accounts to consider nature, an omission which encourages us to pollute, burn, extract and chop down its various components with little regard for the environmental consequences. This problem—which had been recognised but not yet adequately addressed in 2010—suggested to me that something new was brewing in the world of accounting. So I continued to think about it and to wonder: *can* accountants save the planet?

This question implicitly addresses one of economics' key conundrums: the concept of 'externalities'. The fact that neither nations nor corporations account for the damage their lawful activities inflict on nature and society is considered by economists to be a problem of externalities. In traditional economics, nature and society are conceived as being external to the workings of commerce and this is reflected in the way we—and profit-driven markets—value the world. The problem of externalities is best expressed by former World Bank economist Raj Patel in his hypothetical '$200 hamburger'. In this thought experiment Patel estimated the real cost of a McDonald's Big Mac to be $200. The reason Big Macs sell for almost one-hundredth of this figure is that their price does not account for their real costs. These include their carbon footprint, their impact on the environment in terms of water use and soil degradation, and the enormous health-care costs of diet-related illnesses such as diabetes and heart disease. Traditional accounting models do not take these costs into account, but they still have to be paid; it is just that the McDonald's Corporation does not pay them. We do. Society as a whole pays, in the form of environmental disasters, climate change, the depletion of natural resources and higher health costs. For Patel, the fact that corporations do not pay the environmental and social costs they rack up amounts to corporate subsidy on a massive scale. As he remarks, 'You'd be forgiven for thinking that this ongoing bailout from nature and society to private enterprise is what puts the "free" into free markets—despite its protests, corporate capitalism has yet to prove that it can operate without these kinds of subsidies.'

The biggest accounting scandal of all in terms of externalities concerns our failure to account for nature. Economist Pavan Sukhdev, the author of the United Nation's 2010 report *Global Biodiversity Outlook 3*, says that unless we value the goods and services currently provided by the natural world for free and factor them into the global economic system, we will continue to destroy the planet. He believes the changes required will entail a wholesale revolution in the way we do business, consume and think about our lives. This is why accounting was on the agenda at the 2010 UN Biodiversity Conference, bringing concepts like natural capital, biological resources and eco-financing into the heartland of nature. And this is why Watts was suggesting that accountants might be the one last hope for life on earth: because they have the potential to hold nations and corporations accountable for their impact on nature. In effect, accountants have the power to reconceive nature (and society) not as an externality but as an *internality*, as an acknowledged component of economies and business.

One other economic problem continued to bother me after I had completed *Double Entry*: the nature (or personality) of the chief commercial agent of modern times: the corporation. This organisational form was born when Elizabeth I granted a royal charter to the merchants of London to pursue their commercial ends in the East Indies. It was a tool of empire which went on to accrue enormous power during the industrial revolution, particularly in America, where in the late nineteenth century the corporation became a legal person, entitled to the same rights as flesh-and-blood people. But the modern corporation so created has few corresponding responsibilities beyond that of max-imising profits. In a human being, the entitlement to all rights with few responsibilities apart from self-aggrandisement might be deemed to be psychopathic. Which is just what professor of law and author of *The Corporation* (2004), Joel Bakan, and his colleagues Mark Achbar and Jennifer Abbott discovered about the corporation when they decided to treat it as the person it legally is and test its psychological profile. Using the American Psychiatric Association's *Diagnostic and Statistical Manual of Mental Disorders* (DSM-IV), they found that the corporation shares many of the charac-teristics that define psychopaths. That is, corporations break the law if they can, they hide their behaviour, sacrifice long-term welfare for short-term profit, are aggressively litigious, ignore health and safety codes, and cheat their suppliers and workers without remorse. And despite its obligation to give a 'true and fair view' of its operations in its annual accounts, the corporation has in several instances so spectacularly failed to do this that investors have lost millions and in 2008 the global economy was brought to its knees.

One has only to remember the collapse in 2001 of the 1990s 'It Company' Enron, along with the demise of its auditor Arthur Andersen, to appreciate the potentially destructive power of the modern corporation. This is the cause célèbre of a corporation behaving badly while failing to account for its activities. Within seven months Enron went from being 'America's Most Innovative Company' and 'No. 1 in Quality of Management' (according to *Fortune* magazine), with its profits booming and its sales soaring, to bankruptcy. It collapsed amid charges of greed, bribery, corruption, deceit, insider trading, tax avoidance, environmental destruction, human rights abuses, theft of workers' entitlements, and more. Its fantastic profits were shown to be fantasy indeed, dependent on massive debts not recorded on the company's books. Its actual debt was not US$13 billion as it appeared in its accounts, but a whopping US$38 billion. But this was nothing compared to the financial crisis unleashed in 2008.

With the rise since the 1980s of multinational corporations, some of which today wield the sort of power once reserved for states, these psychopathic organisations have now become monstrous. In 2000, it was estimated that 51 of the largest 100 economies in the world were not countries but multinational corporations. And as we were continually told by governments and economists to justify their vast injection of public funds into the private sector in the aftermath of the global financial crisis, these beings are now 'too big to fail'. Such scandals made me wonder if the psychopathic and monstrous modern corporation might be in need of a psychological intervention, so to speak.

Following the publication of *Double Entry* in November 2011, with these two big questions still on my mind—can accountants save the planet, by making us account for so-called externalities? And is it time for a psychological intervention in the modern corporation?—I was given several unanticipated opportunities to enter the world of contemporary accounting and find answers to them. I discovered that these were hot topics, and thus began my ongoing investigations into accounting that eventually became this book.

Four meetings were decisive in directing my thinking. The first came in May 2012, when I was invited by Lee White, chief executive officer of the Institute of Chartered Accountants in Australia, to a round-table discussion on the future of accounting. Specifically, it was 'to explore the challenges and opportunities for the profession in the area of corporate sustainability'. ('Sustainability' is the new business and economic catchword used to denote long-term thinking with a view to the future viability of business in the context of the planet's various and increasingly obvious environmental and social crises.)

At the round table I met Michael Bray, Chairman of Energy and Natural Resources at KPMG, who told me about an embryonic international accounting initiative which was in the throes of formulating a new corporate reporting framework. The proposed system encompasses six capitals, adding to accounting's traditional focus on financial and manufactured capital four new categories of wealth, or capital, including 'natural capital'. Bray also mentioned an article written in 1992 by accountant Robert K. Elliott of KPMG New York which argued that our accounting systems are breaking down because they were designed for the industrial era and cannot cope with the new intangible wealth of our information age. The new accounting initiative and the possibilities opened up by Elliott's argument seized my imagination. I was particularly intrigued by the conception of 'six capitals': financial, manufactured, intellectual, human, social and relationship, and natural capital. At that round-table meeting I realised that the changes I had felt simmering in 2010 when I was finishing *Double Entry* were now cooking at lightning speed.

The second meeting was in London in September 2012, with accountant Jeremy Osborn, who had worked with the Prince of Wales' Accounting for Sustainability project. By then I had become obsessed with Raj Patel's $200 hamburger. Why couldn't we cost every component of what we produce, including its effects on nature, in the same way the pioneers of industrial accounting had learnt to cost labour and the other factors of production during the late eighteenth and nineteenth centuries? In my travels I had taken every opportunity to ask accountants: Do you think companies will ever put a money value on the environment? Osborn was the first to have a substantial answer to that question. He told me it had just happened. The German sporting goods company Puma had just priced its impact on nature in the world's first ever 'environmental profit and loss account'. This account was Puma's pioneering attempt to consider the full impact on nature of its activities, from head office right down its supply chain to the providers of rubber for its running shoes. In order to do this, it put a monetary value on the environmental costs of doing business, such as air pollution and waste.

Although Osborn said that he personally did not think it necessary to put a price on nature in order to account for and protect it, the man to whom I next put this question, in London in April 2013, was a passionate advocate for calculating the monetary value of nature for its protection. Leading environmentalist Tony Juniper, who has also worked with the Prince's Accounting for Sustainability project, argued his case in his 2013 book *What Has Nature Ever Done for Us?*, which gives compelling examples not only of the economic value of the various unpriced components of the natural world, such as soil, bees and mangroves, but also of the persuasive effect—in nature's favour—of pricing them. One nation leading the way in preserving nature by pricing it is Costa Rica, which has successfully used the conversion of natural wealth into monetary measures to direct government policy and protect its forests since the early 1990s.

The last meeting was in New York in May 2013, when I was invited by accountant Stanley Goldstein to join the New York Hedge Fund Roundtable discussion on corporate social responsibility and sustainability. Conversations with Goldstein, and with Andrew Park from financial data and media giant Bloomberg—as well as the overflowing room of investors, academics, accountants and others, including a ratings agent from Moody's—convinced me that a new accounting paradigm was actually in formation. Why? Because this new thinking had penetrated the very core of global capital, Manhattan.

And so I found that I had stumbled into what I would soon realise was a revolution. A quiet revolution taking place in the least likely realm of all—our accounting systems—which had been brewing for some thirty years. The 'revolutionaries' were not the usual sort; instead they were accountants, a former judge, a Harvard professor. Their mission was the overthrow not of kings, tsars or states, but of capitalism itself. In the name of capitalism. The need for such a revolution—for a new accounting paradigm—was clearly expressed at the European Accounting Association's conference in Paris in May 2013, where one speaker claimed that corporate accounts now convey only 20 to 30 per cent of a firm's value, whereas 40 years ago accountants could capture up to 90 per cent.

So what is going on? Where is the missing value? *What* is the missing value? Just as physicists and geneticists have found that dark matter (said to comprise some 84 per cent of matter) and 'junk' DNA contain crucial information and are critical for the working of their respective universes, so accountants are beginning to consider and map these missing 'dark regions' of corporate wealth which are not conveyed by financial reports and yet contain information essential for human commerce—and perhaps for the future of human life on the planet. This information has emerged for two key reasons: the advent of the information age, which has brought new categories of wealth held in what are called 'intangible assets' such as brands, patents and customer interactions; and the plethora of new, narrative company reports that have appeared since the 1990s effectively to encourage corporations to consider their externalities, notably environmental, social and governance reports that are broadly referred to as 'non-financial' or sustainability reporting.

To capture this new information in corporate reports, accountants are defining new areas of value, or 'capitals'. Similar work is being done to consider the natural world in the accounts of nations, by refiguring nature as 'natural capital', its products as 'ecosystem goods' and its work as 'ecosystem services'. And so this accounting revolution appears to break a cardinal rule of traditional economics, a law most famously expounded by Chicago school economist Milton Friedman: it denies that so-called externalities—the effects of business on society and the environment—are external. In other words, it literally takes account of the world beyond the firm, and, analogously, of the planet beyond the economy. It is an attempt to account for society and nature in addition to accounting's traditional terrain of financial profits and losses.

I did not set out to write another book about accounting. But by accepting the invitation to that first round table—and by allowing questions of accounting, corporations and nature to plague me—I had unknow-ingly embarked upon this book. Because this is a breaking story, when I came to write it much of my research was conducted through interviews with its key players. Chief among them was former South African Supreme Court judge Mervyn King. At Nelson Mandela's insistence, King had helped to construct the corporate and accounting architecture which made possible South Africa's trans-ition to a post-apartheid economy from 1994. When I met him, in February 2014, King had taken his thinking about corporate governance and accounting to the world. He was now chairman of the new 'integrated reporting' initiative Michael Bray had spoken about in May 2012, the International Integrated Reporting Council (IIRC). King's claims for the powers of accountants in the new millennium are as supercharged as those proposed by Jonathan Watts in 2010. He told me that if integrated reporting is adopted by corporations around the world, then accountants will become '*the* profession that enabled homo sapiens, human society, to move as a sustainable society into the twenty-second century'.

But these mooted—and by the look of it inevitable—changes to our accounting systems to include nature and society are controversial. Despite the apparent logic of fully costing, say, a $200 hamburger so we are forced to pay its hidden costs to society and the environment, such moves are double-edged, morally contentious: they effectively endorse the further encroachment of capital into the natural and social worlds. And they are vehemently opposed by those who deem their concepts and corollaries, such as 'natural capital', 'green economics' and 'sustainable growth', to be oxymorons and who argue that the living systems of the earth are infinitely valuable, for ethical, aesthetic and metaphysical reasons that go far beyond their economic utility, and cannot be priced. And they wonder, as I do, how those very entities most responsible for the destruction of the planet—corporations, the rule of financial capital, economic growth—can suddenly be held up as its saviour. But what systematic forces beyond democratic protest can we invoke to stand against the creep of capital into every sphere of life, including nature? Or, given that corporations look set to be the principal economic organising entities of the twenty-first century, how can we at least tip the balance of power towards nature? There are two promising initiatives on the horizon, one pertaining to the corporation, the other to nature, and, aptly enough in this era of programming and code-writing, both entail tinkering with their code.

Because accounting is the primary language of corporations, the accounting revolution also acts as a psychological intervention: by requesting the corporation to speak differently—to consider more than its own self-aggrandisement, more than its own short-term profits—it is attempting to alter the corporation's behaviour. But I also discovered two other broad endeavours aimed more deeply at the psyche of the corporation. If the accounting revolution is an attempt to make the psychopathic corporation relate to the wider world by asking it to change the way it speaks, then the other two interventions are attempting to alter the corporation's very being. One aims to redesign it conceptually in an attempt to change its DNA (a metaphor popular with these reformers), but the other, more promising initiative seeks to mess with the corporation's literal DNA, to rewrite its actual code, to genetically recombine it in order to make it evolve. The other promising sign on the horizon is the movement to enshrine the rights of nature in law, to give nature the legal power to contest the might of corporations.

This book traces the rise of the new accounting paradigm from its appearance in the accounts of nations in the 1990s to its use by activists from the 1980s to hold corporations accountable for their impact on the environment and society. It examines its emergence in South Africa to govern business as it moved into the new democratic society, and its simultaneous appearance in business reporting and thinking across the globe, which came together with the founding of the International Integrated Reporting Council in 2010. It then turns to recent moves to rethink the corporation itself before considering the rise of the rights of nature as another way of giving value to the earth. This, then, is the story of accounting in the early twenty-first century.

1

THREE WAVES OF WEALTH CREATION AND THE RISE OF ACCOUNTING

Information technology is changing everything.
It represents a new, post-industrial paradigm of
wealth creation that is replacing the industrial
paradigm and is profoundly changing the way
business is done.

ROBERT K. ELLIOTT, 1992

Better measurement leads to better management.

SARAH BOSTWICK, UNITED NATIONS GLOBAL
COMPACT, 2013

IN 1992, ROBERT K. ELLIOTT OF ACCOUNTING FIRM
KPMG in New York published a paper called 'The
Third Wave Breaks on the Shores of Accounting', which
argued that each new 'wave' of wealth creation—agricultural, industrial, information—requires a new form
of accounting. He drew the idea of 'waves' of wealth
creation from writer and futurologist Alvin Toffler's
1980 book *The Third Wave*, which refigures human

history into three broad categories based on the way we generate wealth. In this model, each new form of wealth creation acts like a wave, crashing and colliding, causing conflict and tension, eventually sweeping away the previous society.

The first wave came around 8000 BC when a hunter and gatherer first planted and nurtured a seed, giving birth to agriculture. The agricultural age made possible the creation of a surplus and the amassing of wealth, and gave rise to the first settlements, as humans became attached to the land they were cultivating and so developed defences, governments and codes of law. The second era of wealth creation was the industrial age, which Toffler dates to the Enlightenment ideas of Descartes (1596–1650; the mind–body split, analytical geometry) and Newton (1642–1727; physics, calculus, classical mechanics). It came into its own in the ensuing centuries with machinery powered by fossil fuels, and with factories, railways, sprawling cities, corporations, vertical hierarchies and assembly lines.

The prevailing principle of the industrial era was mass: mass production, mass consumption, mass markets, mass education, mass entertainment, mass media, mass culture, and weapons of mass destruction. It was founded on secularism, the nation state, the nuclear family, and the disenfranchisement of women and non-Europeans. In agricultural societies based on the extended family, people largely consume what they produce within the home, but in the industrial era, women generally stayed home, managing household consumption, while men went out to the factory or office to produce or to manage production. Taken up by the emerging discipline of economics, the split between these two broad spheres of human activity—consumption and production— informed the concerted push from the 1920s to measure national wealth and became the basis of Keynesian macroeconomics. Keynes called consumption 'the sole end and object of all economic activity'. (Elliott does not consider national accounting in his essay, focusing instead on the firm, but Toffler's scheme applies equally to nations and to the problems of GDP accounting.)

The Third Wave charts the death of the industrial era starting in the 1950s with the emergence of a new tool of wealth creation, the networked computer. In Toffler's view, the various changes the developed world has witnessed in the postwar era—the breaking down of belief systems, nation states, two-party politics, the nuclear family and mass culture—are all symptoms of the turbulent transition to the 'third wave', the information age. While the industrial era produced material things we can touch, the wealth of the new era is contained in 'intangibles' such as knowledge, design, planning, research and development, branding and advertising. And unlike the physical world on which the industrial age was founded—land, labour and capital (such as plant and machines)—which is subject to diminishing returns, or used up in production and consumption, electronic wealth is cumulative. When we download a file, the original file remains.

By 1992, the advent of this information age was being felt by those people whose task it is to categorise and measure wealth: accountants. Elliott's essay was one of several attempts to describe the way these changes were affecting management and accounting, but it was the only one to frame them in such broad historical terms. He argued that just as each wave of wealth creation is associated with its own physical technology—plough, machine, computer—so it has its own form of communication and, most importantly for this story, its own particular method of accounting. Elliott's use of Toffler's three waves provides a fruitful framework within which to rethink the history of accounting and its associated technologies, as well as a way of understanding one aspect of the current failures of our various measures of wealth, such as profits and GDP. (The two other key components of this breakdown—the environmental crisis and the rise of the multinational corporation—will be considered later in this chapter and in Chapter 3, respectively.)

In Elliott's view, today's accounting systems are breaking down because they were designed for the industrial era. 'Information technology is changing everything,' his essay begins. 'It represents a new, post-industrial paradigm of wealth creation that is replacing the industrial paradigm and is profoundly changing the way business is done.' The information age requires managers to make very different sorts of decisions from those made by industrial managers attempting to coax the most from factory workers so they could shift the greatest number of identical physical goods, such as Ford motor cars, in the shortest amount of time and at the lowest cost. And because the decisions of managers are guided by accounting information, 'it is natural to expect accounting to change'. And yet it has not.

Before exploring the sorts of accounting information required for third-wave business, Elliott gives a brief overview of the history of accounting in terms of Toffler's three waves to show the interrelated development of accounting, wealth creation and communications technology. In order to grasp the problems of the present, it is worth revisiting this history.

THE FIRST WAVE—AGRICULTURE, WRITING AND SINGLE-ENTRY ACCOUNTING

~

The first wave of wealth creation, agriculture, brought the first form of accounting and its associated information technology. The earliest accounting records date back to around 7000 BC when settled farming communities first appeared in Mesopotamia (now Iraq) and people began to keep track of their agricultural produce and exchanges by recording them with fired clay tokens. The archaeologist who extrapolated this ancient accounting system from the surviving tokens, Denise Schmandt-Besserat, found that each of the tokens' various shapes—cones, spheres, ovoids, cylinders—represented a different produce: a cone was a small measure of grain, a sphere was a large measure of grain, a cylinder was an animal, and so on.

When cities emerged in around 3500 to 3100 BC— and with them bronze smithies, the potter's wheel, mass production kilns, merchants and large-scale trade—the tokens suddenly changed. A complex accounting system emerged. Now there were three hundred shapes to record a wide range of goods, including bread, honey, textiles and metal. The account-keepers began to store their tokens in hollow clay balls—which Schmandt-Besserat calls 'envelopes'—imprinted with the signature seals of the parties involved in the exchange, and eventually also with the imprint of the tokens they contained.

And then in around 3300 BC the ancient accountants transformed the token-and-sealed-envelope system into something utterly new: they flattened out the clay balls and pressed the tokens into their surface, thus creating the world's first clay tablets. With the next step they took, the proto-accountants invented writing: they realised they could simply draw the tokens' shapes on the wet clay tablets with a stylus, thus bypassing the tokens altogether. And so the 3-D tokens were replaced by 2-D symbols; cones became triangles, spheres became circles, ovoids became ovals and so on, and thus writing was invented. The coevolution of accounting and writing was prompted by the need to record agricultural assets and obligations, which formed the basis of a single-entry accounting system.

THE SECOND WAVE—THE INDUSTRIAL REVOLUTION, THE PRINTING PRESS AND DOUBLE-ENTRY BOOKKEEPING

~

The second wave of wealth creation in Toffler's scheme relates to the industrial age. This dates from the late eighteenth century with the rise of machine production in England, with its factories, wage labour, burgeoning cities, and large-scale capital investment in railways and canals made possible by joint-stock companies. However, this era's associated communications technology and its accounting method had both emerged centuries earlier. The former was movable type printing, which was invented in Europe around 1450, probably by Mainz metalworker Johann Gutenberg. The latter was medieval double-entry bookkeeping, which emerged in northern Italy around 1300 to allow merchants to record their increasingly complex business dealings and was codified by Luca Pacioli in 1494 with the publication of his printed bookkeeping treatise *Particularis de computis et scripturis,* or 'Particulars of reckonings and writings'. Elliott calls these two advances 'necessary (though not sufficient) conditions' for the next massive technological change, which brought the industrial era.

The printing press made possible a revolution in the presentation and distribution of knowledge on a scale not equalled until the invention of the computer in the twentieth century. With the mass production of identical texts, knowledge could come out of the libraries of monasteries and castles, where it had been held in unique handwritten manuscripts that were read by a small educated elite. Within three decades of its invention, the printing press had made books more than three hundred times cheaper than they had been with the agricultural communications technology, handwriting. Books rapidly became widely available and affordable to a new class of readers. With printing came an explosion of DIY books explaining the previously esoteric arts of everything from playing musical instruments to keeping accounts in double entry. This new availability of knowledge eventually led to the development of modern science and machine technology.

Double-entry bookkeeping had similarly appeared long before the industrial revolution. The earliest surviving records of double entry date to 1300. Following the Crusades, there was a commercial boom in the emerging city states of northern Italy: Genoa, Pisa, Florence and Venice. As trade flourished on ever greater scales, merchants needed to record new kinds of information to cope with the growing complexity of their business dealings. Because of their unprecedented concentrations of capital, their many partners who each required their individual capital contribution and responsibilities to be recorded, and their vast credit networks spanning

Europe, the merchants of Florence were at the forefront of these new developments in business records. Accounting historians agree that the ledger of the Florentine merchants Giovanni Farolfi & Company dated 1299–1300 is the earliest example of double-entry bookkeeping. The system was further developed by the merchants of Venice, and when itinerant mathematician Luca Pacioli published his encyclopaedia of mathematics in Venice in 1494, he included in it a 27-page exposition of Venetian bookkeeping. Pacioli's was the first printed treatise on double-entry bookkeeping, and thanks to the printing press, it made possible the spread of Italian bookkeeping across Europe and to America over the next two centuries.

The Venetian system Pacioli codified was distinguished by its bilateral form, recording debit and credit entries in two opposing columns. As Pacioli said, 'if you make one creditor, you must make someone debtor'. Or, as Elliott wrote five hundred years later of the system still in use today: 'In double-entry accounting, the debits equal the credits. The debits represent the benefits to the company and the credits represent the sacrifices.'

THE CORPORATION AND THE RISE OF ACCOUNTING

Double-entry bookkeeping came into its own during the industrial revolution, first for the internal management of business and then, with the rise of the joint-stock company in the nineteenth century, for reporting externally to its investors. One of the first to realise its potential as a management tool was Josiah Wedgwood, who built the world's first industrialised pottery manufactory in the north of England and whose mass-produced ceramics took Britain's upwardly mobile middle classes by storm. In 1769, Wedgwood described the public's insatiable appetite for his vases as a 'violent Vase Madness'—but later the same year, Wedgwood and his partner Thomas Bentley found they had serious cash-flow problems and an accumulation of stock. They needed to find a way to reduce their merchandise.

Wedgwood turned to his accounts to solve his dilemma: should he cut production—or reduce prices? His investigations led him to discover the distinction between fixed and variable costs. As he told Bentley, their greatest manufacturing costs were modelling and moulds, rent, fuel, bookkeepers and wages: 'Consider that these expences move like clockwork & are much the same whether the quantity of goods made be large or small.' Thus he continued 'you will see the vast consequence in most manufactures of making the greatest quantity possible in a given time'. By analysing his accounts, Wedgwood had uncovered the commercial benefits of mass production. His detailed costings also revealed something unexpected: a history of embezzlement, blackmail and dissipation. He discovered that his head clerk had been fiddling the books and his cashier had been fiddling with the housekeeper, and fired both men.

This is one of the earliest instances of the use of double entry to analyse business accounts and apply the financial information it yielded to guide business strategy and decision-making in the new industrial world. It is now known as cost accounting. But despite Wedgwood's early foray, a huge shift in outlook was required to move this medieval accounting system beyond its mercantile origins in an exchange economy (where it recorded the exchange of goods, owing and being owed, paying and collecting debts) to manufacturing, where the emphasis is on the production of goods (the conversion of materials and labour into products). Early attempts to do so show the conceptual difficulties posed by the need to incorporate new elements—labour and materials per unit of production—into an enterprise's accounting system so managers could calculate the cost of each unit of production. The challenge lay in the fact that the transactions needed to incorporate the manufacturing of products into the existing double-entry system were not financial transactions: they did not involve the exchange of goods, but rather such manoeuvres as adding the cost of labour acquired or materials bought, or transferring the costs of materials from the storehouse accounts to the factory account. These sorts of 'non-financial' transactions had not been seen before in double entry's 300-year history. It took a century of factory production before these accounting problems were better grasped and the two spheres—commerce and manufacturing—were brought together in one coordinated set of books.

In 1887, Emile Garcke, an electrical engineer, and John Manger Fells, an accountant, published *Factory Accounts: Their principles and practice*, the most influential work on cost accounting in the nineteenth century. It provided for the first time to English readers a systematic statement of the principles of factory accounts. Their double-entry system combined the elements both of factory production and of exchange—wages, stock, goods in process, produce in the warehouse, costs, sales, profits—so that the flow of price data through the ledger accounts was concurrent with the corresponding flow of work through the manufacturing processes that converted labour and raw materials into commodities. Garcke and Fells were among the first to advocate keeping all cost accounts in double entry and integrating them with the financial records. This is the essence of industrial-age internal accounting practices.

The industrial revolution also brought about the first legislation requiring the external reporting of accounting information. This was prompted by the challenge of managing the vast investments needed to build railways, which were financed not through the reinvestment of their own profits as with smaller-scale industries of the time—pottery, cotton, wool, iron—but by private investors on stock exchanges and managed by joint-stock companies. Repeated cases of railway fraud and corporate failure in Britain led creditors and investors to demand that the government regulate joint-stock companies. In 1844, the British government responded with the Joint Stock Companies Act, which required companies to keep publicly available financial statements based on reliable accounting records. A series of acts, including the Limited

Liability Act of 1855 and the Companies Act of 1862, required accountants at every phase of a company's life and established the basic architecture of the modern corporation. This architecture includes the idea of a corporation as a legal entity; the idea that a corporation is an ongoing concern that yields an income as 'dividends' (not a series of separate speculative ventures with profits and losses paid out as 'divisions' of capital at the end of each new venture, such as with the sea voyages of the mercantile era); the idea of limited liability; the concept of depreciation; the practice of cost accounting; and the formal establishment of auditing.

Double entry proved to be the perfect mechanism for generating the financial statements that underpinned the modern corporation. It could accurately record business transactions; distinguish between capital and income, and between private expenses and corporate costs; and it could produce data that helped to evaluate past investment decisions. By 1900, annual financial statements had become the raison d'être of double-entry bookkeeping, and most businesses across the planet were using it to keep their books. As Elliott says, the debits and credits of double entry 'provide a very convenient way of keeping track of a large number of contracts in various stages of execution—committed, partially executed, and fully executed. A simple accounting entry could record each stage of the contract'. Double-entry bookkeeping thus made possible the expression both of a corporation's financial position and of the change in that position over a period of time.

It was from government intervention in errant corporate activity in the nineteenth century that the accounting profession—and its regulation—evolved, and this pattern of scandal and regulation continued in the twentieth century. Various corporate wrongdoings led to a new Companies Act in Britain in 1929, with which the reporting of a profit and loss account—or income statement—became legally required. In the United States the Wall Street Crash of October 1929 prompted Roosevelt's New Deal, the first full-scale, systematic government intervention in a market economy, and the Securities and Exchange Acts of 1933 and 1934, which mandated audited financial statements for all publicly traded companies. The US Securities and Exchange Commission (SEC) was created in 1934 to regulate the securities industry and enforce federal laws. By the end of the 1930s, the income statement had become the focal point of accounting practice and reflected the growing importance of equity markets and shareholders as the providers of finance in the economy.

As the modern corporation grew more complex in the postwar era, new standard-setting organisations were established in the United Kingdom and United States: what would become the UK's Accounting Standards Committee (ASC) was set up in 1970, and three years later the Financial Accounting Standards Board (FASB) was established in the US. These bodies increasingly codified accounting practices, especially the meaning of 'true and fair view' (one of accounting's fundamental principles, thought to be achieved when a company's accounts give a correct and complete picture of its financial position) and 'generally accepted accounting principles' (or GAAP, accounting standards within any particular jurisdiction). The globalisation of capital markets and the growing need for internationally accepted accounting standards led to the creation of an international accounting body in 1973, the International Accounting Standards Committee, which was replaced in 2001 by the International Accounting Standards Board (IASB).

National accounting

A similar movement to measure the wealth of nations began in the seventeenth century with English polymath William Petty. During an illustrious career in medicine, music and politics, Petty made the first quantitative analysis of the national income and wealth of England. As a landowner, he set out to prove mathematically that England could use its land, labour and capital more effectively to raise more revenue to fund its 1664–67 war against the Dutch without further taxing his own class of landowners. In his 1665 book *Verbum Sapienti* ('A Word to the Wise'), Petty demonstrated that, contrary to common belief, land produced only a small portion of England's national income—and therefore that landowners made up only a small part of its potential tax base. By estimating the wealth and national expenditure of England and Wales, Petty found there was a much larger and as yet untapped source of income to tax: labour. His analysis showed that labour produced three times more income than land.

This was the first quantitative analysis in the history of economics, and Petty wrote of his innovative approach: 'The method I take to do this, is not yet very usual; for instead of using only comparative and superlative words, and intellectual arguments, I have taken the course . . . to express myself in terms of number, weight and measure.' Petty's method exemplified another innovation of the age: the increasing use of numerical argumentation, especially in science, made possible by the gradual rise of Hindu–Arabic numerals and algebra as the global lingua franca, which allowed sophisticated reasoning with numbers.

Although national income statistics had been periodically collected since the nineteenth century, the Great Depression of the 1930s made the need for this information more urgent. National accounting techniques were pioneered in Britain by economist Colin Clark at Cambridge University from 1931, and economist Simon Kuznets applied Clark's methods in the United States. The first set of national accounts—Kuznets' *National Income 1929–1932*—was presented to US Congress in 1934. It was a set of industry-by-industry estimates that amounted to national income and allowed Roosevelt to show that from 1929 to 1932 the income of the United States had shrunk by more than half.

When the US economy was forced into wartime production in the 1940s, policymakers needed a different sort of information. They needed figures for national production and spending—according to the types of products and purchases made—so they could determine their wartime budgets. The income statistics made for the Depression era did not provide this information. This led to the first estimates of gross national product (GNP), which were calculated to give the government a picture of the overall productive capacity of the economy and show the impact of a shift from civilian spending on consumer products to government spending on the weapons of war. When they were consolidated in 1947—the national income accounts inaugurated during the Depression and the production accounts prompted by the war—these two accounts made the United States' first double-entry books of national economic accounts.

Meanwhile in Britain, economist John Maynard Keynes had responded to the Depression by developing his revolutionary approach to market capitalism, his theory of effective demand. Published in 1936 as *The General Theory of Employment, Interest and Money*, it became enormously influential because it provided a theoretical basis for the measurement of national income, consumption, investment and savings at the same time as the first moves towards their calculation were being made in Washington. Keynes was the first to offer a systematic way of thinking about the behaviour of an entire economy, picturing it as an aggregate quantity of output resulting from an aggregate stream of expenditure.

As war became imminent, Keynes was able to demonstrate that his new aggregate approach to a national economy could be applied not just to the problem of unemployment but also to the problem of managing a wartime economy, with the accompanying risks of inflation due to the sudden surge in government spending that war necessitates. His method of combating inflation required the construction of national income statistics to manage aggregate demand. That is, assuming the extra government spending (or increased demand) in the wartime economy would cause inflation, Keynes wanted to control the economy's total demand (made up of demand from various sectors, including consumers, business and government). To do so he needed a way to measure this total or aggregate demand, which can be approximated through national income statistics.

In February 1940, Keynes published his pamphlet *How to Pay for the War* as an appeal to the British Treasury to consider his radical ideas and gather statistics on the national economy so it would have a map to guide its financing of the war. It was for this landmark pamphlet that Keynes first developed a system of national accounts for the United Kingdom based on double-entry bookkeeping, a system which was published as the pamphlet's appendix 'A Budget of National Resources'. It was based on his *General Theory* concepts of aggregate demand and aggregate supply and measured in prices. In 1941,

Britain's first set of national accounts was presented by a team led by James Meade and Richard Stone in their paper 'National Income, Saving and Consumption'. The government budget that followed in April 1941 was shaped largely by these statistics and the influence of Keynes.

Following the war, under the aegis of the newly created United Nations, Stone was put in charge of producing a standard system of national accounts which could be applied to all countries. The United Nations published the work of Stone and his colleagues in 1952 under the title *A System of National Accounts and Supporting Tables*, as part of its Standardised System of National Accounts, or SNA. Over the next decades, national accounts were gradually constructed in most nations across the globe, inaugurating a new field of national accounting, its accompanying theories of economic growth, and the rise of the GDP as *the* measure of national progress.

This is where we are today, with a system of measures of corporations and nations which has been applied with apparent success to measuring physical production in the industrial era and the vast material wealth it has generated for large parts of the globe.

Two further legacies of double-entry bookkeeping

Before we move to the third wave, it is worth briefly considering two further legacies of industrial-age accounting: its inherent flaws and the concept of capital.

Our industrial accounting system based on double-entry bookkeeping is founded on uncertainty. Its most fundamental concepts and practices, such as income measurement and asset valuation, are based on ambiguities. Accountants still cannot agree on how to define income, the measurement of which remains one of the most intractable problems in financial accounting theory and practice. The valuation of assets only becomes more complex and more fiercely debated as modern global corporate structures and financial instruments become increasingly labyrinthine, and income measurement, the key to determining profits and therefore dividends, is inextricably linked to this contentious, elusive practice of asset valuation. Nor is the crucial measurement of costs an objective process: costs are also highly contestable figures and may result as much from the collusion or rivalries of firms as from any other actuality. Accrual (or corporate) accounting—the need to allocate revenues and expenses between accounting periods and to value assets and liabilities at the end of an accounting period—raises problems which have never been solved and are probably incapable of solution.

The era of double-entry bookkeeping also created a new category of wealth called 'capital', and gave us a way to formulate and quantify its fluctuations in numbers. Pacioli called capital 'that amount of wealth which is used in making profits and which enters into the accounts'. The term had evolved from *capitale*, a Late Latin word derived from *caput*, meaning both 'chief' or 'head', and 'property'. By the end of the thirteenth century, 'capital' was used in bookkeeping to describe the productive wealth of the proprietor—the capital assets of a firm. The calculation of capital is central to the double-entry system: from the capital account, Pacioli said, 'you may always learn what your fortune is'.

Double entry provided the means of discarding all information extraneous to decision-making, leaving behind only numbers that pertained to capital. It then translated these numbers into a common measuring tool for changes in the stock of capital called 'profit' (for increases in capital) and 'loss' (for its decrease), which allowed a relatively precise evaluation of business activities in hard numbers. Double entry thus transformed business books from memory aids equivalent to diaries written in various vernacular languages into records which allowed the calculation of the universal concept of profit—and which could therefore be used to measure the success in financial terms of each individual transaction and of business generally. And so it allows us to compare an enterprise's total assets at the beginning of a profit-making venture with its total assets at the end— and thereby to value and determine the potential success (purely in terms of profit) of any potentially profit making activity, even when non-calculable goods are at stake, such as education or the natural environment.

In my travels into the world of twenty-first-century accounting, everywhere I went I heard the received accounting wisdom, 'Better measurement leads to better management,' or 'You can't manage what you can't measure.' It seems we are a measuring and calculating species. And now we need new measures with which to count and manage our wealth, which we call capital, because it is changing. Or, we need to rethink exactly what we consider our wealth to be, what it is that we value, and whether it can or should be expressed only in terms of numbers and money. But for the moment, the extension of the idea of 'capital' to include new categories—of nature, human brain power, relationships and society—is the language in which our rethinking about wealth is taking place. It is as if we can imagine no other way.

THE THIRD WAVE—THE INFORMATION AGE, DIGITAL TECHNOLOGY AND . . . ?

Two big new forces have thrown traditional financial reporting into turmoil, making novel and unprecedented demands on it. These are the networked computer and the various crises of the natural world, from environmental degradation and resource depletion to extreme weather events and climate change. The first has given rise to the idea of intangible value or immaterial wealth, such as intellectual capital, image, confidence, brand recognition, fashion; the second to the idea of sustainability. The first of these has preoccupied accountants since the 1990s and is the focus of Elliott's 1992 article.

The second formally entered the world of accounting more recently through external pressure from activists, ethical investors and others since the 1980s.

The third great wave of wealth creation is the information age, which began with the invention of the transistor in 1947 and of the first commercial computer in 1951. As with the previous waves of wealth creation, the information age is also bringing massive social and economic change. In this new era, our economy is driven not by the physical labour of agriculture, nor by the machines of industry, but by data. The information technology of the third wave is the digital computer, which makes possible fast, inexpensive information storage, transfer and processing. When harnessed to its full potential, with software, databases, networks and cables, the computer opens up vast new realms of what is often termed 'knowledge work'. And yet we struggle to capture its new form of wealth in our accounts. The conundrum of the information age is expressed in a remark made in 1987 by economist Robert Solow: 'You can see the computer age everywhere but in the productivity figures.'

Despite being greater in scale than the railways and canals of the industrial revolution, the infrastructure required to build this new information age is as invisible to us as its measurable effects on productivity. Geographer Nigel Thrift calls the investment in cable, wireless, server farms and the new kinds of workers required by information technology 'a moment in the human history of engineering just as significant as the construction of the Great Wall, or of the pyramids'. But we do not see it. The invisibility even of our age's physical infrastructure is due to the fact that a huge 99 per cent of our international communications is delivered through undersea cables, which can carry vast quantities of data compared to satellites and have been our main information carriers since the first commercial use of the internet in the 1980s.

French economist Yann Moulier-Boutang, who calls this new age 'cognitive capitalism', captured some of the unprecedented nature of our epoch shift when he said in 2007:

> The political economy which was born with
> Adam Smith no longer offers us the possib-
> ility of understanding the reality which is
> being constructed before our eyes—namely
> the value, wealth and complexity of the world
> economic system—and it also does not enable
> us to deal with the challenges that await
> humanity, whether ecological or social.

Today we need a new political economy derived from a new system of measuring and valuing, a new system of accounting.

We are living in a rift between epochs. As Elliott says, there is 'a cost involved in switching from one technology to another, and that cost is technological discontinuity'. When he was writing, in 1992, the workforce of the

United States had already begun to make the shift to knowledge work: 2 per cent of people were growing food, 10 per cent were making things in factories, and 60 per cent were working in the primary and secondary information sectors. The primary information sector includes organisations mostly concerned with producing or using information and knowledge, such as computer manufacturers, universities, law and accounting firms, and the publishing and entertainment industries. In the secondary sector are non-information businesses that produce or use information, such as engineering and marketing departments in an industrial firm.

Elliott argued that when managers grasp the significance of information technology, they use it to do something radically different from the old way of doing business: they use it to get close to their customers. Information technology literally closes the time and space gaps between customers' demands and businesses' response to them—and businesses respond by improving quality and by 'demassifying', or making their products more specialised. This is the opposite of the thinking of the industrial era, from Josiah Wedgwood to Henry Ford, which relied on the mass production of identical products to reduce costs. (As Ford remarked about the Model T in 1909, 'Any customer can have a car painted any color that he wants so long as it is black.') Demassification can be seen, for example, in the vast range of cable and satellite television networks that now provide specialised channels for entertainment, news, music, shopping, sports and movies, compared to the old model of three or so networks, such as NBC, CBS and ABC in the United States.

Another feature of information technology is that it allows business to be managed on a global scale, coordinated by electronic networks, databases and messaging. This presents managers with very different issues from those encountered by industrial managers. In particular, it challenges the old hierarchical organisational structures designed like an inverted tree, with the chief executive officer at the top and the various departments branching off it, each with their own sub-branches. Modelled on the church and the military, these hierarchies made it easier for a few people to control a large number of employees. But they were also ungainly, because each branch is separated from the next into 'stovepipes' or 'silos': distinct departments such as marketing, engineering, manufacturing, sales, accounting and finance. This prevented communication between the various branches of the organisation, which slowed change and brought enormous inefficiencies, including time wasting, work replication and overlooked talent. The third-wave structure is the digital network, which allows any two or more people to work together on one task and communication to flow unimpeded in any direction via various electronic messages.

One of the hardest tasks of the information age is 'the conversion of the human resource base from the old model (white collar–blue collar) to the new model:

knowledge workers'. The old accounting systems measured whether the blue-collar workers did what they were
told to do. But the change and innovation the third-wave
organisation thrives on are best encouraged by allowing
everyone to participate, which requires a better-educated
workforce. The primary focus of knowledge and information organisations has also shifted from the product to
the customer, as is evident in the growing number of
requests for and the increasing responsiveness of business
to customer feedback.

These changes raise two kinds of accounting issues:
those related to internal accounting information, the sort
first used by Josiah Wedgwood to manage his pottery
manufactory; and those related to external accounting
information, which is reported to capital providers.

Internal accounting information

In industrial-era business, internal accounts are used
to manage and control an organisation. They focus on
the firm's tangible assets, including inventory and fixed
assets, such as land, buildings and equipment. They
measure increases and decreases in assets, liabilities,
income and expenses. That is, they measure activity,
not the rate of change in activity (or how systems and
products change and improve over time, information
which is crucial to managers in the fast-moving electronic
age). With industrial accounting, the general ledger
replicates the departmentalised hierarchy of the organisation, locking the firm into the inverted-tree structure.

If in its move to accommodate the new imperatives of the information age the organisation tries to become networked and break through the silos, its accounting structure snaps it back into the hierarchical form. It has no way to deal with shared costs and benefits between departments, so open exchange between them is formally suppressed. In this way the account structure acts as 'a powerfully conservative force trapping the organization in the second wave'. The information produced by these accounting structures remains similarly limited. One chief executive officer of a successful software company described the effect of this to Elliott: 'trying to run my organization with the output of our accounting department is like trying to fly an airplane that has only one dial—a dial that shows the sum of airspeed and altitude. If it's low, I'm in trouble, but I don't even know why.'

In 1992, Elliott speculated on the sort of accounting systems that were needed for third-wave managers. Among other things, such systems would embody a shift from tangible to intangible assets (such as research and development, employees' knowledge and experience, data and capacity for innovation), from products to customers, from replicating the hierarchy to enabling the network, and from accounting based on events that have taken place to real-time tracking of processes. Electronic accounting systems would become more responsive to change, they would be able to evolve as new phenomena were encountered without having to be totally redesigned. This would make it easier for companies to access, analyse and disseminate new information, such as customer feedback, and add it to the accounting system.

At the time Elliott was writing, accounting firms and academics were already beginning to conceptualise new accounting systems aimed at shifting the treatment of financial figures as the foundation for measuring corporate performance to treating them as just one among a broad set of measures. One such approach was the Balanced Scorecard, a term coined in 1992 by Harvard Business School's Robert S. Kaplan and director of the Palladium Group David P. Norton, which attempted to bring together financial information with non-financial information in order to link a company's current activities to its long-term strategy. As with the CEO who compared the running of his business to flying an aeroplane, Kaplan and Norton conceived of managers as pilots who needed a range of measures to guide them, not just the aggregate of speed and altitude provided by the old measures.

External accounting information

Like management accounting, 'financial accounting' is a second-wave concept that limits a firm's accountability to the provision of financial information. In the new era, however, organisations need to provide other sorts of information for investors and other interested parties, such as that pertaining to their capacity for innovation, research and development, knowledge and long-term strategy. As Elliott puts it:

Much of what users want to know about the
company is nonfinancial. For example, its
mission and goals, its strategy, the industries in which the company participates, the
competitive position of the company within
these industries, relative levels of quality and
customer satisfaction, progress in product-
design, development of the company's
human assets.

And none of these are recorded in a company's financial
numbers.

Non-financial value

These issues of accurately measuring and reporting
corporate value are no longer the concern solely of an
elite class of capital providers. Since the 1980s, they have
been increasingly important for all of us, in a global
economy where most people—through superannuation
and other annuities and entities such as local government—have funds invested in or are influenced by stock
markets. This was made spectacularly clear by the 2008
financial crash. In 2001, J. Frank Brown, then Global
Leader of Assurance and Business Advisory Services at
PricewaterhouseCoopers, remarked on the rise of the
so-called 'universal investor'. He claimed that the world
of external corporate reporting is 'ripe for a revolution'
because 'things have changed':

For better *and* for worse, the common man
and woman have evolved into *Homo investus*.
In the United States, more than half of the
adult population now owns stock, directly
or indirectly through pension and mutual
funds. In the United Kingdom, the number is
25 percent, and in Europe it's more than 12
percent and growing rapidly.

One of the most significant consequences of the emergence of the universal investor is a shift in the relative
wealth of corporations and nations: in many developed
countries, the market value of all listed companies (or
stock market capitalisation) is similar to or greater than
the size of the domestic economy. Corporations increasingly rule the world. And so the way they value their
wealth—*our* wealth—is of critical importance.

According to KPMG accountant Michael Bray, Elliott's
speculative model of third-wave accounting is the 'bare
bones' of the new (six capitals) integrated reporting model
that Bray is backing. Many of the problems Elliott can-
vassed in 1992 are still being faced today, and Bray sums
these up as 'corporate reporting that's not conducive to
capital investment'—in other words, a reporting model
that does not give investors and analysts a full picture of
the state of a company because it is still founded on financial reporting, which only accounts for tangible assets.
The missing information is broadly covered by the term

'non-financial value', which, by definition, is not conveyed by financial reports. (Although the term 'non-financial value' is widely used, Paul Druckman, chief executive officer of the new integrated reporting movement chaired by Mervyn King, argues that ultimately this information bears upon a company's financial health and viability so it is misleading to call it 'non-financial'.)

The advent of non-financial value was being widely felt in the 1990s—especially, not surprisingly, among those working with the new technology companies whose share prices soared despite the fact that they had few or no earnings, let alone made an accounting profit. For example, on 27 March 2000, 'third-wave' technology company Cisco Systems had a market capitalisation of US$555.44 billion, over six times more than that of 'second-wave' General Motors (US$88.19 billion). This contradicted all the received wisdom of the old accounting paradigm. General Motors had earned more than twice the amount of Cisco in its previous accounting periods and had ten times its assets. The staggering difference in their share prices was the result of non-financial value, or intangibles, which were not required to be valued or disclosed, even if they could be. The value of technology companies, from Cisco to Twitter, lies in the minds of their creators and employees, their intellectual property.

Nick Ridehalgh, partner at KPMG Sydney, experienced this first hand. In the late 1990s, Ridehalgh, then with PricewaterhouseCoopers, worked on the audits of telecommunications companies, including preparing prospectuses for a few dotcom technology companies for stock market listing. This brought him face to face with their missing or non-financial value: there was, he told me, 'nothing on their balance sheets, nothing on their profit and loss [accounts], just a cash burn—and yet they were listing the most significant dollar values. You can't see their value in traditional financial reporting'. Sophisticated analysts and specialist investors realised this and were responsible for the firms' astronomical share prices, but the fact that capital was being allocated to organisations that had few tangible assets on the balance sheet went against the rationale of corporate reporting, which is supposed to provide a 'true and fair view' of a company. The value of these technology companies was held in some other form of wealth or 'capital': the human capital, the knowledge of the individuals in the organisation, as well as the intellectual property (or intellectual capital) they had developed—'some tech geeks and their software', in Ridehalgh's terms—none of which had a value on the traditional balance sheet.

At the time, Ridehalgh was part of a global team at PricewaterhouseCoopers working to develop a new reporting model they called ValueReporting. This model was their attempt to find ways of reporting the new intangible assets—such as knowledge, brand recognition and market share—of the information age. It was driven by the realisation that the corporate reports companies were preparing and they were auditing did not reflect the companies' true underlying value. This breakdown of the reporting measures was frustrating: as an auditor, Ridehalgh's aim is to provide information to investors and potential shareholders through a 'robust assurance process', so that if and when they invest their money they 'understand the key value drivers of the business and they're comfortable that those value drivers are being enhanced over time'.

'Value driver' is a term widely used by those involved in the new reporting initiatives. It refers to those things that increase the value of a product or service by improving our perception of it and giving the company a competitive advantage. Value drivers include things like advanced technology, brand recognition, reliability and customer satisfaction. These things are not included in traditional corporate reporting. Because the technology companies were locked into the industrial reporting paradigm, in most cases their reported value and stock market value diverged spectacularly; they met their legal obligation to provide financial reports, which showed negative assets, major losses and huge cash outflows, and yet their share prices were often stupendous. As mentioned, the market was understanding value not contained in these financial reports: the value of these companies was in their technology developers, the chief technology officer, the chief executive officer; in their technology and their belief in the future value of that technology. But the assurance profession (auditors) was not providing any assurance of that information.

Ridehalgh found that this crucial missing information was being provided in mediums and forms other than annual financial reports, which were 'very generic, very regulatory driven'; instead, non-financial information tended to be given in narrative form, rather than numerical, and in specialist investor briefings.

Harvard Professor of Management Practice Robert G. Eccles has been working to find ways to account for non-financial value for some twenty-five years. He is particularly focused on corporate reporting, the boundary between the firm and the market. In 1989, he started a research program on improving corporate reporting. He found that one of the key pieces of information companies were not reporting and investors wanted to know was corporate strategy. When Eccles published an article discussing these findings, PricewaterhouseCoopers, who were working on ValueReporting at the time, asked him to replicate his study around the world. Wherever he went he found the same reporting gaps, the missing non-financial information. His work with PricewaterhouseCoopers on ValueReporting led Eccles to co-author *The ValueReporting Revolution: Moving beyond the earnings game*, which was published in 2001 and called for a revolution in corporate reporting. The authors argued that unless managers begin reporting on all the non-financial measures they use to manage their companies, they will continue to be locked by financial markets into the short-term 'earnings game' which compels them to pursue quarterly earnings increases at the expense of all else, including long-term strategy and social and environmental responsibility.

This leads us inexorably to the concept of sustainability, because long-term thinking and social and environmental responsibility are its central concerns. Like Eccles, Ridehalgh spoke about the development of his thinking from a focus on non-financial value to the idea of sustainability, which among other things forces a change in business perspective from the short to the long term. In the industrial paradigm, management is focused on short-term performance, particularly on short-term financial performance, to the detriment of longer-term considerations such as the health of the environment. Corporations are realising that sustainability issues which were once considered irrelevant now have a significant bearing on the viability of their operations. These issues, which Ridehalgh called 'megatrends', include climate change, increasing urbanisation, population growth, and water and food shortages, and they all bear on the ability of organisations to 'create value'—or function profitably—in the medium and long term. According to Ridehalgh, these issues lead managers to ask new questions which pertain to the long-term viability of their business, such as 'Will I have to change my business model? Will I have to change my supply chain? Will I have to change my products and services? Will I have to change my location?'

A BRIEF HISTORY OF SUSTAINABILITY

~

The term 'sustainability' first emerged in a business context in the 1980s. In 1987 one of the pioneers in the field, John Elkington, co-founded the London consultancy SustainAbility with environmental campaigner Julia Hailes. Together they wrote the bestselling *Green Consumer Guide*, which was published the following year. As Elkington remarked in 2009, when they founded their think tank in 1987 almost no one had heard of the term sustainability or knew what it meant. 'In the intervening decades, however, the concept has gone viral.' And yet, he said, 'it remains a challenge to define the concept in meaningful, consensual and operational ways'.

According to sustainability expert Wayne Visser:

> At one level sustainability is simply about the ability to survive (and thrive) over a given period of time, preferably the long term. However, sustainability has come to have a much more specific meaning linked to human development and environmental agendas.

Even as recently as 2013, Eccles and his Harvard colleague George Serafeim wrote that although sustainability is now part of the business lexicon, it is a controversial term and its meaning is not well defined. They give the word a corporate dimension:

> We define sustainability in terms of a company's *strategy* and the relationship between this strategy and the society that grants companies their license to operate. A sustainable strategy is one that enables a company to create value for their shareholders, while at the same time contributing to a sustainable society.

Their definition introduces the idea of value creation for shareholders, and so refers to a sort of 'sustainable capitalism', which is how sustainability is most commonly used by those working with the new accounting paradigm. They define a sustainable society as 'one that meets the demands of the current generation without sacrificing the needs of future generations'. As is common, here they allude to the landmark report *Our Common Future* released in 1987 by the World Commission on Environment and Development, chaired by former Norwegian prime minister Gro Harlem Brundtland. Known as the Brundtland Report, it introduced the idea of 'sustainable development' which it defined as 'development which meets the needs of current generations without compromising the ability of future generations to meet their own needs'. In accounting terms, according to Eccles and Serafeim, a sustainable strategy is one that attempts to minimise the negative effects on the environment and local community (or negative externalities) of a company's activities, without 'significant losses in productivity and value creation'. And so the responsibility of business is now seen to extend beyond profit max-imisation alone to its impact on the broader realm of society and the environment. In other words, in this new conception of business and accounting, externalities become internalities. This is in stark contrast to the ideas outlined by leading postwar economist Milton Friedman in his influential 1970 essay 'The Social Responsibility of Business is to Increase its Profits' (which I return to in Chapter 3).

Whatever its exact definition, sustainability concerns the challenge of sustaining a world population forecast to reach more than nine billion people in the twenty-first century. As Elkington says, this is 'simply not going to be workable if we cling to current economic and business models, technologies and governance systems'.

Concerns about the impact of corporate activity and economic growth on the environment and society are often dated to the publication in 1962 of *Silent Spring*, Rachel Carson's account of the damage done to the natural world—especially to birds—by pesticides; while the birth of planetary consciousness is frequently attrib-uted to the first photograph taken of the earth from space (by *Apollo 8*) in 1968. Another landmark event in this history was the global think tank Club of Rome's 1972 report *The Limits to Growth*, which has sold 30 million copies around the world and become the best-selling environmental book of all time. *The Limits to Growth* was the first systematic investigation into the long-term impact on the planet of the industrial mode of resource use and of economic and population growth. It found they were not sustainable. In the same year, the United Nations held a Human Environment conference to discuss the state of the planet; this gave birth to the UN Environment Programme, created to promote sustainable development and be 'the voice of the environment' within the United Nations.

In 1982, the important and previously neglected (by traditional economics) relationship between the economy and the natural world was addressed at a workshop in Sweden on the 'Integration of Ecology and Economics', which led to the creation of the International Society for Ecological Economics (ISEE). Ten years later, following its conference 'Investing in Natural Capital—A Prerequisite for Sustainability', the society laid out the tenets of a new sort of economics founded on the paradigm-shifting assertion that the economic system is a subsystem of the global ecosystem. Its two other precepts made an equally radical break from mainstream economics: that 'fundamental uncertainty is large and irreducible and certain processes are irreversible'; and that there are limits to 'biophysical throughput', or the amount of natural resources we can mine, cut down, burn and consume. As a result of these insights they argued that nature—or 'natural capital' (a term first explicitly used in 1973 by British economist E.F. Schumacher in his book *Small is Beautiful*)—needs to be conserved, and that economics needs to include a broader range of values, such as ethics, equity and concern for future generations. As leading ecological economist Robert Costanza said in 1991, this worldview 'treats humans as part of and not apart from the processes and functions of nature'.

Because they extend the concept of wealth beyond that of conventional economics to include nature, ecological economists distinguish three different sorts of capital: natural capital, human (or cultural) capital and traditional manufactured capital. And they think of all three capitals in economic terms, as stocks of wealth that produce a range of ecological and economic goods and services that are used by the human economy. Costanza has defined 'natural capital' as the extension of the economic idea of capital to environmental 'goods and services'. There are two sorts of natural capital: non-renewable resources, such as oil, coal and minerals; and renewable resources such as ecosystems. In accounting terms, natural capital is the stock, which yields a flow of ecosystem goods (such as fish, honey and trees) and services, such as atmospheric regulation, flood control, water catchment and purification, nutrient recycling, erosion control, waste processing and pollination. To make us aware of the extent of our dependence on ecosystems for our survival, these economists argue that we must internalise the costs of our economic activities (a similar way of thinking to Raj Patel's $200 hamburger). In other words, rather than treating them as externalities, we must include nature's goods and services in our accounting systems: we must take them into account. While this was not so pressing in the early industrial period, when natural resources were more abundant and the population was relatively small, this is no longer the case. In order to achieve sustainability, these economists claim, we need to incorporate ecosystem goods and services into economic accounting. And to do this we must find a way of giving value to natural capital.

In 1997, the journal *Nature* published a paper called 'The Value of the World's Ecosystem Services and Natural Capital' by a group of authors led by Costanza, which put a dollar value on the annual contribution of seventeen ecosystem services. Many of their valuation techniques were based, either directly or indirectly, on attempts to estimate individuals' willingness to pay for ecosystems services. As a result, they estimated for the entire biosphere a value in the range of US$16–54 trillion per year, with an average of US$33 trillion per year. This was roughly equal to the 1998 'Gross World Product' (the total amount of goods and services produced in the world's economy in a year) of US$39 trillion. Yet one form of value—the Gross World Product—we count and husband. The other, more critical one—natural production and provision—we ignore and deplete. This is because in our medieval accounting systems adapted to the industrial age we measure only financial and manufactured capital. Natural capital is only accounted for when it is destroyed, transformed for our consumption into factories, railways, roads, buildings, clothing, food and other things.

One of the first books to outline this new conflation of business and environmental thinking was *Natural*

Capitalism: Creating the next industrial revolution by Paul Hawken, Amory Lovins and L. Hunter Lovins, published in 1999. In line with the tenets of ecological economics, the authors argue that the economy is part of the larger 'economy' of the natural world. They take up the concepts of natural capital and ecosystem services to argue that nature provides not just raw materials for industry but also services that are invaluable to the human economy but are not yet valued by our accounting systems because we consider them to be free. The authors extend the idea of three capitals to four: human capital (including labour and intelligence, culture and organisation), financial capital (cash, investments and monetary instruments), manufactured capital (infrastructure, machines, tools and factories) and natural capital.

Because we treat the wealth of nature as free, the authors of *Natural Capitalism* argue, our current form of capitalism is 'a financially profitable, nonsustainable aberration in human development' which does not obey its own accounting principles: 'It liquidates its capital and calls it income'—in other words, it is the greatest Ponzi scheme ever perpetrated. (The term 'Ponzi scheme' describes companies that illegally use capital assets rather than profits to pay returns to investors. Such fraudulent behaviour is a criminal offence.) Today's industrial capitalism uses up the stocks of the natural and social worlds without valuing them or accounting for their depletion. And so we are exhausting the bounty of the natural world and the health of our societies. As *Natural*

Capitalism says: 'While there may be no "right" way to value a forest or a river, there is a wrong way, which is to give it no value at all. If we have doubts [as to] how to value a 700-year-old tree, we only need to ask how much it would cost to make a new one. Or a new atmosphere, or a new culture.'

The authors of *Natural Capitalism* ask some of the driving questions behind my interest in the new accounting paradigm:

> What would our economy look like if it fully valued *all* forms of capital, including human and natural capital? What if our economy were organised not around the lifeless abstractions of neoclassical economics and accountancy but around the biological realities of nature? What if Generally Accepted Accounting Practice booked natural and human capital not just as a free amenity in putative inexhaustible supply but as a finite and integrally valuable factor of production?

And what if we started to behave as if such principles were in force?

Dealing with non-financial value is the key accounting problem of the new age. It pertains both to the intangible assets of the information economy, such as instant brand recognition or an outstanding workforce, and to issues of sustainability, such as long-term access to clean water for a beverage company. There are two broad challenges in dealing with non-financial value: the first is how to find meaningful ways to measure it, the second is how to find a way of integrating it with financial information so that its effects on the bottom line and a company's long-term viability are evident to investors and others. The first challenge is being taken up by a number of independent groups; the second is being addressed by the International Integrated Reporting Council. But the first systematic attempts to measure both the intangible value of the information age and the factors that pertain to sustainability were made in GDP accounting by the United Nations in the revisions to its System of National Accounts (SNA) in 1993. We turn now to national accounting and the troubling implications of natural capital accounting.

BEYOND GDP: THE 'NEW' WEALTH OF NATIONS—AND THE GREY AREAS IN GREEN ACCOUNTING

Effectively measuring progress, wealth and well-being requires indices that are as appealing as GDP but also more inclusive than GDP—ones that incorporate social and environmental costs or benefits.

BEYOND GDP CONFERENCE, 2007

We need a revolution in measurements to go along with our digital technology and digital economy revolutions.

IRVING WLADAWSKY-BERGER, 2013

Economics cannot function as a reliable guide until natural capital is placed on the balance sheets of companies, countries, and the world.

PAUL HAWKEN, AMORY LOVINS AND L. HUNTER LOVINS, 1999

In 2007, the European Commission, together with the European Parliament, the Club of Rome, the Organisation for Economic Co-operation and Development (OECD) and the World Wildlife Fund, hosted a conference called 'Beyond GDP'. Their aim was to work out the most appropriate ways of measuring national progress, because the old measure—GDP— cannot address the global challenges of the twenty-first century, such as climate change, resource depletion and poverty. Opening the conference the president of the European Commission, José Manuel Barroso, said: 'We cannot face the future with the tools of the past. It's time to go beyond GDP.'

The following year, France's then president, Nicolas Sarkozy, established a commission to consider alternatives to GDP that would accommodate the conflicting demands of economic growth and environmental protection. Led by Nobel laureate Joseph Stiglitz, with economists Amartya Sen and Jean-Paul Fitoussi, the Commission on the Measurement of Economic Performance and Social Progress recommended at least seven different measures to assess national quality of life: health, education, environment, employment, material wellbeing, interpersonal connectedness and political engagement. Its report *Beyond GDP*, published in 2009, noted the critical importance of getting these measures right: 'What we measure affects what we do; and if our measurements are flawed, our decisions may be distorted.' It said:

47

Choices between promoting GDP and protecting the environment may be false choices
once environmental degradation is appropriately included in our measurement of
economic performance. So too, we often draw
inferences about what are good policies by
looking at what policies have promoted economic growth; but if our metrics of economic
growth are flawed, so too may be the inferences that we draw.

Forty years on, their findings capture in economic
terms the impassioned words spoken in March 1968 by
Senator Robert F. Kennedy about the Gross National
Product of the United States, which concluded: 'It measures everything, in short, except that which makes life
worthwhile.' The GDP measures only those things that
have monetary value—only those things that are legally
bought and sold. Or, in the officialese of the Australian
Bureau of Statistics:

The national accounts are a macroeconomic data set revolving around the central
economic concepts of production, income,
expenditure and wealth. They also comprise a
monetary system, and therefore rely substan-
tially on being able to measure the money
transactions taking place between the various
economic agents in a market economy.

While the OECD's 'beyond GDP' investigations led to its launch in 2011 of the 'Better Life Initiative'—an interactive website with eleven measures deemed essential to wellbeing, including health, education, environment, community and work–life balance, as well as more traditional categories such as income, housing and jobs—such information has yet to rival the policy-directing power of the single GDP statistic. In 2013, the OECD's annual economic report *Going for Growth* did for the first time explicitly advise that growth must not come at the expense of social and environmental objectives, conceding that in some cases 'growth policies are likely to clash with income distribution or environmental objectives', but it merely asked nations to bear these 'policy tradeoffs' in mind so their unintended consequences can be 'identified, measured and managed'.

The moves to go 'beyond GDP' are loaded with such nominal concessions to other values broadly summarised as 'wellbeing', and yet the GDP itself remains intact and dominates policy debates and news headlines. To date, only one measure has been proclaimed GDP's equal: natural capital. In 2012, the United Nations granted natural capital equal status to the GDP and formally launched an era of natural capital accounting. It is in this realm that accountants might be said to have the power to 'save the planet'—but the early manifestations of natural capital accounting, such as the United Kingdom's essays with 'biodiversity offsetting' and the debates that erupted around them, suggest the potential dangers this new field of accounting might pose to the natural world. As we shall see, while many environmentalists and ecologists have worked actively on behalf of such accounting, even they have found that its early practice opens a potentially treacherous new terrain in the hands of a government intent on economic growth.

In case we need reminding of the vast power wielded by national accounting statistics, the recent history of Greece provides a stark example. In February 2013, Andreas Georgiou, the head of its national statistical agency ELSTAT, was charged with falsifying Greece's 2009 official economic data: he allegedly manipulated the country's budget deficit figure as a percentage of GDP. After Georgiou became head of ELSTAT in 2010, the Greek GDP figures produced under his management were approved by the European statistics agency (Eurostat) and the International Monetary Fund for the first time in years. Since 2004, the Greek national statistics had come under intense scrutiny from Eurostat and were regularly given 'reservations', indicating that Eurostat doubted their validity. For his crime of producing figures approved by the statistics agency, Georgiou may be charged with treason. He said: 'That this is happening in the middle of the euro zone is a strange and surreal experience. I am being prosecuted for following the law.' Georgiou's more rigorously constructed, and lower, GDP meant that the 2009 Greek budget deficit rose from 13.4 per cent to 15.8 per cent of the GDP, which is a difference of massive consequence in terms of international politics and a nation's ability to borrow. The availability of bailout money from the European Union to save the shattered Greek economy depends on targets for reducing government spending and borrowing expressed as a ratio of the budget deficit to GDP. And so Georgiou's 'crime' demonstrates the power of the GDP in the twenty-first century: so much hinges on this single figure—including the economic viability of nations—that its alleged mismeasurement has become a treasonable offence.

IS GOVERNMENT PART OF A NATIONAL ECONOMY?

As we have seen, the work done since the 1920s to measure the wealth of the United Kingdom and United States by Colin Clark, Simon Kuznets, Richard Stone and others was the foundation for the accounts kept today by most nations on earth. The United Nations' embryonic System of National Accounts (SNA), the 56-page *System of National Accounts and Supporting Tables* published in 1952, is now a hefty 750 pages, having been periodically updated and expanded as the things that we measure and the ways that we categorise them have changed. The most recent SNA updates, in 1993 and 2008, address the intangible wealth of the information age and the unpriced wealth of nature.

But before we turn to this new wealth it is worth looking briefly at the changing perceptions of government's role in an economy to appreciate the somewhat arbitrary nature of the classifications national accounting makes. That government is part of a national economy is now received wisdom, but this was not always the case. Pioneering political economist Adam Smith (1723–90) excluded both government and services, including banking, from his conception of national income because he did not deem them to be productive. To a certain extent, Smith's view of government was a product of his times: until the twentieth century, not only did 'the economy' refer exclusively to the private sector, but the government's role in an economy was extremely limited. It acted only to fund wars and dispense justice. With the growth of cities in the nineteenth century, however, governments gradually began to extend their role by providing such goods as infrastructure and water to the new urban centres.

It was this very question—the place of government in a national economy—that was the most fiercely contested during the construction of national income measures in the United States in the 1930s. Did government spending, including that on war, contribute to national income or decrease it? For Simon Kuznets, it most definitely decreased it. But Kuznets was on the losing side of the debate. His error was in believing that by constructing national income measures he was designing tools to measure not just pure economic output but also national welfare. As he argued, an enlightened society—rather than a merely acquisitive one—would not consider government spending on armaments as contributing to national income. But with the outbreak of war in Europe in 1939 and the need to sell President Roosevelt's rearmament program to Congress, Kuznets was overruled by Milton Gilbert of the US Department of Commerce, and government was conceptually and statistically recruited into the economy as the 'ultimate consumer', regardless of its purpose. As we have seen, the theoretical underpinnings of this move were provided by Keynes' *General Theory*, which conceived of a whole economy in terms of its various economic 'sectors': households, businesses, governments and foreign economies.

Since the rise of Milton Friedman's free market economics in the 1980s, which advocated privatisation and small government, the actual role of government in national economic life has been slowly diminishing, increasingly outsourced to the private sector (although it remains conceptually part of a national economy). The shift in power from the public to the private domain has been one of the most striking features of the post-1970s information age—prompted by many things, but largely powered by two new global forces that transcend national boundaries and render them increasingly meaningless, governments increasingly impotent: the internet and global capital.

Finance and the SNA 1993

The changing statistical perceptions of the place of finance in a national economy are as telling as those regarding government. Just as he excluded government from his conception of national income, so Adam Smith excluded services, including banking, defining them as inherently unproductive. Smith's view of services was one held by most economists until the twentieth century. Services in general are a problem for GDP because (as with all industrial-age measures) it originated with the measuring of tangible economic resources, and the products of services are intangible. It is relatively easy to measure the value of physical output—stuff like cars, jeans and hamburgers—but much harder to measure the 'output' of teachers, doctors, actors or musicians. Here we meet again the conundrum of measures made for the industrial era being asked to gauge non-industrial value. And yet, even in 1937, just under half the jobs in the British and US economies were in the service sector. Today, services account for over two-thirds of GDP in OECD countries.

The SNA was revised in 1993 because of the increasing complexity of global economic and financial systems, and the myriad changes brought by rapid technological advances, including electronic transfer mechanisms and the networked computer. The redefinition of financial services is one of the more controversial of the revisions made by the SNA in 1993 and is especially significant for this story because it valorises the subsequent ascendancy of capital markets. In terms of national accounting, measuring the contribution of the finance sector is challenging—and changes to the way we measure it have altered our perceptions of its significance. As GDP historian Diane Coyle says, the view that the financial sector comprises an important part of the economy evolved alongside changes in the statistical methodology of its measurement.

In 1953, the SNA showed finance as making a negative or small positive contribution to the GDP. It was seen as an essentially unproductive activity because the interest earned on borrowing and lending was subtracted from the sector's final contribution to GDP. But the financial services industry boomed during the 1980s, and in the subsequent SNA revision a way was found to measure its contribution to a national economy. A new construct which is as inscrutable as its name is awkward, called 'financial intermediation services indirectly measured' (FISIM), was introduced to measure the value of financial services that are not explicitly priced. Its calculation is extraordinarily difficult: it works by separating out the interest earned on borrowing and on lending and defining each independently as a productive activity whose output can be measured, much like the production of Ford motor cars. In effect, it is a concept designed to measure the services banks are said to provide by taking on risk, and so in this new system, increases in risk-taking are recorded as increases in real growth in financial services. As a consequence of its inclusion in measures of national wealth, risk-taking behaviour becomes enormously desirable, glamorous even.

Coyle questions the extent to which assuming risk—rather than managing it—is in itself a productive activity:

'Taking risks is not a valuable service to the rest of the economy, although managing risk is.' It is one thing to assume a risk, and quite another to manage it, and at escalating levels, without running the entire international economy into the ground. But this subtle distinction is not made by FISIM. According to Coyle, because of the way we measure the financial sector following the 1993 SNA revisions, its contribution to the UK national economy has been overstated by at least one-fifth, and perhaps as much as a half. And this overstatement of its contribution to national wealth—to GDP and therefore, under the logic of traditional economics, to economic growth and jobs—has given the finance sector an unprecedented ability to direct government policy, especially regarding its own regulation, or, more significantly, its lack of regulation. Even the sober Coyle, whose view of the GDP is generally positive, argues that the statistical approach to valuing the finance sector is 'mistaken', especially given that during the global financial crisis the sector's contribution to national wealth was shown to have made big increases to GDP.

In 2011, the Bank of England acknowledged that the astronomical growth recorded in the UK financial sector in the decade before the 2008 crash—when it grew twice as fast as the UK economy as a whole—may have been overestimated: 'There is some evidence that financial services output grew less quickly over the recent past than the official data suggest.' This overstatement is significant because it suggested the sector's productivity was extraordinarily high (especially given that there was little corresponding growth in employment in the financial sector over the same period) and further enhanced its prestige and influence. And if this overstatement artificially raised the UK's GDP figures—so opaque are these measures that the Bank of England could not determine to what extent this might have been the case—it would have affected the government's monetary policy regarding inflation.

THE WEALTH OF ELECTRONIC INFORMATION—'INTELLECTUAL CAPITAL'

As it has for company accounts, the intangible wealth of the information age has also proved challenging to GDP measures. They cannot capture the value of the essential qualities of the age: the effects and pace of innovation, the complexities of the global networked economy and production chains, and the increasing proportion of intangibles that contribute to our economic wealth, including online activities with no price, such as YouTube videos, Wikipedia, or Linux software.

GDP measures do not capture the phenomenal improvement of computers and other electronic technology such as mobile phones since the 1990s. Because the prices of computers, laptops, notebooks, tablets and other digital devices have fallen dramatically—and this technology has therefore become widely available to most

people on earth (it is estimated that of the global population of some seven billion people, around six billion
have access to mobile phones and the internet)—the
vast growth in their sales and use is registered by GDP
figures as negligible or declining wealth, when clearly
the reverse is true.

The increasing availability of purely digital products
and services with zero price—such as online music,
search engines, apps, crowd-sourced information or
software, and social media—further scrambles GDP
figures, which measure only monetary transactions.
Massachusetts Institute of Technology's Erik Brynjolfsson
has demonstrated just how far GDP is from capturing
the value of the information age: according to US GDP
figures, the percentage of national wealth made up by
the information sector—software, TV and radio, movies,
telecommunications, data processing and publishing—has
remained unchanged for twenty-five years, at about 4 per
cent of GDP. In fact, Brynjolfsson says, over the last ten
years, access to free online services alone has been worth
an average of some US$300 billion a year. He estimates
that monetary measures of digital goods and services may
underestimate their value by as much as 95 per cent. To
capture this value, Brynjolfsson proposes measuring the
impact of digitisation according to the time consumers
spend: 'Consumers pay with time, not just money, and
where they choose to spend their limited time and attention online is a form of voting. Increasingly, the digital
economy is the "attention economy".' One early finding

using such measures shows that free goods and services contributed the equivalent of US$139 billion to the US economy in 2010, more than 1 per cent of the GDP. In 2009, Brynjolfsson and his colleague Adam Saunders captured the puzzle of the information age in their riff on Solow's paradox when they said: 'We see the influence of the information age everywhere, except in the GDP statistics.' The anomalies created by the advent of digital technology have prompted economic strategist Michael Mandel to suggest that our definition of economic output—or GDP—needs to be expanded to include not just goods and services but 'data', or information, as well.

Information technology has also proved confounding to 'development economics', a field that burgeoned with the advent of GDP accounting and the corresponding boom in statistics on economic growth. This branch of economics attempts to work out the factors that contribute to economic growth and development in order to foster them. Because the presence or absence of new technology seemed to explain variations between different countries' rates of economic growth, development economists began to ask how technology 'happened'. This led them to theorise about 'intellectual capital', which encompasses such things as education, skills, knowledge and ideas, as the 'cause' of technology, and so the interest in this new category—intellectual capital—was sparked.

The latest revisions to the SNA, made in 2008, have attempted to deal with the intangible value of the 'new economy', as it calls the information age. The SNA 2008 creates new categories of intellectual assets, including reclassifying 'research and development' from an expense to a capital asset. The output of research and development thus becomes 'intellectual property products'. This means that any expenditure on research and development in developing intellectual property, such as a song, movie, cancer drug or piece of software, is counted as investment—and so enhances profits and hence GDP—rather than a business cost. Before these changes, spending on R&D and on the creation of entertainment and artistic originals was not measured in GDP. As the SNA 2008 says, many of these assets, 'often seen as a hallmark of the "new economy", are associated with the establishment of property rights over knowledge in one form or another'.

The wealth of nature—'natural capital'

In 2012, nature was given the greatest honour traditional economics could grant it: it was formally declared 'natural capital' and brought into the embrace of economic life when the United Nations System of Environmental–Economic Accounting (SEEA) was officially adopted as a statistical standard and natural capital was given equal status to the GDP. Although the SEEA does not (yet) provide monetary measures for nature, instead measuring it in physical terms (such as by volume of water), this idea of natural capital has brought with it new financial concepts and made possible their pursuit in national economic policy, as we shall see. Nature is now so big in the eyes of global finance and economics that at Rio+20 (the United Nations Conference on Sustainable Development held in Rio de Janeiro in 2012, twenty years after the first Earth Summit was held there) it was given its own 'Natural Capital Declaration' (NCD). Launched by the United Nations and the Global Canopy Programme (which protects forests as natural capital), the NCD was signed by the chief executive officers of forty financial institutions. Its purpose is to integrate natural capital reporting into private-sector accounting—into the realm of the corporation. But it was at the national level that the importance of such environmental accounting was first acknowledged, when in 1993 the United Nations first recommended that 'satellite accounts' for the natural environment be added to regular GDP accounts.

One of the serious problems with GDP measures is that they have absorbed the concepts of Keynes' *General Theory*, which sees the economy in terms of flows—of income and expenditure—rather than stocks, of capital. This has enormous consequences for the maintenance of 'infrastructure', both manufactured and, increasingly urgently, natural: it encourages us to use it without maintaining it. Unlike businesses, nations are not required to set aside an amount for the depreciation of their capital assets. This is what authors Paul Hawken, Amory Lovins and L. Hunter Lovins are referring to in *Natural Capitalism* when they argue that our current economic system 'liquidates its capital and calls it income'. Just as we are using up our stocks of existing manufactured infrastructure, like transport systems, buildings and sewage systems, so we are using the earth's stock of nature—such as fresh water, soil and clean air—without guarding against its depletion. This leads us to the greatest accounting omission of all: the wealth of nature.

In terms of nature, the main challenge accountants face is in defining, quantifying and valuing its currently unpriced contribution to the economy. As we saw in the last chapter, to make this conceptually possible, ecological economists have applied to nature economic terms such as 'capital', 'goods' and 'services', giving us concepts like 'natural capital' and 'ecosystem goods and services' to understand the way the environment feeds our economic wealth. For the moment we will accept these terms in order to explore how GDP accountants intend to use them, but we will also be asking what the implications are—for nature and for ourselves—of translating nature into such cold hard abstractions.

Following discussions about sustainable development after the release of the Brundtland Report in 1987 and in response to requests made at the 1992 Rio Earth Summit, in 1993 the United Nations published its first environmental accounting guidelines. These embryonic guidelines—the System of Integrated Environmental and Economic Accounting—recommended that the GDP and other systems of national income measurement include supplementary environmental and social information. The system they outlined was based on approaches to environmental accounting pioneered by the UN Environment Programme and the World Bank. The guidelines were issued as a work in progress and opened to a long process of global consultation which led to their further development and enshrining as a statistical standard in 2012.

Many countries responded to the United Nations' 1993 recommendations by attempting to expand their national accounts to include such satellite accounts. The United States was one such country. But when it published its first environmental satellite accounts in 1994, adjusting its GDP for the depletion of its stocks of oil and other non-renewable resources, their downgraded view of US wealth proved so controversial and so politically explosive that Congress shut down the program almost the moment the revised numbers were published. US economist Everett Ehrlich highlighted the Orwellian nature of this move when he said that by putting a stop to the US environmental accounts, 'Congress made thinking about a Green GDP a thought crime.'

But thinking about a so-called 'Green GDP' did not go away.

Millennium Ecosystem Assessment

Six years later, in 2000, UN Secretary-General Kofi Annan established the Millennium Ecosystem Assessment in response to demands from scientists and policy-makers who wanted to calculate the value of the world's ecosystems and bring the vast amount of new scientific research on ecosystems out of specialised journals and into mainstream policy debate. Taking its cue from ecological economics, the assessment focused on 'ecosystem services', which it defined as 'the benefits people obtain from ecosystems'. These are divided into four categories: provisioning services such as food, water, timber and fibre; regulating services that affect climate, floods, disease, wastes and water quality; cultural services that provide recreational, aesthetic and spiritual benefits; and supporting services such as soil formation, photosynthesis and nutrient recycling.

The assessment's report *Living Beyond Our Means: Natural assets and human well-being*, published in 2005, found that over the past 50 years we have changed the earth's ecosystems 'more rapidly and extensively than in any comparable period of time in human history', mostly to supply our increasing demands for food, fresh water, timber, fuel and fibre. But only now are the corresponding costs of our demands on nature becoming clear. And not only have we failed to see the costs of destroying the earth's ecosystems, but these costs are often felt most acutely far from the places where their benefits are enjoyed. As the report remarked: 'Shrimp on the dinner plates of Europeans may well have started life in a South Asian pond built in place of mangrove swamps—weakening a natural barrier to the sea and making coastal communities more vulnerable.'

The authors found that unless we change our attitudes and actions, we will continue to deplete the natural world. They also found that much of the technology and knowledge needed to reduce our impact on ecosystems is already available, but that we are unlikely to use it until we stop thinking of ecosystems as free and limitless—in other words, until their full value is accounted for. The Millennium Ecosystem Assessment found that the degradation and depletion of our ecosystems was a problem of accounting. The challenge lies in finding new measures for the things we have never before taken into account. The report states: 'In the midst of this unprecedented period of spending the Earth's natural bounty . . . it is time to check the accounts. That is what this assessment has done, and it is a sobering statement with much more red than black on the balance sheet.' In order to protect the 'natural capital assets' that we have run down to reap the benefits 'from our engineering of the planet', the report concluded that we must put a value on nature in all its multiple roles in human life, from the economic to the aesthetic and spiritual.

The Economics of Ecosystems and Biodiversity

In 2007, a global initiative called The Economics of Ecosystems and Biodiversity (TEEB) was launched to do just this. Led by economist and banker Pavan Sukhdev, it was proposed by a group of environment ministers at a meeting in Potsdam, Germany, who were inspired by the Millennium Ecosystem Assessment and by the British government's 2006 *Stern Review on the Economics of Climate Change*, authored by economist Nicholas Stern, which made an economic case for early action on climate change. The ministers wanted to make an equivalent case for the economic valuing of the earth's ecosystems. Hosted by the UN Environment Programme, TEEB aims to provide both a better understanding of the economic value of ecosystem services and the practical tools to allow us to account for this value.

Sukhdev has been promoting TEEB around the world since its inception. In a TED talk given in July 2011, he spoke of his concern that the enormous costs of degrading ecosystems and biodiversity are invisible because they do not appear in our economic accounts. He said: 'The bad news is, Mother Nature's back office isn't working yet, so those invoices don't get issued. We need to do something about this problem.' In other words, we need to account for nature.

When Sukhdev was recruited to lead TEEB in 2008, he was working at Deutsche Bank in India, where he had founded a similar project, the Green Accounting for Indian States Project. In 2000, Sukhdev and some colleagues became concerned about India's 'gung-ho' attitude to GDP growth, an attitude inspired by and which hoped to replicate China's then growth of a remarkable 8.9 per cent per annum. Sukhdev and his associates believed that such economic growth would bring more costs than benefits to society. 'So we decided to do a massive calculation—and started producing green accounts for

India and its states.' This project gave rise to Sukhdev's interest in—and belief in the power of—green accounting, and eventually led him to TEEB.

TEEB's interim report was published in 2008, just when the meltdown of the global economy was making headlines with losses of some US$2.5 trillion worth of financial capital. TEEB's report showed that we—and the global economy—were losing natural capital at a comparable rate: around US$2–4 trillion worth of natural capital per annum. Here was a problem of equal magnitude to and with far greater long-term consequences than the global financial crisis—and yet policymakers have been slow to act on it.

This is enormously frustrating for Sukhdev, who both understands the urgency of the ecological problem and believes in the potential of accounting to address it. As he says, 'Economics has become the currency of policy', and he believes we must convert the problem of our use of nature into this currency if we are to solve it. As an example of the way this can make nature economically visible, Sukhdev tells a story of shrimp farms in Thailand. Commercial shrimp farming, which requires clearing mangroves, at first appears to be a more profitable use of land than leaving the mangroves intact: the annual profits of shrimp farming are US$9632 per hectare, while the annual private profits of the mangroves are US$584 per hectare. But once government subsidies to shrimp farmers equivalent to US$8412 per hectare are removed, profits fall to US$1220 per hectare. And when the coastal destruction caused by the shrimp farms is priced, the numbers become very different. The shrimp farms are now worth minus US$9318 (after subtracting the public costs of restoring the mangroves after five years, when the farms are abandoned because their production declines), and the mangroves are worth US$12,392 (US$10,821 per hectare for coastal protection against storms, US$987 per hectare for fish nurseries and US$584 per hectare for wood and forest products). For Sukhdev, this example demonstrates that the problem of our destruction of nature is in part due to our failure to distinguish between public benefits and private profits—and that private profits take precedence over public benefits because the latter are not priced. As he argues, seen through the lens of public benefit— rather than the narrower one of private profit—in this case of Thailand's mangroves, conservation clearly makes more sense.

WEALTH ACCOUNTING AND THE VALUATION OF ECOSYSTEM SERVICES

According to World Bank Group Vice President Rachel Kyte, natural capital accounting is a perfect fit with the bank's core mission of 'ending poverty and boosting shared prosperity'. In 2010, the World Bank launched its own initiative to develop natural capital accounting. Called Wealth Accounting and the Valuation of Ecosystem Services (WAVES), it was designed to promote sustainable development by encouraging natural capital accounting, and to help develop ecosystem accounts, in the belief that they would ensure that both development planning and national economic accounts consider natural resources. By 2013, eight countries—Costa Rica, Botswana, Colombia, Madagascar, the Philippines, Guatemala, Indonesia and Rwanda—had signed up to WAVES and were developing natural capital accounts for resources like forests, water and minerals.

At the national level, natural capital accounting has spawned its own world of complex environmental–economic transactions. Among them is a system called 'payments for ecosystem (or environmental) services' (PES), a broad term for a wide range of economic arrangements that attempt to assign a price to ecosystem or environmental services in order to conserve them. PES was devised to offer landowners incentives to manage their land to provide an environmental service, such as maintaining forest cover. The longest-running ecosystem services scheme is the Conservation Reserve Program in the United States, which was officially established in 1985 but dates to the 1950s. Under this scheme the US government pays out over US$1.5 billion a year to landowners such as farmers to encourage them to protect endangered wildlife habitats and environmentally sensitive land. Like so many of these initiatives designed to account for nature, it appears to work in nature's favour, as the experience of Costa Rica also demonstrates.

Costa Rica and payments for ecosystem services

In 1997, Costa Rica became a pioneer in the developing world when it introduced its own payments for ecosystem services scheme, *Pago por Servicios Ambientales* (PSA), to pay landowners for the services provided by the forests on their land. The Forestry Law of 1996 on which Costa Rica's PSA program is based defines ecosystem services as 'those offered by the forests and forest plantations for the protection and enhancement of the environment'. The four main services its forests provide are greenhouse gas mitigation, watershed protection, biodiversity conservation and preservation of scenic beauty. Home to an extraordinary variety of plant and animal life— more than 500,000 species, or almost 4 per cent of the world's estimated number of species—Costa Rica is one of the twenty countries in the world with the greatest biodiversity. But during the 1970s, with the fast-food industry booming, it effectively bore much of the social and environmental cost of our '$200 hamburgers' when it cleared vast tracts of forest to make way for cattle ranches to supply the growing world demand for beef. For the next ten years, Costa Rica had the highest deforestation rate per capita in the world. To help maintain the country's forest cover, the government established national parks. But this was not enough.

In the mid 1990s, Costa Rica's Carlos Manuel Rodríguez—then director of national parks and later vice-minister (1998–2000) and minister (2002–06) of energy and environment—attempted to persuade the government to act more decisively to preserve the country's forests. Initially he convinced the government to use such tools as subsidies, tax relief and payments to encourage the preservation of the forests. But the enormous financial cost of these strategies meant that they were not politically feasible for long, especially without any way of measuring the benefits gained by the forests' preservation. Without such metrics, the finance ministry could not see the value of maintaining healthy ecosystems and the environmental services they provided.

Rodríguez realised that forest conservation was only possible if the value of the standing forest was seen to be equivalent to the money lost by not clearing it for cattle ranching. He had to start translating nature into the language of economics: 'We needed to generate some information about the economic benefits of protecting nature.' So he and his colleagues started to look for ways of putting an economic value on the standing forests. They soon saw that they could estimate the financial contribution of the protected forest areas from the amount of income Costa Rica was earning from ecotourism and also by calculating the value of the water the forests preserved for its hydroelectricity industry. Armed with economic valuations of the forests, Rodríguez returned to the finance minister accompanied by some economists. As Rodríguez later explained to environmentalist Tony Juniper: 'When [the finance minister] saw these guys with me, he began to talk to them and they were speaking the same language. This was a turning point, and now the economics of nature is institutionalized in Costa Rica.'

Costa Rica's PSA program is funded by government and private interests. It receives between US$10 and US$45 per hectare annually from businesses that want to protect water services, and the government matches these amounts using funds from various sources, including a fossil fuel tax and a water tariff. More than 7000 private landowners receive the payments, which range from around US$41 per hectare a year for forest regeneration to over US$980 per hectare over a five-year period for new forest plantations. The results have been impressive. Not only have Costa Rica's forests and natural areas been protected since the launch of the program in 1997, but large tracts of ruined land have also been restored. In the late 1980s, only 21 per cent of Costa Rica was covered by forests; by 2010 that had risen to 52 per cent. This was accompanied by improvements in the country's living standards and energy savings. In 1985, only half of Costa Rica's energy came from renewable sources. By 2010, this figure had risen to 92 per cent.

The success of Costa Rica's early exercise in valuing nature set it on the path to accounting for natural capital. It helped its policymakers to realise that, as Rodríguez puts it, 'there is no long-term economic growth without protecting the health of the ecosystems. If we can show that economic and social health is dependent on the health of nature, then most politicians see the case we are making'. For Costa Rica, the benefits of showing the interdependency of nature, society and the economy seem clear. Juniper, who has worked with Rodríguez on a series of sustainability programs with the World Bank, calls Costa Rica's experience with PES 'a kind of integrated reporting, applied to a nation state' and says that the power of such monetary accounting for nature 'is clear in the outcomes seen in this remarkable country'. While its program has been criticised for favouring large absentee landowners as opposed to small landowners and for being based on short-term contracts of five years, it has nevertheless fostered conservation among private landowners and made forests valuable in their own right.

Endorsing natural capital

~

As we have seen, the question of how we protect nature against rampant economic development has become so critical in terms of national accounting that in 2012, after almost two decades of consultation, the United Nations adopted a new international standard to give natural capital equal status to the GDP: the System of Environmental–Economic Accounting (SEEA). Two earlier versions had been published, the first as mentioned in 1993, but neither had the status of an international standard. The Australian Bureau of Statistics, which along with many other bodies contributed to the new standard's development, called it 'a significant milestone in the on-going development of information to support the needs of government, industry and the general public in the area of environmental policy'. The sorts of policy areas to which the SEEA is designed to contribute include energy use, water consumption, depletion of natural resources, mitigating and adapting to climate change, green growth and solid waste management.

The SEEA is the result of the growing realisation among economists, politicians and other policymakers that economic activity affects the environment and vice versa. It allows a wide range of disparate data to be brought together for the first time and translated into various statistics that highlight the connections between the environment and the economy. The final, official version—the SEEA *Central Framework*—was published in February 2014. The framework, its concepts and classifications are consistent with those of the SNA economic accounts so that the two sets of accounts can be compared and used jointly to direct economic and environmental policy.

As with the development of comprehensive national accounts from the 1930s, this first comprehensive environmental and economic standard has been designed in response to a crisis—the unchecked depletion of natural resources, damage to ecosystems, greenhouse gas emissions and pollution—and with a particular policy aim in view: sustainability. And given that the issues of the twenty-first century hinge on the interaction of economic activity with the natural world, the new measures have been designed to focus on this relationship. The SEEA does not produce one number as GDP accounts do. Rather, it is a broad, flexible system which produces a variety of measures and indicators that can be applied to many different circumstances. It covers a wide range of natural and economic phenomena, including water, minerals, energy, timber, fish, soil, land and ecosystems, pollution and waste, production, consumption and investment. The environmental information is measured in physical terms but is not given a monetary value. Instead, it is their shared framework that allows the new environmental accounts to be integrated with the economic information for the first time.

The United Nations expects that countries will adopt the framework gradually and according to their own policies. There is no imperative (as there was with the implementation of the Marshall Plan) compelling various nations to construct such accounts. As yet no government has made an integrated set of national accounts, one that clearly shows the relation between the economy and the environment. But since Rio+20, change is in the air. Governments have started to commit to valuing ecosystem services and to measuring natural capital and using it to guide policy. By the end of 2013, 68 countries around the world were working to measure ecosystem services in various ways, from research to policy development. But these moves to account for nature have been far from universally endorsed, both in principle and, as with the UK's early forays into implementing 'biodiversity offsetting', in practice.

THE PEOPLE'S SUMMIT AND
RESISTANCE TO NATURAL CAPITAL

~

While the logic of natural capital accounting appears persuasive from the point of view of Raj Patel's $200 hamburger and Pavan Sukhdev's Thai shrimp farms, its implications have been widely criticised. Such moves to price and therefore internalise market externalities are seen to be consistent with the neoliberal agenda of privatisation and market rule. Essentially, critics assert that this approach to the environmental crisis concedes to the increasing dominance of financial capital as the organising principle of life on earth, of markets rather than governments as the drivers of change. They see natural capital accounting as a twenty-first-century version of the eighteenth-century British enclosure movement (when traditional rights to common land were subsumed by the rights of individual owners) and a further extension of the market into the realm of nature.

In 2012, during the official United Nations Rio+20 Earth Summit, a rival meeting, called the People's Summit, was held to protest against the United Nations' and World Bank's conception of nature as capital and their idea of a 'green economy'. It also aimed to canvas ways other than green economics of responding to the many related crises we face in the new millennium: ecological, financial, social, political, and particularly issues related to poverty, food and energy. The UN Environment Programme has defined the green economy as one whose growth in income and employment is driven by investments in systems to reduce carbon emissions and pollution, enhance energy and resource efficiency, and prevent the loss of biodiversity and ecosystems. A green economy is also supposed to 'maintain, enhance, and, where necessary, rebuild natural capital . . . especially for poor people whose livelihoods and security depend strongly on nature'. While 'maintaining, enhancing and rebuilding' natural capital sound like laudable activities, they contain a world of new meaning, especially the idea of 'rebuilding' natural capital, which has spawned the concept of 'ecosystem (or biodiversity) offsets', as will be examined below.

Some two hundred groups gathered at the People's Summit, ranging from Greenpeace and Bill McKibben's global climate movement 350.org to unions, indigenous groups, religious groups, Oxfam, the international peasant movement Via Campesina, Brazil's national movement of *catadores* (garbage collectors) and the survivors of the 2011 Fukushima nuclear disaster. They were all frustrated by the lack of progress that had been made in responding to the environmental crisis since the inaugural UN Earth Summit in 1992. While the 1992 summit saw the birth of the UN Commission on Sustainable Development, in the commission's first twenty years, the People's Summit pointed out, biodiversity losses and climate change have only accelerated, and the need to address them has become even more urgent. The two major achievements of Rio 1992's Declaration on

Environment and Development—the UN Framework Convention on Climate Change (signed by all major countries) and its Convention on Biological Diversity— have had little impact on the rates of global ecological destruction and resource degradation, or on the rise of greenhouse gas levels, which have increased by over 40 per cent since 1990.

The People's Summit was also concerned by the dominance of private interests in the green economy. While the original Earth Summit had acknowledged the role of privatisation and neoliberalism in contributing to the threats humanity faces, the People's Summit argued that Rio+20 was now presenting these same forces as part of the solution to these problems. As their Final Declaration candidly put it:

> At Rio+20 we have seen the repetition of the failed script of false solutions proposed by the very same actors who have caused the global crisis. As this crisis deepens, corporations continue to advance in a growing attack on the rights of the peoples, democracy and nature, seizing control over the commons of humanity to save the economic–financial system.

It argued that the 'so-called "green economy" is just another facet of the current financial phase of capitalism', which is characterised by the concentration of ownership, the overstimulation of consumption, the exacerbation of private–public debt, carbon and biodiversity markets, public–private partnerships and increased foreign ownership of land. According to the People's Summit, multinational corporations have not only increasingly taken control of local natural resources and ecosystems, which they fear will be further privatised under the new regime of natural capital, but of the United Nations itself. The United Nations has indeed increasingly turned to collaborations with corporations and the private sector, which is as much as anything an acknowledgement of the vast resources private interests now command. The declaration advocated the power of 'organized and mobilized' people to free the world from the control of corporations and financial capital.

The declaration also denounced the historical environmental debt incurred mostly on 'the oppressed peoples of the world' and argued it should be assumed by the highly industrialised countries, because they are the ones who caused today's multiple planetary crises. As well as polluting their own lands, rich countries also outsource their pollution, which according to Raj Patel is estimated to cost poor countries more than US$4.32 trillion in ecological damage. This dwarfs the entire third-world debt owed by poor countries to rich ones, which is only US$1.8 trillion. The fruits of this environmental debt are mostly enjoyed by people in wealthy nations (such as the shrimp on the dinner plates in Europe), but the costs are usually 'paid' in ecological disasters by the nations who can least afford them, such as the desertification of Bolivia, the mudslides of Pakistan and the deforestation of the Amazon and Indonesia. In this context, the protection of land rights and compensation for ecosystem services (despite its connection to natural capital accounting) were considered important by the People's Summit, as was the need to recognise the cultures and knowledge of indigenous peoples. As Waratan from Brazil's Pataxó tribe said: 'Native people preserve nature . . . Native culture needs to be preserved like the environment.'

The most substantial alternative response offered by the People's Summit to Rio+20's promotion of green economics was the idea of creating legal rights for nature, an initiative that has been most comprehensively led at a national level by Bolivia. Speaking at the UN General Assembly in April 2011, Bolivia's UN ambassador Pablo Solón argued that the environmental crisis presents us with a stark choice: 'Humanity finds itself at a crossroads: we can commercialise nature through the green economy or recognise the rights of nature.' Bolivia has chosen the latter path.

NATURAL CAPITAL AND
BIODIVERSITY OFFSETTING

The United Kingdom is one country leading the way with the former approach. At the Rio+20 forum in June 2012, UK Deputy Prime Minister Nick Clegg said that his government was committed to including natural capital in its national accounts by 2020 and had established a Natural Capital Committee to provide advice on the state of the UK's natural capital. Two months after Clegg's commitment to natural capital accounting at Rio+20, journalist and environmental activist George Monbiot wrote a scathing attack in the *Guardian* on the idea of natural capital and the concept of biodiversity offsets.

Like many of those at the People's Summit, Monbiot sees the new regime of natural capital accounting as nothing more than an extension of the enclosure movement, a means of 'privatizing and commodifying' those parts of nature that still lie beyond the market: 'nature is being valued and commodified so that it can be exchanged for cash.' And like many of its critics in Rio, Monbiot also contends that this new order asks us to believe the unbelievable, that those responsible for the crisis in nature might be able to fix it: 'Commodification, economic growth, financial abstractions, corporate power: aren't these the processes driving the world's environmental crisis? Now we are told that to save the biosphere we need more of them.'

In August 2012, Monbiot's wrath was prompted by a series of UK initiatives to account for nature. The first, begun in 2009, was the National Ecosystem Assessment, which released its report in June 2011. It analysed the value of the UK's natural environment, taking account of the 'economic, health and social benefits we get from nature'. As the world's first such assessment to be conducted on a fully national scale, it put the UK in the vanguard of the natural capital movement. While acknowledging that putting monetary values on nature is 'theoretically challenging' and that some ecosystems may 'in fact be infinite in value', it found that inland wetlands provide benefits to water quality worth some £1.5 billion a year to the UK. It estimated that bees and other pollinators are worth £430 million a year to British agriculture, and the 'amenity benefits of living close to rivers, coasts and other wetlands' is worth some £1.3 billion a year. According to the report, these costings show 'that the tendency to focus only on the market value of resources we can use and sell, such as timber, crops and fisheries, has led to the decline of some ecosystems and habitats through pollution, over-exploitation, and land conversion'.

The report was followed by the launch in November 2011 of the UK Ecosystem Markets Task Force, led by businessman Ian Cheshire, to explore the business possibilities of 'green goods, services, products, investment vehicles and markets which value and protect nature's services'. The aim of the task force was, as Cheshire put it, to find 'new ways for business to profit from valuing and protecting nature', including the vast savings that can be made by using raw materials and energy more efficiently. In May 2012, the Natural Capital Committee was launched with the aim of helping the government understand how the state of the natural environment affects economic performance and individual wellbeing, as well as advising it on how to manage its national environmental wealth.

In his response, Monbiot acknowledged that the rationale behind this thinking is 'coherent and plausible': 'Business currently treats the natural world as if it is worth nothing. Pricing nature and incorporating that price into the cost of goods and services creates an economic incentive for its protection.' But he railed against the implications of thinking about nature as 'natural capital'; of natural processes as 'ecosystem services', existing only to serve us; of forests, hills and river catchments as 'green infrastructure'; and of biodiversity and habitats as 'asset classes' within an 'ecosystem market'. For Monbiot, these phrases are a sure sign that these various manifestations of the natural world will be assigned a price, and 'all of them will become exchangeable'.

This potential exchangeability—in which nature and ecosystems become 'fungible', or tradeable—is something Monbiot especially opposes, particularly where it concerns the idea of ecosystem offsetting, an offshoot of natural capital accounting. He rejects ecosystem offsetting in principle, calling it 'replacing habitats you trash with new ones created elsewhere'. And if the European Union's use of carbon offsetting is any guide to how ecosystem offsetting will unfold, Monbiot also opposes ecosystem offsetting in practice. He attributes the breakdown of Europe's Emissions Trading Scheme in April 2013 (following the European Parliament's rejection of a proposal to make the burning of fossil fuels by companies

more expensive) to the failure of governments—swayed
by the intervention of business—to put a proper price on
carbon. And he fears the same will happen in the sphere
of ecosystem offsets, especially because the commodification of nature paves the way for it to be colonised
by financial services and traders, which opens up the
possibility of financial speculation in nature.

That this is indeed part of the UK's plan for nature
is indicated in the report by its Ecosystem Markets Task
Force on the new business opportunities the National
Ecosystem Assessment will make possible. Among the
eight main types of business opportunities—which
include ecosystem offsetting and payment for ecosystem
services—are 'financial and legal services'. Financial
services would make it possible to invest in ecosystem
products and attract a return through various financial
manoeuvres such as offsetting and permit trading, or
natural commodity markets; and legal services would
create the necessary legal structures to privatise ecosystems, to make possible their legal ownership so their
goods and services can enter the market.

In August 2012, Monbiot warned against the
destructive possibilities hidden in the ecospeak of 'ecosystem services'. He argued that although the government
says these ecosystem offsets 'must not become a licence
to destroy', once the principle is established, nature will
become as tradeable as everything else. His fears were
tested soon after in a case of nightingales in Kent.

Nightingales, forests and ecosystem services

By December 2012, Medway Council in Kent had slated a housing development for Lodge Hill, which has one of the UK's highest concentrations of nightingales, a threatened species whose numbers dropped by 50 per cent between 1998 and 2011. The development would require destroying the nightingales' forest, despite the fact that similar destruction elsewhere had exacerbated the decline in England's nightingale population. In the new era of natural capital accounting, the developers were required to adhere to the idea of ecosystem offsets by considering alternative accommodation for the nightingales. In its November 2012 report on the proposed development, commissioned by Medway Council, the Environment Bank (a private company that brokers biodiversity offsetting agreements for developers) found that 'offsetting could work in principle for nightingales in Kent—it is technically feasible but it is neither straightforward nor guaranteed'. In other words, the Environment Bank found that in principle the nightingales' existing forest habitat could be destroyed if another similar forest habitat were created elsewhere (should such a reconstruction even be possible), but that such a manoeuvre was difficult and not assured of success. Such offsetting would require 300 to 400 other hectares—'of the right sort, of the right quality, of the right size, with the right management, and in the right place'—to be found and revamped as a nightingale habitat in the hope that the nightingales might settle down there. In response, Monbiot argued:

> Accept the principle of biodiversity offsetting and you accept the idea that place means nothing. That nowhere is to be valued in its own right any more, that everything is exchangeable for everything else, and nothing can be allowed to stand in the way of the graders and degraders.

Eventually, however, Medway Council's housing strategy was found to be 'unsound' when the government's wildlife watchdog Natural England declared Lodge Hill to be a Site of Special Scientific Interest because of the nightingales. As a result, the development plan was rejected in 2013 by a government inspector. The decision sparked enormous protests—especially about the loss of the £27 million that the housing strategy had apparently cost to prepare—and claims that the nightingales who frequented the forest only stayed for four months a year. Rodney Chambers of the Medway Council said it was 'very disappointing news to receive from unelected quangocrats at Natural England', and added that 'this won't just cost public money—it will cost local people 5,000 much needed new homes, and 5,000 jobs'.

The concept of biodiversity offsetting was designed to deter development by adding to the monetary costs of environmental destruction, and in the case of the

Lodge Hill development it seems to have worked in the nightingales' favour. But by formalising the idea that one habitat can be replaced by another elsewhere, the concept of biodiversity offsetting can also become the means by which to justify environmental destruction. The policy ignores the fact that habitats are unique and place-specific and that ecosystems are extremely difficult to re-create. It also ignores the interrelationships of human communities with natural ones, and the rich histories and human cultures that are embedded in them. These factors are made clear in a second case of proposed biodiversity offsetting in the UK.

In March 2014, motorway developers Extra MSA Group submitted a planning application to build a petrol station, hotel, restaurants and car park to service a motorway near Sheffield. As part of their development, they would destroy some twelfth-century woodland known as Smithy Wood. To offset the destruction, they have pledged to replace the 21 acres (8.5 hectares) of ancient woodland with 60,000 new trees in a new 39-acre (16-hectare) space open for public recreation. The proposed project is a crucial test case for the new principle of biodiversity offsetting. It is being fiercely contested by conservationists and locals who argue that the woodland is priceless and irreplaceable. As well as its value for its own sake and that of the plants and animals it houses, the wood also has a rich and unique heritage. When Monbiot wrote about the case in April 2014, he spoke of its cultural value: 'For local people, Smithy Wood is freighted with stories. Among the trees you can imagine your way into another world.' But in this new era of biodiversity offsetting, the developers are making a case for its destruction, because they will 'replace' it elsewhere. The decision on this development is yet to be made, but it shows that what was designed to be a means of safeguarding nature is potentially an opportunity for developers to destroy it.

Monbiot regards the very idea of giving the natural world financial values as a sign of defeat, a way of framing an argument for the inherent value of nature and its preservation in the terms of the opposition, those who seek to destroy it in the name of economic development. He writes:

> Costing nature tells us that it possesses no inherent value; that it is worthy of protection only when it performs services for us; that it is replaceable. You demoralize and alienate those who love the natural world while reinforcing the values of those who don't.

Monbiot's argument against biodiversity offsetting stopped me in my tracks. It fed into my growing misgivings about how nature would benefit from its reconception as natural capital in the six capitals model and sparked a dawning realisation of the full implications—moral, aesthetic and spiritual—of these persuasive (in economic terms and in the context of the planet's 200-year industrial history) moves to price nature in order to save it. The very fact that natural capital accounting is being driven by organisations designed to foster financial capital, such as financial institutions, corporations and accounting bodies, should have suggested to me its potential to serve interests other than nature's. But I was in thrall to the $200 hamburger and the way business externalities allow us to destroy the planet by blinding us to the real costs of our food, our t-shirts, our smartphones, of everything we buy. From that moment, the concept of natural capital was for me filled with ambiguity and opened a complex moral and metaphysical terrain which demanded the most finely calibrated negotiations between earthy pragmatism and the moral refusal of financial capital's rule. It brought home to me the full force of Keynes' 1933 remark—'once we allow ourselves to be disobedient to the test of an accountant's profit, we have begun to change our civilisation'—and of the true bankruptcy of that civilisation, which has so lost its bearings in the universe that its only apparent common measure of value, and of right or wrong action, is the rule of money. If we make ourselves and the planet over in the name of financial capital we might find one day that we have nothing left at all. Just a stash of electronic dollars. For me the prospect of green accounting was now irrevocably tainted with grey.

THE GREY AREAS IN GREEN ACCOUNTING

~

Long-time environmental activist Tony Juniper has found that natural capital accounting and its offspring, such as biodiversity offsetting, have the power to make real change. In August 2012, Juniper responded in the *Guardian* to Monbiot's attack on what Juniper termed the 'new discourse' on natural capital. Calling Monbiot's arguments a 'one-sided picture' and 'a dangerous game', he wrote with the frustration of one who had endured years of relatively fruitless campaigning for the environment and has found in the moves to account for nature a tool with teeth. While Monbiot's 25 years of environmental activism have taught him that the only real change comes from organised people power on a large scale, Juniper has been working closely with accountants because he has found that their numbers give him the robust language he had been searching for—a language that, unlike moral arguments, has the force to sway the sceptics who consider nature 'an economically costly distraction that gets in the way of economic "growth"'.

For Juniper, there is no alternative for the preservation of the natural world other than the path of natural capital. He explains: 'I have spent the past 25 years campaigning for nature for its own sake, because it is beautiful, because it should exist for its own reasons and because we have no right to destroy it', but in those years he has found that not everyone agrees with that line of thinking, especially those set on development and economic growth.

And in the decades during which Juniper attempted to convince them otherwise, they continued their ceaseless construction, mining and clearing. He now believes that strategy was a road to destruction—'more forests are cleared, oceans polluted and greenhouse gases released'— and says that we cannot continue with our 'ideological purity preserved'. Knowing that the verbal rhetoric of conservationists, steeped in beauty and ethics, is impotent against the numerical rhetoric of economic growth and development, he argues that the only alternative is to 'open a new discourse, one that requires the sceptics to meaningfully engage, and on the field where future environmental battles will be won and lost—the field of economics'. And so he has adopted the language of economics because it is economists, not environmentalists, who have misunderstood the real costs of growth on a finite planet, and the only way to get this news to economists is by speaking their own language. These two worlds are so alien to each other—economics steeped in economic growth, environmentalism in conservation— that they need a new language in order to communicate. The terminology of natural capital and environmental accounting gives these two worlds a way to speak to each other for the first time. So while for Monbiot this concession to economics is already a diminishment of the beauty of nature, for Juniper it is nature's only hope, as the experience of Costa Rica attests.

But while Juniper is an advocate of biodiversity off-setting and sees its potential as 'a tool of great benefit', he is also aware of the dangers opened up by this new paradigm of green accounting. In June 2014, he commented on the potential misuse of biodiversity offsetting by governments in relation to the Smithy Wood case, saying: 'Where there is no alternative, biodiversity offsets can be useful. But offsetting can be abused. If governments want to use this as a window-dressing for a pro-growth agenda, as I fear that Britain does, it can be very dangerous.'

Many environmental economists who advocate biodiversity offsetting and believe it is the best way to protect nature also acknowledge that in practice it is open to abuse. In August 2012, economists Robert Costanza, Simone Quatrini and Siv Øystese also responded to Monbiot's opposition to biodiversity offsetting. They argued that the unfair (mis)appropriation of ecosystem services he fears might happen if they are *given* financial value is in fact happening already—but this is because they are *not* given a financial value. As they said, these valuable ecosystem services are 'embedded in virtually every product we buy, but their contributions are often neglected and unvalued'. In other words, as we have seen, ecosystems are already implicitly valued in our economic models—but this value is zero. They also argued that the move to put a dollar value on ecosystem services to make their value visible does not necessarily imply, as Monbiot suggests, that they will then become tradeable, any more than human beings become tradeable when we put a dollar value on human life in the many decisions we make about health care, highway safety, insurance and so on. In such cases human life is often expressed in monetary terms—but 'this certainly does not mean that we can or should exchange humans in markets'. This argument is also persuasive.

These authors concede that Monbiot is right to be concerned about privatisation and commodification, but claim that the valuation of nature, even in monetary terms, does not in itself necessarily lead to privatisation. 'Many natural capital assets are, and should remain, common property and should be managed as public goods.' And to deal with this, they say, we need to create new institutions, such as common assets trusts, which allow us to 'propertise our common assets' on behalf of everyone and not just private interests. This would mean that we in the current generation would become trustees—or stewards—of the earth for future generations, and would have an interest in maintaining and increasing the long-term value of these assets.

One example of such thinking, backed by Costanza, is the Vermont Common Assets Trust, which was proposed in 2011 in the US state of Vermont when legislation was introduced that would use state assets to benefit every citizen of the state as well as to protect its natural environment. The idea for the Vermont trust was first raised in 2004 by Professor Gary Flomenhoft of the Gund Institute of Ecological Economics at the University of Vermont, and Costanza encouraged then state senator Hinda Miller to introduce the relevant legislation. A common assets trust is a powerful way of establishing collective rights to certain shared resources rather than granting private ownership of them, with any profits made from their use to be shared by all rather than accruing exclusively to business interests.

The legislation—which in mid 2014 is still pending—is based on the public trust doctrine. If passed, the law would declare certain natural resources to be common assets that belong to all state citizens; these resources would then be protected by the Vermont Common Assets Trust. The public trust doctrine dates back to Roman civic law and was first codified by Emperor Justinian in 529 AD. It says: 'By the laws of nature these things are common to all mankind—the air, running water, the sea, and consequently the shores of the sea.' US courts have deemed this doctrine to be a 'high, solemn and perpetual duty' and Vermont has adopted it in its proposed common assets trust legislation as a way of preventing bottling companies from exploiting its groundwater. The trust would protect the state's commons for present and future generations, and any revenues it earned—for example, by selling rights to extract water—would be invested in the trust fund and then paid out as dividends to the citizens of Vermont. This would echo the practice of the Alaska Permanent Fund, which pays its citizens between US$1000 and US$2000 a year from oil earnings. The Vermont Common Assets Trust legislation stipulates that a minimum of 25 per cent of the funds must go directly to each citizen. The rest of the money would be spent on improving the state's common assets, which include natural assets such as air, water, forests, undisturbed natural habitats and entire ecosystems, as well as social assets such as the internet, public education, libraries, transport infrastructure, science and technology, health care, city parks, and grants to minors when they turn eighteen.

Joining the debate around the UK's biodiversity offsetting scheme, ecologist Mark Everard of the Institution of Environmental Sciences argued in April 2014 that Monbiot had missed the point of the scheme—and in so doing, undermined the work of the scientists who developed it. The problem, he stated, was not the *principle* of putting a value on the work of nature; rather, the fault lies in the way it is being interpreted in the case of Smithy Wood. Like Costanza and others, Everard pointed out that if we do not value things, their default value is zero, and that putting a price on nature is merely an indicator to help us compare essentially incomparable values and bring them to the negotiating table.

But he concurred strongly with Monbiot over the way governments—especially the Cameron–Clegg coalition government in the UK—appear to be ignorant of the value of nature or 'utterly dismissive' of the importance of protecting that which remains. An expert in this complex new area of environmental accounting, with its many hair's-breadth distinctions, Everard argues that in terms of the costs borne by those people who do not make immediate profits from these initiatives to offset nature—particularly the young and future generations —'the current dominant political mantra is revealed essentially as one of liberalisation from "green tape" to drive largely unreconstructed Thatcherite/Reaganomic economic exploitation justified under "austerity measures"'. In Everard's estimation, such neoliberal approaches to biodiversity offsetting seem to surrender long-term interests 'in the headlong pursuit of short-term profit'. He said of Monbiot's example of Smithy Wood:

> The most generous thing that can be said for
> this misplaced watering down of the concept
> of 'Biodiversity Offsetting' is that it is at least
> one step more enlightened than thinking of
> the wood as merely equivalent to a timber
> stack at the local builder's merchant.

In light of his concessions, Everard's concluding riposte —'if economic values are the best we have got today, let's use them'—seems cold comfort indeed.

THE PROBLEMS WITH MARKET RULE

As suggested in the discussion above and in Everard's own reservations about the apparent use of the new natural capital accounting paradigm by the UK coalition government, opposition to 'green economics' is motivated by concerns about its implied shift of power from governments to the market. Monbiot's attacks on accounting for nature—on the offloading of the care of nature to the market—are fuelled by the same urgent and unprecedented phenomena that prompted the advent of natural capital in the first place: our relationship with nature is broken, nature is in crisis; and corporations now wield vast power at the expense of the nation state. Monbiot calls the twenty-first-century nation state 'self-hating' because it has handed its authority to the private sector—and it is this state against which his most passionate rebukes are directed. For him, the solution to the environmental crisis lies in the exertion of power by governments and their responsibility for reining in markets. In his view, governments must make tough decisions—such as setting a meaningful price on carbon—and have the spine to implement them rather than outsourcing these difficult moral and ethical choices to the market. The problem with allowing the apparently cool hand of the market to resolve with a column of figures all 'those messy, subjective matters, the motivating forces of democracy', is that, as Monbiot puts it, it is a fickle master and 'unresponsive to anyone except those with the money'.

Although Monbiot concedes that markets are not always wrong, he does believe 'they fail to solve the problem of power'. He cites the flawed and ineffective European carbon market as one example of this. By bowing to pressure from business and not putting a substantial price (of, say, €30 to €40 per tonne, rather than the €2.63 to which it slumped in 2013) on carbon, the European Parliament rendered the European Emissions Trading Scheme impotent. For Monbiot, 'All systems of government are flawed. But few are as flawed as those controlled by private money'—or, held captive to the machinations of global financial markets to which they increasingly concede their power through privatisation and deregulation.

In his 2012 book *What Money Can't Buy: The moral limits of markets*, philosopher Michael J. Sandel explored this encroachment of markets into every avenue of twenty-first-century life, probing its moral implications. He argues that there are two broad dangers with handing power to markets: first, that it makes inequality more acute because life becomes harder for those without money; and second, that markets tend to corrupt. Sandel says that although this second problem is more difficult to describe, most of us have a sense of it—and it relates to the fact that pricing 'the good things in life' can taint them. This is because 'markets don't only allocate goods; they also express and promote certain attitudes towards the goods being exchanged'.

One of the simplest and most telling examples Sandel gives of the way in which things—and our attitudes to them—are altered by their pricing is his story of the late pickup of children from childcare centres in Israel. When the childcare centres introduced a fine for parents who were late to collect their children at the end of the day, keeping the staff back and the centre open, they found to their surprise that it did not provide the deterrent they had intended; instead, the late pickups actually increased. Why? Because the parents perceived the fine as a monetary payment for a new late-pickup service and so more of them began to make use of it. To them, the fine was an additional fee for a new service.

Sandel finds that the same logic—or illogic—also applies to tradeable pollution permits. This approach to reducing emissions 'says in effect that emitting pollution is not like littering but [is] simply a cost of doing business'. When he argued this point in *The New York Times* in December 1997, the paper was flooded with scathing letters accusing him of not understanding the virtue of markets. This prompted Sandel to reconsider his views about emissions trading to some extent—'though not for the doctrinal reasons the economists put forward'. He based his revised view on the following reasoning: unlike tossing litter out of a car window, emitting carbon dioxide is not in itself objectionable ('We do it all the time when we exhale'). What is objectionable is doing it in excess. Sandel says that the simplest way of putting a price on pollution and therefore of curbing it is to tax it—but this is also the most politically difficult to enact. And when market thinking gained its hold in the 1980s, environmentalists themselves began to favour market-based approaches to saving the planet, such as putting a price on carbon and letting the market do the rest.

However, Sandel pinpoints the moral problem with a global market in pollution permits: it allows rich countries to avoid meaningful reductions in their own energy use by buying the right to pollute from others. As he sees it, this entrenches an instrumental attitude towards nature (as Monbiot argues over ecosystem off-setting) and undermines 'the spirit of shared sacrifice' required to establish a global environmental ethic. This matters morally and politically, because in allowing rich countries, corporations and individuals to 'buy their way out of meaningful changes in their own wasteful habits' we bolster the belief that nature is a dumping ground for those who can pay. As Sandel says, whatever the efficiency of a global market in buying and selling the right to pollute, it 'may make it harder to cultivate the habits of restraint and shared sacrifice that a respons-ible environmental ethic requires'. Here Sandel makes a crucial point, one that will be taken up in Chapter 6. What is needed to address global warming is not so much economic incentives as a change of mindset: 'Global action on climate change may require that we find our way to a new environmental ethic, a new set of attitudes toward the natural world we share.'

A similar danger to that posed by pollution permits is raised by the advent of carbon offsets (the trading of a reduction in carbon emissions in one place to compensate or 'offset' an emission made elsewhere)—that those who buy them may feel that in doing so they have done their bit towards averting climate change, effectively paying to pollute rather than changing their behaviour. The risk is that carbon offsets will become 'a painless mechanism to buy our way out of the more fundamental changes in habits, attitudes, and ways of life that may be required to address the climate problem'. Like the fines at the childcare centre, carbon offsets could thus encourage more polluting behaviour rather than less. Due to this moral conundrum, they have been compared to medieval indulgences, which allowed sinners to buy their way out of their sins.

As these examples make clear, while economists might assume that markets are 'inert'—that they do not affect the goods they exchange nor the people who exchange them—this is not so. As Sandel puts it, 'Markets leave their mark.' And sometimes 'market values crowd out nonmarket values worth caring about'.

This grey and explosive ground—where morals meet markets in a political vacuum—is where many environmental scientists and activists, economists, international organisations and others dare to tread today. So if governments have outsourced their power, who or what is the new source of power in the twenty-first century? Everyone I spoke to about the new accounting paradigm had one single answer: corporations. We must now deal with the might and reach of the corporation in the twenty-first century.

3

DEALING WITH THE CORPORATION AS MONSTER AND PSYCHOPATH—AND OPENING A WINDOW ONTO ITS CHARACTER

Modern Society is a Frankenstein which has created a new monster—the corporation of overwhelming size and unrestrained power.

PROFESSOR I. MAURICE WORMSER, 1931

But the real question [for companies] is can you ever care about anything other than maximizing profits?

DAYLIAN CAIN, YALE SCHOOL OF MANAGEMENT, 2009

[Non-financial reporting] will succeed because it offers stakeholders what financial reporting alone fails to offer: a window on the character and competency of the reporting company.

ALLEN WHITE, 2005

I N FEBRUARY 2010, THE BP CORPORATION, FORMERLY known as British Petroleum, released its 2009 annual report, which declared that it was 'the largest producer and leading resource holder in the deepwater Gulf of Mexico'. Two months later, having successfully dug the deepest well ever recorded (the Tiber prospect), BP moved its leased drilling rig, the *Deepwater Horizon*, to a new location in the Gulf of Mexico and began a new well. Named Macondo after the fictional town in Gabriel García Márquez's 1967 novel *One Hundred Years of Solitude*, the well soon yielded oil. On 20 April 2010, as the crew attempted to seal the well, a mix of petroleum and gas escaped and blew up the rig, killing eleven workers and unleashing a monstrous underwater oil gusher. Over the following three months, some 4.9 million barrels of oil and a similar volume of gas spewed out into the Gulf of Mexico. The toxic waste polluted the sea, rivers and other waterways, killed thousands of animals (more than six thousand birds alone washed up) and caused abnormalities in countless others, including shrimp born with no eyes or eye sockets. It damaged beaches, and the health and lives of people along the coast, and ruined the local fishing and tourism industries.

In May 2011, a year after the BP oil spill, eighteen Nobel laureates met in Stockholm to prepare a communiqué for the Rio+20 Earth Summit on the long-term implications of human activity on the environment. In his 2012 book *Corporation 2020*, Pavan Sukhdev tells the story of this meeting, which he attended as an expert witness on the green economy and the invisible economics of nature. As a way into their discussion, the laureates held a mock trial between the plaintiff Planet Earth and defendant Humanity. The charges were serious damage done to Planet Earth by Humanity. For several hours, the defence did their best to mount a case for Humanity, but the judges found in favour of the plaintiff and declared Humanity guilty on most counts. Among the 'punishments' meted out to the guilty party was a thousand years of community service.

Although the trial was intended as an amusing prelude to the serious proceedings, for Sukhdev it left some 'worrying undertones hanging heavy in the air'. It made him wonder if humanity is even capable of changing its ways, let alone willing to. It made him ask: 'Was there something *pathological* about humanity's suicidal intransigence?' Well might we ask. But rather than leaving the question hanging, Sukhdev goes on to point out that the proceedings were somewhat pointless anyway, because Humanity's invisible co-defendant had not even been called to testify. And yet this co-defendant has conspired with Humanity for the past 60 years during which the offences against Planet Earth took place. The missing agent is, of course, the corporation. Sukhdev calls the unaccounted role of the corporation in the destruction of the earth the biggest agency problem of our times.

But the problem with today's corporation in terms of this trial for the destruction of the earth—which was after all about real not mock damage to the planet—is as much about its unprecedented monstrous size and power as it is about its agency or actions. In 2000, it was estimated that 51 of the largest 100 economies in the world were not countries but multinational corporations. In 2013, the 2000 largest publicly listed companies in the world employed 87 million people and generated around half the world's GDP. Giant US retailer Walmart alone employed 2.2 million people, the equivalent of half the population of New Zealand. The 2008 global financial crisis has left countries messed up, broke and confused—but business is booming. And corporations have spread so seamlessly through our lives, in the way that governments began to in the nineteenth century, that, confounded by the ambiguous nature of these global beings—are they with us or against us?—George Monbiot could write in April 2014 of the multinational consumer-goods company Unilever:

> I can think of no entity that has done more to
> blur the lines between the role of the private
> sector and the role of the public sector. If you
> blotted out its name while reading its web
> pages, you could mistake it for an agency of
> the United Nations . . . Sometimes Unilever
> uses this power well. Sometimes its initiatives
> look to me like self-serving bullshit.

There is a long history of attempts by governments, organisations and individuals to rein in the power of corporations, dating from the first emergence of the concept of limited liability. The Boston Tea Party of 1773 was itself an act of defiance against the world's first truly multinational company, the British East India Company. From the late 1960s, on the tide of anti-war and civil-rights protests, activists have also increasingly targeted the all-power little-responsibility modern corporation, qualities that led professor of law I. Maurice Wormser to liken them after the Wall Street Crash to Frankenstein's monster, and Joel Bakan, Jennifer Abbott and Mark Achbar (in their 2003 film *The Corporation*) to diagnose them in the wake of the Enron debacle as psychopathic. To understand the nature of the modern corporation, we must understand its evolution—and the profound transformation that occurred in our legal understanding of it during the industrial era.

A STORY OF CORPORATIONS

Corporations are no modern invention. The idea of sharing risk and pooling capital may date back to as early as the third millennium BC in Ancient Mesopotamia, where the earliest accounting records have been found, but the concepts of limited liability and corporate identity first emerged in ancient India and Republican Rome. From 800 BC to 1000 AD, India's *sreni*—which were groups of merchants and artisans, or guilds—acted as proto-corporations with shares that could be sold and shareholders who were liable for the *sreni*'s debt in proportion to their investment. Because of their immense power, the *sreni* were strictly regulated by India's dynastic rulers. In Republican Rome (509 to 27 BC), *societates publicanorum* (societies of government leaseholders) were created to carry out state contracts. These contracts covered a wide range of activities, including the provision of grain; tax collection; building public infrastructure such as roads and temples; leasing mines for gold, silver and iron; and making weapons. Groups of investors could bid on government contracts to carry out these services for the state. Shareholders were granted limitations on liability by the government and could trade their shares. When Rome became an empire in 27 BC, the imperial state gradually took over the societies' public works programs, and by the time the Western Roman Empire fell in the fifth century the *societates publicanorum* had disappeared.

The next significant move in the corporation's genesis came in 1600, when England's East India Company which would become the world's first truly multinational corporation was founded, and was followed by the Dutch East India Company in 1602. Both became so influential they were able to direct their countries' foreign policy for two centuries. By the 1760s, the British East India Company was a titanic enterprise with bases around the globe, including in England's North American colonies. But in these colonies the local entrepreneurs resisted the company's power and undermined its monopoly by bringing tea directly into America. The British Tea Act of 1773 was designed to bolster the foundering East India Company by extending its monopoly over the American tea trade; in other words, to enhance the profits of its shareholders and put its competitors out of business. The colonists' opposition to the Act came to a head on 16 December 1773 when, disguised 'in the costume of a Indian' (as one first-hand account expressed it), a group of them boarded three British ships moored in Boston harbour and tipped their cargo of tea into the water. In his history of the corporation, US journalist Thom Hartmann discusses a rare first-hand account of the 'Boston Tea Party' by Boston shoemaker George Robert Twelve Hewes, who led one of the revolutionary groups. Hartmann writes:

> Reading Hewes's account, I learned that the Boston Tea Party resembled in many ways the growing modern-day protests against transnational corporations and small-town efforts to protect themselves against chain-store retailers or factory farms. With few exceptions, the Tea Party's participants thought of themselves as protesters against the actions of the multinational East India Company.

The colonists' defiance led to armed conflict at Lexington and Concord in April 1775, which sparked the American

Revolution. In Hartmann's telling, that war—which would grant the American colonies their independence from Britain—was triggered by the attempts of a transnational corporation and its government patrons to deny American colonists 'a fair and competitive local marketplace'.

It is ironic that, as Hartmann puts it, the American 'nation was founded in an anti-corporate-power fury', because it was in America in the next century that the modern corporation really came into its own. In England from 1720 to 1825, joint-stock companies were prohibited by the 'Bubble Act' unless authorised by royal charter. This Act—promoted by the South Sea Company ostensibly to quell a surge of speculation and spectacular losses, but more likely to protect its monopoly—meant that the growth of joint-stock companies was stymied in Britain for a century. But in America, joint-stock companies were actively encouraged. By the early nineteenth century, every state in America could issue corporate charters, and the corporation flourished. The world's first limited liability law was enacted in the state of New York in 1811. But the dangers inherent in this new business form were already evident to Thomas Jefferson, who warned in 1816 of the 'aristocracy of our moneyed corporations'.

In 1819, in the landmark case of *Trustees of Dartmouth College v. Woodward*, which pertained to the contract clause of the American Constitution, the Supreme Court recognised corporations as having the same rights as humans to make contracts. Chief Justice John Marshall's judgement included the observation that 'a corporation is an artificial being, invisible, intangible' and established the legal principle that corporations can exist separately from the state and so make contracts in their own right. At the time, corporations depended for their existence on state legislatures, which typically granted corporate charters for a fixed period of ten to twenty years, and for a specific purpose, such as building a road or canal. The Supreme Court's ruling attempted to limit the power of states to interfere with private charters, including those of commercial enterprises.

The ascendancy of these artificial beings increasingly freed from the control of state legislatures—and which could therefore exist in perpetuity—was expressed in 1873 by Edward G. Ryan on the eve of his becoming chief justice of Wisconsin's Supreme Court. Speaking to the graduating class of Wisconsin's law school, he warned that there is

> looming up a new and dark power . . . the enterprises of the country are aggregating vast corporate combinations of unexampled capital, boldly marching, not for econom- ical conquests only, but for political power . . . The question will arise and arise in your day though perhaps not fully in mine, which shall rule—wealth or man; which shall lead—money or intellect; who shall fill public

> stations—educated and patriotic freemen, or
> the feudal serfs of corporate capital . . .

This idea of a corporation as an independent artificial being was extended some seventy years after *Trustees of Dartmouth College v. Woodward* in an extraordinary episode which now underpins US corporate law but which was based on a judge's throwaway line. The case was *Santa Clara County v. Southern Pacific Railroad,* tried in 1886, during which a court reporter overheard the chief justice say that the court was of the opinion that the Fourteenth Amendment—regarding the legal protection of any person—also applied to corporations. The Fourteenth Amendment was one of three Reconstruction Amendments adopted between 1865 and 1870 to eradicate from the US Constitution the implicit approval of slavery: the Thirteenth Amendment explicitly abolishes slavery, and the Fifteenth Amendment forbids any government from denying a citizen the right to vote based on race, colour or previous condition of servitude. The Fourteenth Amendment concerns citizenship rights and equal protection of the laws for 'all persons'—and herein lies its loophole. By not distinguishing such persons as natural or artificial, the Fourteenth Amendment has been held to apply to both. US law is based on British common law, which recognises two types of 'persons': 'natural persons' and 'artificial persons'. The latter include governments, churches and corporations. The concept of 'artificial persons' was created so the law could be applied to them and they could make contracts and be taxed. Most laws relating to humans specify 'natural persons', while those that relate to artificial persons either say so or refer to them by name. But the Fourteenth Amendment does none of these things. While the case of *Santa Clara County v. Southern Pacific Railroad* is said to have established—and in terms of US case law *did* establish—corporate personhood, legally it did not, because the judge's purported remark was only added by the court reporter in his headnote, and headnotes do not have legal standing. The history of US corporate personhood is founded on this anomaly.

Two years later, corporate personhood was affirmed in *Pembina Consolidated Silver Mining Company v. Pennsylvania*, when the US Supreme Court held that in applying the Fourteenth Amendment, 'Under the designation of "person" there is no doubt that a private corporation is included.' Following this decision, in his December 1888 State of the Union address, President Grover Cleveland warned of this burgeoning corporate power: 'Corporations, which should be the carefully restrained creatures of the law and the servants of the people, are fast becoming the people's masters.'

And in the ensuing half century following the adoption of the Fourteenth Amendment to ensure citizen rights and equal protection of the law for freed slaves, it had been used more often for artificial than for natural persons. As US Supreme Court Justice Hugo Black noted in 1938, 'of the cases in this Court in which the

Fourteenth Amendment was applied during the first fifty years after its adoption, less than one-half of one percent invoked it in protection of the Negro race, and more than fifty percent asked that its benefits be extended to corporations.'

And so in just over one hundred years, corporations in America had gone from being the spur of a revolutionary war of independence to the burgeoning masters of its people. Not surprisingly given this history of granting corporations the same rights and protections as humans in the eyes of the law, the corporation prospered, and by 1890 there were almost half a million of these corporate persons in the United States.

In the early twentieth century, US case law seemed to enshrine another principle governing corporations, apparently requiring a company to operate exclusively for the profit of its shareholders and not for the benefit of its employees or the community. The case was *Dodge v. Ford Motor Company* of 1919, brought by shareholders John and Horace Dodge, who owned 10 per cent of Ford. In 1916, Henry Ford had decided to spend some of his US$60 million capital surplus reinvesting in new plant rather than paying dividends. The Dodge brothers, friends and business rivals of Ford's, did not approve of this use of their potential funds: they wanted their dividends, not new Ford factories and employees. So they took Ford to court to demand the money as rightfully theirs.

At the trial, Ford described his vision for his company in terms of the social good, calling it 'an instrument of service rather than a machine for making money'. He explained: 'My ambition is to employ still more men, to spread the benefits of this industrial system to the greatest possible number, to help them build up their lives and their homes. To do this we are putting the greatest share of our profits back in the business.' He said that his company was 'organized to do as much good as we can, everywhere, for everybody concerned . . . [a]nd, incidentally, to make money', and testified that if you gave workers a good wage and sold inexpensive cars 'the money will fall into your hands'. But the Michigan Supreme Court rejected this reasoning and decided in favour of the Dodge brothers, ruling that Ford could not be run as a charity and holding that a business corporation is organised primarily for the profit of its shareholders. The court ordered the payment of a large dividend (some US$19 million), and the Dodge brothers used the money to build up their own car business, the Dodge Brothers Company.

This case is frequently cited to argue that US law requires company boards to maximise shareholder wealth, or profits, to the exclusion of all else. While this reading has been refuted by some legal scholars, the case went on to shape corporate practice and popular perceptions of the role of business in modern America, the heartland of industrial capitalism and home of the industrial corporation, and its spirit was enshrined in mainstream postwar economics, as stated most clearly by Milton Friedman.

In September 1970, in an essay emphatically titled 'The Social Responsibility of Business is to Increase its Profits' and published in *The New York Times Magazine*, Friedman responded to 'businessmen' who speak about the social responsibilities of business in a free-enterprise system, including 'providing employment, eliminating discrimination, avoiding pollution and whatever else may be the catchwords of the contemporary crop of reformers'. In Friedman's influential opinion, there is 'only one social responsibility of business—to use its resources and engage in activities designed to increase its profits so long as it stays within the rules of the game, which is to say, engages in open and free competition without deception or fraud'.

Friedman's view reflects the long history of the development of corporate rights without a corresponding acceptance of their responsibilities. From their early beginnings as joint-stock companies, corporations have increasingly acquired rights—such as limited liability, and rights to due process, to merge and to acquire—without attracting many corresponding obligations. The result was 'an accountability deficit in which all company stakeholders—investors and non-investors—were essentially excluded from the knowledge, oversight and control associated with rapid industrialization', as Allen White of Boston's Tellus Institute (founded in 1976 to address social and environmental issues) put it. We have created corporations as entities driven mostly by narrow, profit-seeking self-interest and with such little regard for the communities in which they operate that their behaviour can verge on the psychopathic, as in the 2010 BP *Deepwater Horizon* oil disaster and its devastating effect on the Gulf of Mexico, and the many sins and omissions of Enron, from environmental destruction to the theft of worker entitlements. And yet, as Sukhdev points out, 'This corporation became the main agent of modern, market-centric economies in the twentieth century, a poster child and champion of free-market capitalism.'

This profit-seeking self-interest has had the additional unfortunate consequence of propelling corporations to focus on ever diminishing periods of time in their decision-making, driving them to maximise profits for the next quarterly report to appease stock markets bent on maximising their wealth. This culture of short-termism has driven profitmaking to manic new heights at the expense of sound business. A 2013 study found that 75 per cent of US chief financial officers would not take the decisions that were in the best interests of their business if the decisions would result in missing the quarterly guidance—that is, if it meant the business would not meet their own prediction of near-term profit expressed as an amount of money per share, usually given in a quarterly report. This is rule by numbers taken to the extreme.

The publication of the Brundtland Report in 1987 made clear that modern society with its rule of economic growth founded on short-term considerations was not sustainable over the long run on this one planet. As we have seen, that report introduced the term 'sustainable development', which brought together the previously antithetical ideas of environmental protection and economic development, and so the idea of sustainability entered the language of economics and eventually became common parlance. It also gave sustainable development a widely adopted definition: 'Humanity has the ability to make development sustainable to ensure that it meets the needs of the present without compromising the ability of future generations to meet their own needs.' The Brundtland Report's concern for unborn generations broke with the short-term thinking of postwar economics predicated on economic growth at all costs, most notably in Friedman's mantra of optimising short-term profits and the primacy of shareholder value creation.

Laws governing corporate disclosure—from the first British law requiring joint-stock companies to disclose financial information in 1844 to the US Securities and Exchange Commission's mandating of audited financial statements in 1934—have obliged the poster children of free-market capitalism (corporations) to speak to the outside world in the language of financial accounting. But in the twenty-first century, even the language of corporations is found to be breaking down. Had they been summonsed to testify at the mock trial of Planet Earth versus Humanity, with no means of expressing their own role in the damage inflicted on the natural world and society, these monstrous legal persons would have been incapable of uttering a single intelligible word.

REFORMERS OPEN WINDOWS ONTO THE
CHARACTER OF THE CORPORATION

~

Friedman's 1970 dismissal of the 'contemporary crop of reformers' and their 'catchwords' did little to dampen such campaigners' desire to cure corporations of their singular focus on profit at the expense of society and the environment. Working at the interface between social and environmental activism and business and investment, these energetic reformers called for corporations to acknowledge their impact on the wider world, especially given the enormous power they now have. To do so, they marshalled the forces of accounting. One model in their drive to hold business environmentally accountable was the movement to dis-invest—or divest—from apartheid-era South Africa that began in the late 1970s. The anti-apartheid divestment movement aimed to put pressure on the South African regime by asking investors to withdraw their funds from businesses in South Africa. Their thinking was directed by the Sullivan Principles, developed in the US in 1977 by the Reverend Dr Leon Sullivan, a black preacher on the board of General Motors, the largest employer of blacks in South Africa. The principles demanded equal treatment of employees regardless of their race. The US divestment activists lobbied institutional investors—such as universities, pension and retirement funds, mutual funds and faith-based funds—to withdraw their investments from South African companies as well as from

US businesses operating in South Africa that had not adopted the Sullivan Principles.

US politician and long-time social activist Bob Massie was a student campaigner in the anti-apartheid divestment movement. According to Massie, the movement's power came from unleashing 'a whole set of disturbing ideas and questions into institutions that had never thought of them or did not want to think about them'. Initially, he says, investors responded with scepticism and saw the movement to direct funds for social purposes as threatening to bring about the end of capitalism. But the tide turned when pension funds worth billions of dollars joined the movement. For example, one bank that had been 'violently' criticising the idea of divestment from South Africa did a sudden about-face and created a 'South-Africa-Free' equity fund when it realised that people were demanding it.

If there is a founding mother for this socially responsible investing movement, it is Joan Bavaria, who in 1999 was named a 'Hero for the Planet' by *Time* magazine. While working as an investment officer at the Bank of Boston from 1969, Bavaria realised that many investors wanted to include social and environmental values in their investments but that financial institutions were not designed to make this possible. So in 1981 she co-founded the Social Investment Forum, dedicated to advancing socially and environmentally responsible investment, applying the lessons of the South African divestment movement. The following year, Bavaria founded Trillium

Asset Management to help investors allocate their funds according to their social and environmental values.

Her next move was prompted by an environmental catastrophe. On 24 March 1989, the *Exxon Valdez* oil tanker ran aground in Prince William Sound off the coast of Alaska. It spilled between 260,000 and 750,000 barrels of crude oil into the sound over several days, the most devastating oil spill in US history until the *Deepwater Horizon* disaster of 2010. The spill contaminated 2500 kilometres of coast and killed thousands of birds, otters, fish and other creatures. The region was so profoundly damaged that 25 years later it has still not fully recovered. Suddenly the environmental cost of doing business was made shockingly clear. Bavaria brought together a group of environmental activists and social investors to ask companies to practise what she termed an 'environmental ethic', which required going beyond the profit-focused principle of US case law established with *Dodge v. Ford Motor Company*. The group was named Ceres (the Coalition for Environmentally Responsible Economies) after the Roman goddess of agriculture and fertility. Its aim was to bring together environmentalists, businesspeople and investors to create a business model with the ideal of ensuring the health of the planet and the prosperity of its people. Adopting Ceres' environmental ethic included agreeing to the 'Valdez Principles', named in memory of the oil spill and inspired by the Sullivan Principles and the MacBride Principles. (The latter were created in 1984 for corporate issues regarding religious discrimination in

Northern Ireland.) The Valdez Principles, later renamed the Ceres Principles, are a set of ten guidelines that govern corporate environmental behaviour, including protecting the biosphere (or all the earth's ecosystems), using natural resources sustainably, and reducing waste and energy use. Its tenth principle asks corporations to report periodically on their progress; these reports are independently audited and made available to the public. To make this possible, Ceres developed an accounting framework for environmental measurement and reporting.

When Ceres was launched in 1989, the idea of corporate environmental reporting was so new that after five years only fifteen companies had signed on. Divestment activist Bob Massie, who was director of Ceres from 1996 until 2003, said on its twenty-fifth anniversary in 2014:

> [In 1989,] the whole idea of having an environmental ethic or measuring your performance above and beyond your legal requirements was considered completely insane. And a few visionaries, like Joan Bavaria and others, believed it could happen and should happen. Sustainability was considered to be a shockingly difficult thing that no company would ever voluntarily take on as a goal.

Since then Ceres has mobilised dozens of companies and hundreds of institutional investors to take account of the environment in their decisions and practice.

As part of this new thinking on extended corporate accountability, in 1994 John Elkington (co-founder of London think tank SustainAbility) coined the term 'triple bottom line', a concept he explored in his 1997 book *Cannibals with Forks: The triple bottom line of 21st century business*. The 'triple bottom line' enlarges the focus of business beyond its traditional 'bottom line' of financial performance to include society and the environment. Elkington's approach is reflected in the now much-touted phrase 'people, planet, profit', which multinational oil and gas company Shell used as the title of its first sustainability report in 1997.

Ceres' next initiative was informed by this triple-bottom-line thinking. According to Massie, from 1996 a lot of different organisations were beginning to think about how to measure the environmental impact of business: 'One of the problems was that every group had a different idea about how to do that, every NGO had an idea, different corporations had ideas.' At the time, US corporate culture was heavily influenced by Chicago school economics and the views of free-market funda-mentalists such as Alan Greenspan, Chairman of the US Federal Reserve from 1987 to 2006, whose thinking made clear that the environment lay beyond the realm of corporate responsibility.

One night in 1997 in a Chicago bar, Massie was talking to his colleague Allen White of the Tellus Institute. They had just left yet another of their dispiriting meetings with US companies in their quest to promote environmental disclosure. As White tells it, that night they had 'an epiphany over a couple of beers and a profound sense of frustration'. Their revelation was this: 'Don't wait for the US to catch up with the idea of environmental disclosure. Be bold. Go global.' So they came up with the idea of creating a global framework for reporting the environmental and economic impacts of corporations—and the Global Reporting Initiative was born.

GLOBAL REPORTING INITIATIVE

The aim of the Global Reporting Initiative (GRI), established by Ceres and the Tellus Institute, was to create a generally accepted system of corporate environmental measurements and disclosure, the sustainability equivalent of the generally accepted accounting principles for financial reporting. And as with financial reporting, its founders envisaged a system that would be managed and improved by a standard-setting body like the US Financial Accounting Standards Board. The breathtaking magnitude and ambition of this undertaking was expressed by one of Massie's relatives when asked to contribute money to the scheme: 'Let me get this straight,' he said, 'you are suggesting that if we give you $100,000, you are going to bring about a complete transformation of the global system of accounting?' Yes, that was their plan. Ceres eventually raised millions of dollars and the first GRI framework was created online through inclusive global consultation with a wide range of interested people, including businesspeople, accountants, United Nations representatives, and human rights and environmental activists. Through this hyper-democratic process, the GRI's initial environmental focus was extended to include social issues such as human rights and workplace safety, as well as corporate governance.

This concept of 'corporate governance'—or the way corporations are directed and controlled, including the duties and responsibilities of company directors—became a hot issue in the 1990s. Unlike laws governing corporations' accountability to shareholders, no comparable codes about how corporations should be directed were created during the corporation's adolescence in the nineteenth and early twentieth centuries. It took a series of corporate scandals in the UK in the early 1990s to prompt the first code of corporate governance. The failure of the Bank of Credit and Commerce International and the sudden collapse of textile company Polly Peck International led to the formation in 1991 of the Committee on the Financial Aspects of Corporate Governance, chaired by Adrian Cadbury, to create a code for the financial dimension of British corporate governance. Published in 1992, the Cadbury Report—*Financial Aspects of Corporate Governance*—became the first of a number of voluntary codes of corporate governance established around the world and influenced governance codes in Europe and the United States, including the World Bank's. As a result, a governance strategy became a key component of running a company, and the twentieth-century focus on management shifted to a focus on directors and governance. (It is worth noting that despite the marked increase in the number of corporate governance codes, such voluntary guidance did not prevent the systemic failure of corporate governance which contributed to the 2008 global financial crisis.)

And so it was natural that the first GRI guidelines, released in 2000, would include corporate governance along with environmental and social responsibility. These three aspects of turn-of-the-millennium corporate life have become widely known by the initials ESG (environmental, social and governance). Like software, the GRI guidelines continue to evolve. An updated version, G2, was launched in Johannesburg at the United Nations World Summit on Sustainable Development in 2002. The same year, by now no longer part of Ceres, the GRI came under the aegis of the UN Environment Programme and was established in Amsterdam as a non-profit organisation, where it continued its mission of making social and ecological reporting as normal as financial reporting.

With the expansion of global capital markets and the commercial use of networked computers and the internet from the late 1980s, international codes such as the GRI have become increasingly important as regulators of corporate activity. As a result of the internet and social media, consumers are becoming aware of corporate behaviour and are beginning to expect it to be sustainable, and capital markets are realising the long-term benefits of environmental, social and governance issues and their connection with other non-financial corporate values like brand, image and reputation. In 2009, White said:

> We built GRI in the belief that a globalized
> world needs a generally-accepted global
> standard for nonfinancial reporting to
> achieve the accountability and transparency
> that all stakeholders need and deserve. A
> decade after its conception and in the wake
> of a global economic crisis driven in large
> measure by a breakdown in accountability
> and transparency, this core belief has never
> been more compelling.

Today, thousands of organisations around the world report information on sustainability performance using the GRI's guidelines, which have become the world's de facto sustainability standard. In 2013, their fourth iteration, G4, was released. The G4 guidelines define a sustainability report as one that 'conveys disclosures on an organization's most critical impacts—be they positive or negative—on the environment, society and the economy'. A sustainability report also presents an organisation's values and governance model, and 'demonstrates the link between its strategy and its commitment to a sustainable global economy'. The G4 further claims that

> expectations that long-term profitability
> should go hand-in-hand with social justice

and protecting the environment are gaining ground. These expectations are only set to increase and intensify as the need to move to a truly sustainable economy is understood by companies' and organisations' financiers, customers, and other stakeholders.

The G4's 'specific standard disclosures' cover the three categories of economic, environmental and social disclosures, the last of which includes labour practices and decent work, human rights, society (the impact an organisation has on local communities and society more broadly) and product responsibility (which concerns the products and services that directly affect stakeholders, notably customers). Within the social category, the G4 includes such measures as the total number and rates of new employee hires and employee turnover by age group, gender and region; return-to-work and retention rates after parental leave, by gender; type of injury and rates of injury, occupational diseases, lost days and absenteeism, and the total number of work-related fatalities, by region and by gender; the average hours of training per year per employee by gender and by employment category; the ratio of basic salary and remuneration of women to men by employee category; total number of incidents of violations involving rights of indigenous peoples and actions taken; and operations with significant actual and potential negative impacts on local communities.

The environmental dimension of sustainability in the G4 concerns the organisation's impact on living and non-living natural systems, including land, air, water and ecosystems. It covers 'inputs' such as energy and water, and 'outputs' such as emissions, effluents and waste. It also covers biodiversity and transport, as well as environmental compliance and expenditures. For example, it asks organisations to report on the percentage of materials used that are recycled; the organisation's energy consumption according to non-renewable and renewable sources, as well as its total energy consumption and energy sold, and its reduction of energy consumption; its total water used, water sources significantly affected, and the percentage and total volume of water recycled and reused; the habitats it has protected or restored; and its emission of greenhouse gases.

By fostering reporting on these many aspects of an organisation's activities, social, environmental and financial, the GRI intends to make abstract concepts tangible so that organisations can better plan and measure their effects on the wider world. Massie explained their purpose in 2009: 'The GRI was built on the notion that transparency would allow everyone to see—and thus to accept intellectually and morally—their own responsibility for the choices we face today and in the future.'

As former GRI director Ernst Ligteringen said in 2014, the evolution of sustainability reporting has been 'phenomenal'. In 2000, just over thirty companies worldwide prepared reports using GRI guidelines. By 2012, the number had grown to more than 11,000. So successfully has the GRI agitated for non-financial reporting that by 2013 even bastions of financial capitalism such as the NASDAQ Stock Market and the New York Stock Exchange were issuing their first GRI reports. But now its success in encouraging business to issue environmental, social and governance reports has created a new problem: a plethora of non-financial information that is yet to be related in any systematic or meaningful way to regular financial reporting and whose existence has had questionable real effects on the serious issues it seeks to address. (The proliferation of this information is partly driving the move to integrated reporting.)

United Nations Global Compact

At its 1992 Earth Summit in Rio de Janeiro, the United Nations set the scene for its greater involvement in corporate activity, acknowledging that although corporations were responsible for damaging the environment, they were also capable, along with governments and other organisations, of contributing to its care and maintenance. This was the beginning of its rapprochement with the corporate world. The 2012 People's Summit's charge that the United Nations had newly aligned itself with the private sector and its market thinking was not without grounds. In 2000, the United Nations formally acknowledged the growing significance of the private sector and the importance of fostering collaborations with business when it founded the Global Compact, the first

UN initiative in its 55-year history created with a specific focus on the private sector. This turn toward the private sector was an acknowledgement that corporate activities bear enormously on the world beyond the economic sphere as traditionally understood. Given this, the UN Global Compact serves as a voluntary complement to regulatory frameworks, as a way to help guide business practices and to build private–public sector partnerships.

By signing the Global Compact, businesses signal their commitment to sustainability, agreeing to its ten principles across four areas: human rights, labour, the environment and anti-corruption. As an integrity measure, the signatories must file a Communication on Progress (COP) on their achievements within the four areas, including a measurement of their results, and provide this to their stakeholders. If a business continually fails to publish a COP, it is expelled from the Global Compact. Unlike the GRI, the Global Compact is not developing its own reporting framework; signatories can choose their own reporting framework for their COP. In 2000, the Global Compact had just 44 signatories. Today it has over 12,000 participants, including more than 8,000 businesses in 15 countries, making it the largest voluntary corporate sustainability initiative in the world.

Before I spoke to the Global Compact's reporting manager Sarah Bostwick and investor relations manager Danielle Chesebrough in New York in October 2013, I had considered the United Nations mostly in terms of its work with national accounting standards through the

SNA. The fact that the Global Compact is addressing corporate reporting and working with the private sector on development issues seemed to mark a new era in UN standard setting. Bostwick explained that the Global Compact grew out of the realisation that business could play a critical role in contributing to global discussions about and action on globalisation, development and sustainability. Chesebrough added that the whole philosophy of development has evolved over the past twenty years. Previously, private companies and multinationals would not have been considered suitable partners for non-government organisations or governments, while today most big development projects are based on partnerships between international bodies, governments and business.

Both Bostwick and Chesebrough see the Global Compact as part of a broader movement working to transform capitalism from within and introduce new notions of value related to the environment and society. Bostwick described the rise of sustainability accounting frameworks over the past two decades as a movement to redesign capitalism itself: 'There are a lot of different actors in different fields with different priorities working on this, but ultimately we're all working toward the same goal.' In her view the ultimate goal is to 'drive innovative solutions' and create new forms of capitalism that can 'transform business and set the course for a more sustainable future'.

The initiative has received huge support from business, as was made clear at the United Nations' Rio+20

Summit when the Global Compact hosted a Corporate Sustainability Forum attended by a staggering 3,000 people. As Chesebrough said, 'The private sector really showed up.' In his report on this forum, UN Secretary-General Ban Ki-moon affirmed the place of business as a welcome partner of the United Nations: 'Increasingly, we are looking to business not as a source of problems but as the place to go for solutions.'

UNITED NATIONS PRINCIPLES FOR
RESPONSIBLE INVESTMENT

As part of its new vision of private enterprise, the United Nations has also formed an initiative directed at investors. Called the Principles for Responsible Investment (PRI), it is the investor equivalent of the Global Compact and was the brainchild of James Gifford, an Australian who started out as a computer programmer and social activist. Today the PRI has over 1200 signatories from the global investor community—but when it was founded in 2006 it had only one member of staff, and that was Gifford himself. In a break between his master's degree on socially responsible investment and a PhD on shareholder engagement at the University of Sydney, Gifford worked one winter as an intern at the UN Environment Programme Finance Initiative in Geneva. While there he realised that the United Nations did not have an initiative that promoted responsible investment. When he mentioned this to the UN, they offered him a job and the PRI was born.

Kofi Annan launched the PRI in 2006 at the New York Stock Exchange with signatories representing US$2 trillion in assets under management committed to responsible investment. In April 2014, eight years after its launch, the PRI had more than 1260 signatories representing over US$45 trillion in assets under management, or 15 per cent of the world's total investable assets.

The goal of the PRI is to encourage a more sustainable global financial system by making sustainability central to investment decisions and practices. To do this the PRI has developed six principles of responsible investing which provide a voluntary framework to help investors incorporate non-financial issues into their decisions, as well as creating an international network of like-minded investors. By signing to the six principles, investors pledge to incorporate environmental, social and governance (ESG) issues into investment analysis and decision-making; be 'active owners' and incorporate ESG issues into ownership policies and practices; seek appropriate disclosure on ESG issues by the entities they invest in; promote the principles within the investor community; implement the principles effectively; and report on their progress with the principles. Possible actions investors might take to promote ESG issues according to the PRI include addressing these issues in their investment policy statements; supporting the development of ESG-related tools, metrics and analyses; and asking investment service providers (such as financial analysts, consultants, brokers, research firms and ratings companies) to integrate ESG factors into their research and analysis. The signatories must also encourage companies to develop sustainable strategies, which includes asking the companies they invest in to report on their ESG practices. All signatories must report to the PRI's secretariat. Initially, to protect proprietary information, signatories were not required to publish this information publicly, but in 2013 public disclosure became mandatory. In the first reporting round under the new framework, more than eight hundred investors disclosed how they are using the PRI's six principles to encourage a more sustainable investment practice.

CARBON DISCLOSURE PROJECT

The Carbon Disclosure Project (CDP) is another initiative focused on the relationship between business and the environmental crisis. It was launched in London in 2000 to encourage companies and cities to disclose, manage and share environmental information, with the aim of motivating them to reduce their carbon emissions. CDP's co-founder Paul Dickinson, who studied responsible business practice with the Body Shop's Anita Roddick, believes business has replaced government as the primary shaping force in society. In 2009 he said: 'I have real confidence that the corporations of the world are going to outperform government in terms of dealing with climate change. In fact, they are already.' So CDP works directly with 3000 of the world's largest corporations—including some that have higher greenhouse gas emissions than individual nations—to help them reduce their carbon emissions and other environmental damage. It uses its vast collection of climate change, water and forest-risk information in an attempt to encourage better business practice and investment decisions.

CDP acts on the corporate sector through its investor-led initiative which asks the world's highest-emitting companies to make emissions reductions and publicly disclose their targets. CDP sent out its first round of letters in May 2002, signed by just 35 institutional investors, to press companies to reduce their carbon use and disclose this information. In 2013, CDP sent letters to some three hundred companies in seventeen high-emitting industries on behalf of 767 institutional investors with US$92 trillion in assets. The idea is that when investors worth trillions of dollars put pressure on companies to report on their carbon emissions, the companies are more likely to disclose them and also to change their energy use to minimise them. Like the others involved in this reporting movement, CDP believes reporting can change behaviour and its climate-change reporting framework is modelled on the structure of corporate accounting standards.

Water—now called 'blue gold' by business because of its inestimable value—is CDP's latest focus. Failing infrastructure, pollution and climate change are rapidly depleting the world's water supplies, and just under half the world's population now has inadequate access to water. Meanwhile corporations are beginning to realise the risks water shortages pose for their business operations. These risks have been highlighted by investment failures such as the forced shutdown in 2012 of Newmont Mining's US$4.8 billion Conga gold- and copper-mining project in Peru over fears of water shortages. This project is still active, but its future is uncertain.

CDP also runs the Climate Disclosure Standards Board, which was founded in 2007 by business and environmental organisations, including Ceres, to create an international reporting framework for company disclosure of climate change. It published its first Climate Change Reporting Framework in October 2012.

CDP's chief innovation officer, mathematician and activist Nigel Topping, gave a talk in 2012 at the UK's Schumacher College, named after economist and environmentalist E.F. Schumacher. Speaking of activist groups like CDP, Ceres and the GRI, Topping termed these new kinds of organisations 'private politics': the private sector intervening where politics and the public sector have failed. He described the work CDP does by requiring companies to disclose their carbon emissions as 'throwing a judo move with global capitalism'; that is, it is using capitalism's greatest heft—corporations—to alter its course.

To explain why he believes the disclosure of information such as carbon emissions has the potential to catalyse systemic change, Topping quoted scientist and systems analyst Donella Meadows who proposed a hierarchy of places to intervene in a system to effect change. In a paper published in 1997, Meadows argued that some modes of intervention are more effective than others; therefore the range of possible places to intervene in a system can be scaled according to their potency. Using systems analysis, she suggested that there are 'leverage points' or places within a complex system (such as a firm, city, economy or ecosystem) where a small shift in one element—such as a law—can bring big changes in the whole system. Meadows argued that an understanding of these shifts and how to use them would help us to solve big systemic problems such as hunger, resource depletion, environmental destruction and pollution. At the bottom of the hierarchy are 'constants, parameters and numbers', which include subsidies and taxes. So in this view, fiddling with taxes is the least effective way to bring about systemic change. By contrast, providing new information to a system—which is what accounting does—so that it can reorganise itself is the fourth most powerful way of making change. Complex systems like the global economy have emerging properties that cannot be predicted—and Topping argued that CDP and the other agents of private politics, by introducing new information to the system, can bring about massive changes in the global economy.

(According to Meadows' hierarchy, the second most powerful way of changing a system is to change the mindset or paradigm it stems from; and at the apex of the hierarchy is 'power to transcend paradigms', which we can only do by changing our values.)

Aviva Investors and the Corporate
Sustainability Reporting Coalition

Another group agitating for change in the way corporations do business by enlisting the power of the
investment community is the Corporate Sustainability
Reporting Coalition (CSRC). Created by asset managers
Aviva Investors in 2011, the CSRC represents investors
with some US$2 trillion under management, financial
institutions and others, including the GRI and CDP. Like
these other organisations, it also believes that any move
to sustainable growth must be underpinned by corporate
transparency and accountability, and that this can only
happen through corporate sustainability reporting.

At the Rio+20 Summit, the CSRC asked the United
Nations member states to require all listed and large
private companies to include—or 'integrate' (this word
is key to the new reporting paradigm)—sustainability
issues in their regular annual financial reports, or explain
why they had not done so. This integration or com-
bining of the two reports is significant because most
companies issue their sustainability reports separately
from their financial reports, and often several months
later, which makes the two sets of information difficult
to compare and undermines the potential of sustainability information to influence investment decisions.
But instead of the integrated reporting requirement
requested by CSRC, the United Nations' official report
from Rio+20, *The Future We Want*, granted it a single
paragraph: Paragraph 47 'acknowledge[s] the importance

of corporate sustainability reporting and encourage[s] companies, where appropriate, especially publicly listed and large companies, to consider integrating sustainability information into their reporting cycle'.

Aviva Investors' Steve Waygood has led the push for companies to report on non-financial—or sustainability—information. Not surprisingly, Waygood calls Paragraph 47 'weak'. He argues that non-financial value is inextricably linked to financial value and that non-financial information is therefore essential, not optional, for investors when they are evaluating a company's worth. For example, 'non-financial' information about customer retention, employee retention and government relations gives investors insights into a company's cash flows. Waygood's activism stems from his belief that investors have a central role to play in the transition to more sustainable business—and that in order to play this role, they need the right information. As he says, given that markets work on the basis of data, 'if the information we rely on from companies is short term and thin, then a short-termist view will prevail in the capital markets'.

THE IRRESISTIBLE FORCE OF TRANSPARENCY

This surge of activism to force the industrial-era corporation into the twenty-first century through so-called sustainability reporting has led to a proliferation of non-financial reporting initiatives and information that provide a window into corporate character and make 'transparency' the mot du jour. Like many words in this corporate accounting universe, 'transparency' is a slippery term, but in this context it is concerned with a corporation's disclosure of its internal workings to the outside world. It is about communicating pertinent information to a broad group of stakeholders and denotes clarity and honesty.

The issue of transparency is critical in the moves to rethink accounting by bringing together financial and non-financial information in one report as advocated by Steve Waygood at Rio+20. In his foreword to Robert Eccles and Michael Krzus' 2010 book on the subject—*One Report: Integrated reporting for a sustainable strategy*—Canadian business consultant Don Tapscott raises this distinctive feature of our age of networked intelligence. As he puts it, 'an old force with new power is rising in business'. This force is transparency. Because of globalisation, the internet and other mass communications, and the global financial crisis, business is now being held to account in ways that have never before been possible. Tapscott continues:

> Firms are being held to complex and
> changing sets of standards—from unrelenting
> webs of 'stakeholders' who pass judgment
> on corporate behavior—to regulations, new
> and old, that govern and often complicate
> everyday activities. In an ultra-transparent

world of instant communications, every
step and misstep is subject to scrutiny. And
every company with a brand or reputation to
protect is vulnerable.

Tapscott and others in the new reporting movement believe that companies now have no choice but to share information. As he puts it, 'The irresistible force of transparency has met the immovable object of an outdated and even dangerous model of reporting.' This new age of transparency forces corporations to shape up. In *The Naked Corporation*, their book on the subject published in 2003, Tapscott and his co-author David Ticoll declared: 'You're going to be naked, so you'd better be buff!'

One recent example of a company being forced to get buff due to this new transparency in the networked age is Unilever, the company whose website George Monbiot likened to that of a United Nations agency. In 2007, it launched a campaign for its Dove Self-Esteem Fund; called 'Onslaught', the campaign featured a young girl and an onslaught of beauty propaganda from contemporary media to show the way girls are bombarded with images of supposedly ideal physical beauty. Greenpeace responded to Dove's campaign in April 2008 with their own video clip called *Dove Onslaught(er)* and featuring a young girl called Azizah and a barrage of images of environmental destruction. Created to criticise Unilever's use of palm oil in its products (it is the world's biggest buyer of palm oil), *Dove Onslaught(er)* shows the devastation palm oil plantations have wreaked in Indonesia, where large tracts of forest have been razed to make way for palm trees. The Greenpeace video claimed that at present rates of clearing, 98 per cent of Indonesia's low-lying forests will be destroyed for palm oil production by the time Azizah is 25. It urged viewers to 'Talk to Dove before it's too late'. The video went viral and prompted tens of thousands of protest emails to Unilever's headquarters in just two weeks.

Unilever responded in May 2008 by agreeing to Greenpeace's call for it to play its part in saving the Paradise Forests of South East Asia. It agreed to support an immediate moratorium on further clearing of Indonesian forests by committing to having fully traceable supply chains by 2012 and using only palm oil sourced from sustainable supplies by 2015. In 2013, Unilever announced that 36 per cent of its agricultural raw materials were sustainably sourced in the previous year, and committed to making this 100 per cent by 2020. Such is the power of the internet and the force of public pressure to change corporate behaviour in the name of sustainability and transparency in the twenty-first century.

THE PRINCE'S ACCOUNTING FOR SUSTAINABILITY PROJECT

To gain a better view of the effects of corporate behaviour, the Prince of Wales founded Accounting for Sustainability (A4S) in 2004. As corporate governance guru Mervyn King tells it, the A4S project came about because Prince

Charles wanted to know more about how the companies the Royal Household invested in affected the wider world. So he consulted his then private secretary, accountant Sir Michael Peat, the former treasurer to the Queen and great-grandson of William Barclay Peat, founding partner of accounting firm Peat Marwick (now KPMG). In King's telling, Prince Charles said to Peat: 'The Royal Household is invested in these companies, I get these annual reports, I find them completely incomprehensible. [The companies] must be having an impact on society and the environment, but I don't see where it is.' This led Prince Charles, with Peat, to form A4S with the aim of developing an approach to corporate reporting that showed how a company and its traditional financial report connected to society and the environment. They called this 'connected reporting'.

Like the other organisations agitating for radical change to the way corporations account, A4S believes that a sustainable future depends on holding corporations accountable for their contribution to climate change and use of scarce resources. With this in mind, its connected reporting framework proposed five environmental indicators all organisations should report on: polluting emissions, energy, waste, water and other significant finite resource usage. As Peat said in 2008 of the critical importance of incorporating such non-financial information into business practice by connecting financial and sustainability reporting: 'It's no good just having airy-fairy strategies and policies. You've really got to think about how sustainability is going to be embedded in your organisation. Sustainability isn't just an add-on for marketing purposes. It's got to be part of an organisation's DNA.' He believes accountants have a key role to play in introducing sustainability into the thinking and behaviour of business by providing the practical tools to respond to massive issues such as global warming, water shortages and deforestation. As he says, accountants can develop the information, methodologies and systems to move 'being green' from 'being trendy and fashionable to being core and mainstream'.

Like so many others involved in this new accounting movement, Peat calls it a 'revolution' while acknowledging that, as with all revolutions, no one is exactly sure what to do or how to respond. In particular, he comments on the vast amounts of information created by sustainability reporting, to which accountants have been slow to respond other than by piling on yet more information: 'We all know that annual reports have got longer and longer, and so less and less useful. Giving people huge versions of *War and Peace* isn't the right approach.' Something has to give.

Exacerbating the explosion in non-financial information over the past two decades has been the snowballing of financial information over the same period, as each new corporate scandal brings legislation for new disclosures— for example, in the United States the Sarbanes–Oxley Act of 2002 (after Enron), and the 2010 Dodd–Frank Wall Street Reform and Consumer Protection Act following the 2008 global financial crisis. There is an urgent need to bring these two domains together and make them speak to each other meaningfully, as happened at the national level with the new System of Environmental–Economic Accounting published in February 2014. SustainAbility's John Elkington has called the dream of marrying financial and non-financial information in one report 'the Holy Grail of reporting'.

In the early twenty-first century, versions of such reports were attempted by a handful of companies on different ends of the planet. But they were independently pioneered in the last decade of the twentieth century by an initiative prompted by change of a magnitude rarely seen on the global stage: the release from prison of Nelson Mandela and the end of apartheid in South Africa.

FROM SOUTH AFRICA TO ST JAMES'S PALACE: CONNECTING FINANCIAL AND NON-FINANCIAL INFORMATION

The proper governance of companies will become
as crucial to the world economy as the proper
governing of countries.

JAMES WOLFENSOHN, PRESIDENT OF THE WORLD
BANK, 1999

There is a growing weight of expectation on
organisations to operate as good corporate citizens. This is because of the influence they exercise
on the lives of so many individuals.

THE KING REPORT 2002

ON 11 FEBRUARY 1990, AGED 71, NELSON
Mandela walked out of prison after 27 years and
vowed to end apartheid. He told the crowd: 'Today, the
majority of South Africans, black and white, recognise that apartheid has no future. It has to be ended by

our decisive mass action. We have waited too long for our freedom.' President F.W. de Klerk's announcement earlier that month that he would dismantle the country's apartheid laws culminated four years later in South Africa's first democratic elections. At midnight on 26 April 1994, the old South African flag was lowered and the new rainbow flag raised. The following day, Mandela's African National Congress (ANC) party won 63 per cent of the vote, and on 10 May 1994, Mandela was sworn in as president of a new South Africa.

Apartheid did end. But the system that emerged in its place did not deliver on the ANC's economic program of nationalisation of mines, banks and monopoly industry, as set out by Mandela in a note written in January 1990. Instead of this state-led transition to democracy envisaged by Mandela and the ANC, the creation of the new democratic state was steered by the private sector. During those turbulent years between Mandela's walk to freedom and South Africa's first democratic elections, while the political architecture of the new state was being built, behind the scenes the tedious minutiae of the post-apartheid economy were being thrashed out in negotiations between the ANC and the ruling National Party. But, according to Canadian author Naomi Klein's account of those years, it was in those deadening details that the real machinery of the nascent democracy was being installed. These discussions put together the components of a society founded on the power not of the ruling political party but of private enterprise, the dictates of global capital markets and international treaties. According to Patrick Bond, an economic advisor in Mandela's office during the first years of Mandela's rule, the 'in-house quip' was: 'Hey, we've got the state, where's the power?'

As South African journalist and former student activist William Gumede told Klein in 2006, during the transition to a democratic state the ANC supporters were scrutinising the political negotiations, not the economic ones, which they thought were mere technicalities. They later discovered how wrong they had been; this mistake meant that they had missed the real story. Because, of course, the real story was about economics. Three years after becoming president, Mandela conveyed the relative impotence of political power against capital markets in a global economy when he said at the ANC's 1997 national conference: 'The very mobility of capital and the globalisation of the capital and other markets make it impossible for countries, for instance, to decide national economic policy without regard to the likely response of these markets.' The economic arrangements of the new state meant that business would drive South Africa's transition to a post-apartheid society and capital would fuel it. It was in this protean world that a new vision of corporate governance and reporting was conceived.

In December 1992, during the interregnum, the chairman of South Africa's Institute of Directors, Glynn Herbert, received a copy of the UK Cadbury Committee's report on corporate governance. The following January, Herbert passed it on to the Institute's chief executive officer, Richard Wilkinson, who thought it a very inter-esting document and suggested they could do something similar for South African business. Recalling those days from the vantage point of 2012, Wilkinson said: 'Bear in mind this was in January 1993, when everything was in a state of flux in South Africa.' The talks about the coun-try's future had begun and Wilkinson said to Herbert: 'Well, if the [Institute] wishes to have a meaningful place in the future new South Africa, we should take the lead in developing a code of corporate governance for the new South Africa.' So they took their plan for a set of corporate governance principles to guide the country's post-apartheid development to the Institute's council, who agreed to it. And so began the process of setting up a committee to create the principles. Their code needed to be far broader in scope than the purely financial focus of the Cadbury Committee, because theirs was a society in transition. They approached distinguished former Supreme Court judge Professor Mervyn King to chair the committee.

King initially declined their request. At the time he was busy, serving as executive chairman of the textile giant Frame Group Holdings and of First National Bank's corporate and investment banking group, and chairing various other organisations, including the charity Operation Hunger, which fed two and a half million children every day in South Africa's impoverished rural areas. But then Nelson Mandela intervened. He phoned King and asked, 'How's my favourite judge?' King later

said he thought Mandela used this phrase as 'a motivational tool' to persuade him to take the job. If he did, it
worked, because King then agreed to chair the committee.

Mervyn King had had a stellar career in the law before
he was forced into business by an act of conscience. The
son of a 'simple bookkeeper', King had always wanted to
study law. As a clerk and young attorney in Johannesburg
in the late 1950s and early 1960s, he worked in the
building across from where Mandela and ANC leader
Oliver Tambo practised as attorneys. King says Mandela
and Tambo were his 'learned friends', but that as a young
white attorney in the apartheid state, he could not have
practised in the same firm as them. After Mandela was
imprisoned on Robben Island in 1963, King became
chairman of Operation Hunger (while continuing to
practise law). Mandela's daughter worked with King for
Operation Hunger, and through her Mandela came to
know of King's work. In 1977, aged 40, King became the
youngest ever judge appointed to the Supreme Court of
South Africa. Three years later he became the youngest
Supreme Court judge ever to resign. He clashed—or
'crossed fingers' as he put it—with then prime minister
P.W. Botha over having to impose the government's
discriminatory race laws, and resigned from the bench.
King then embarked on his career as a non-executive
director on various company boards. His experience
of corporate law and his inside view of the workings
of corporate boards gave him an intimate and nuanced

view of the corporate world and awakened his interest in governance.

So King was the right man to chair the committee that would create South Africa's first code of corporate governance. It took the committee eighteen months to write the code, which was named after King and issued on 29 November 1994, six months after the ANC came to power with Mandela as president. When the King Report on Corporate Governance—now known as the King Report 1994 or King I—was released, it was acclaimed in South Africa and around the world as the most comprehensive report on corporate governance to date. It was especially noted for its inclusive 'stakeholder' (rather than merely shareholder) view of the corporation's ambit. Looking back on that moment from 2012, Wilkinson said that when the report was released, 'the decisions had not been made about which way the new South Africa was going to go, whether it was going to follow the communists, socialist or capitalist route. So we stuck our neck out an awful long way in publishing this report before the decisions were made.'

SOUTH AFRICA'S CORPORATE
GOVERNANCE CODES

~

It is worth considering the evolution over two decades of South Africa's three King codes of corporate governance because they show the critical importance of such governance in the electronic age of global capital and multinational corporations, when the power of corporations rivals that of states and most of us are directly implicated in their fortunes. As World Bank President James Wolfensohn pointed out in 1999: 'The proper governance of companies will become as crucial to the world economy as the proper governing of countries.' The truth of this statement was clearly demonstrated when the global economy collapsed in 2008 due in part to the absence of good corporate governance. This evolution also shows that once you extend the mental focus of boards beyond a consideration solely of their company's shareholders to a broader group of 'stakeholders' (including employees, customers, local communities and the natural environment), the reporting of non-financial information becomes critical. As does, in its wake, the need to relate it to the company's financial information in meaningful ways; that is, to integrate the two sets of information, the old, industrial-era financial information and the new electronic-age sustainability information.

This then raises the question of how—in what terms—this non-financial, mostly intangible value is expressed, because (regardless of any moral misgivings about measuring it, such as those expressed by the People's Summit and George Monbiot) much of it is difficult if not impossible to translate into numerical terms that speak to financial data and therefore to investors. In other words, we are talking about attempts to quantify—or make meaningful to capital providers—the possibly unquantifiable: natural systems, humans, human cultures, societies. In South Africa, this non-financial information would extend to the disclosure of critical health and social practices that pertained to its particular socioeconomic circumstances, such as a company's policies to encourage black economic empowerment and strategies for dealing with HIV/AIDS (some 5.7 million South Africans had HIV/AIDS in 2007, possibly the highest incidence in the world).

South Africa's second code of corporate governance, published in 2002 and known as King II, explicitly addressed the critical role of governance in the twenty-first century. Its executive summary says:

> The 19th century saw the foundations being laid for modern corporations: this was the century of the entrepreneur. The 20th century became the century of management: the phenomenal growth of management theories, management consultants and management teaching (and management gurus) all reflected this preoccupation. As the focus swings to the legitimacy and the effectiveness of the wielding of power over corporate entities worldwide, the 21st century promises to be the century of corporate governance.

Together the King codes of corporate governance make two things clear: the growing importance of sustainability reporting and the need to integrate it into the traditional financial report; and the underlying assumption that South Africa's transformation to a post-apartheid society hinged on corporations and their ability to attract global capital.

In the spirit of the free market, the King codes are principles-based and voluntary, not governed by law or regulation. This is a key tenet of the new reporting initiatives, including that of the International Integrated Reporting Council. For King, the reason the King codes are principles-based and voluntary is that 'there are always ways of getting around a rule. It's considerably harder to get around a principle'. And although the Johannesburg Stock Exchange made integrated reporting a regulatory requirement in 2010, companies are given the option to produce an integrated report or 'explain why they are not' doing so.

THE KING REPORT 1994

The first King report on corporate governance recommended standards of conduct for boards and directors of listed companies, banks, financial and insurance companies, and large unlisted companies. While it specifically applied only to these enterprises, it encouraged all companies to adopt its code. It established guidance on the composition of boards, methods for board appointments, directors' remuneration, frequency of board meetings, annual reporting, auditing requirements, affirmative action programs and the implementation of a company code of ethics.

As befitted a corporate culture attempting to include for the first time the majority of its citizens, its distinguishing feature was its inclusiveness. It introduced the idea of stakeholder accountability, encouraging companies to engage with stakeholders, not just shareholders, in what was then a groundbreaking departure from UK and US practice. King has called it 'a big move away from the traditional exclusive approach encompassing the single financial bottom line and the primacy of the shareholder'. This was essential because, as Wilkinson says, one of its major objectives was 'to recognise what the previously disadvantaged could contribute to the new South Africa through business'. King saw the code as a way of educating the newly democratised public about working and doing business in a free economy. Because of these unique historical circumstances, King says, 'we couldn't just cookie-cut what the UK or America had done. Instead we developed an inclusive approach to governance, taking account of the legitimate interests and expectations of the stakeholders in the decision-making process'. In King's words, it would have been 'an act of commercial folly for directors to have directed their companies on an exclusive basis, thereby ignoring all stakeholders other than the providers of capital'.

THE KING REPORT 2002

The King code was revised in 2002 in response to a growing awareness of the environmental crisis, the challenges of scarce resources and other sustainability issues. It emphasised risk management and integrated sustainability reporting. As King describes his expanding view of governance: 'The penny dropped and I suddenly saw that corporations had a huge role to play in making life on earth sustainable. I became passionate about it, and by 2002, when the Earth Summit took place in Johannesburg, we knew we had to rewrite the King Code.' At the time, HIV/AIDS was causing devastation across sub-Saharan Africa, and in South Africa, 1600 people were infected daily with HIV. This became another key focus of the second King report.

In 2002, sustainability reporting was embryonic. The Global Reporting Initiative had issued its first guidelines only two years earlier, and they were tested by a mere 31 companies worldwide. The second King report led the way in its attempt to combine this new information with regular financial reporting; it was the first code of corporate governance to include a section on integrated reporting, which it called 'integrated sustainability reporting'. It established an Integrated Sustainability Reporting task force to analyse a wide range of new and complex areas of non-financial reporting, from stakeholder engagement to ethics and ethical reporting, and from HIV/AIDS policies to black economic empowerment.

As a result, the King Report 2002 recommended that every company report at least annually on its social, ethical, health, safety and environmental policies and practices, following the GRI's sustainability reporting guidelines, and adopted the language of the triple bottom line—'profit, people and planet'—as outlined by John Elkington in 1997. The report broke new ground among corporate governance codes (which were then still primarily focused on financial and not sustainability issues) by stressing that although such social, ethical and environmental issues are referred to as 'non-financial', there is no doubt 'that these so-called non-financial issues have significant financial implications for a company'. And it was clear on the pragmatic economic imperative for South African business to take such a broad approach to reporting: 'Failure to do so might discourage investment', it said, and investment was critical to the nation. The King Report 2002 conceived business as a catalyst not only for economic development but for change in general: 'Increasingly, South African companies are seen as agents of change not only for their own benefit but also for the benefit of their stakeholders.'

On the subject of global capital, the report quoted research which found that institutional investors would pay a premium for shares in well-governed companies. This has profound implications, not only for individual businesses but for the nation itself: by developing good governance practices, managers can potentially increase their share prices; and the creation of good governance 'can make countries, especially in the emerging markets, a magnet for global capital'. And in the information age, as Mandela had found in 1997 and in the words of King II, 'everyone, willingly or not, is a member of the global market place' because 'capital flows across geographic borders as if they were non-existent'.

As with the first King code, the King Report 2002 was internationally acclaimed. It was quoted in US Congress following the catastrophic collapses of Enron and WorldCom, and parts of it were adopted by the New York Stock Exchange and incorporated into the Sarbanes–Oxley Act. After its release in 2002, King was appointed chairman of the United Nations Committee on Governance and Oversight, which produced a governance code for the United Nations in 2006. The following year, he was appointed chair of the GRI, where he became immersed in the latest thinking on sustainability reporting.

Although the Johannesburg Stock Exchange adopted King II's recommendations on sustainability reporting and South African companies began to issue sustainability reports, they did not yet integrate them with their financial reports. In the wake of the 2008 global financial crisis, when King realised that such integration was essential, the King Committee was reconvened to update its code once more.

The King Report 2009

The distinguishing feature of the King Report 2009— or King III—was its clear emphasis on the need for integrated reporting. Despite the fact that the second King code had required companies to adopt sustainability reporting and as a result South Africa became a leader in the field, this sustainability information was issued in isolation and had not yet been connected to the financial reports. So for the 2009 update, King directed his committee on the basis that 'the cornerstone [of the new code] has got to be that governance, strategy and sustainability are inseparable, companies have to integrate them into the very fabric, the very rhythm or DNA of their business'. As the first corporate governance code to recommend integrated reporting, King III stated that 'a key challenge for leadership is to make sustainability mainstream. Strategy, risk, performance and sustainability have become inseparable; hence the phrase "integrated reporting" which is used throughout the Report.'

In March 2010, the Johannesburg Stock Exchange adopted the principles of the King Report 2009, requiring listed companies to apply the new code and therefore to issue integrated reports, or explain why they had not. As a result of this innovation, the Johannesburg Stock Exchange won the World Federation of Exchanges prize for the best stock-exchange regulator in the world in 2010/2011.

In 2014, a report found that since the adoption of King III, South African companies had experienced 'a radical shift in thinking, brought about by the introduction of integrated reporting'. Many companies began to report on sustainability issues for the first time. For example, mining company Impala Platinum Holdings began to report in detail on HIV/AIDS, including in its integrated report figures for the number of employees taking part in voluntary counselling and testing for HIV, and discussing an HIV/AIDS program of 'engaging with sex workers in the informal settlements' around its Zimplats mine. It also began to report on climate change and biodiversity. Cement business PPC and industrial brand-management company Barloworld reported on recycling.

Coal-mining company Exxaro Resources reported on renewable energy and in 2010 made a pledge to become a carbon-neutral group, 'offsetting its carbon emissions in a number of ways from planting trees to cleaner production and energy efficiency'. It also reported details of its biodiversity management, which involved developing 'biodiversity action plans' in five of its seventeen operating units and relocating specific species. One such effort to relocate a species concerned the medicinal flowering plant *Frithia humilis*, which was growing on the site of a coalmine opened in 2008. Because the plant is identified by the World Conservation Union as a vulnerable species, Exxaro relocated it with the aim of helping to protect it. The company moved 3092 plants, 433 of which were adults, 1144 sub-adults and 1515 seedlings. While the adults 'suffered high mortality rates', according to the company, 'seedling recruitment' was high and the sub-adults flourished. Behind these figures are dying adult plants unable to be relocated and some hopeful signs that the younger plants flourished, at least during the period of the report. Not surprisingly, this biodiversity plan suggests that the imperative of financial capital—or the opening of the mine—prevailed.

Gold-mining company Gold Fields also adopted integrated reporting in 2010. Sven Lunsche, Gold Fields' vice president of corporate affairs, was responsible for the move, which he says was prompted by a combination of shareholder feedback, international reporting trends and the King codes. Lunsche said that more and more investors were demanding that companies issue integrated reports and would 'shun' the ones who did not. Until 2010, Gold Fields' annual report had largely been a matter of compliance, reporting the financial information it was legally compelled to. According to Lunsche, the move to integrated reporting has encouraged the company to focus its reports more on the needs and interests of long-term shareholders, whom he sees as representative of—a 'good proxy' for—stakeholders in general, 'because they want information on all the risks facing the company, rather than a narrow focus on financial performance'. He said that fund managers are also beginning to ask questions about the company's approach to social and environmental risks, such as 'Do you have a social license to operate from neighboring communities? Do you have stable labor relations?'

The biggest challenge Lunsche found in moving to integrated reporting was making the new information on the company's health, environment and community investment issues as comprehensive as its financial data. To supply this information, Gold Fields' mine managers now provide monthly reports on safety, energy efficiency, and water usage and quality, as well as on their interactions with local government and communities. In line with the GRI, the company's 2013 integrated report included information on employee health and development, stakeholder relations, human rights and ethics, mine closure (long-term planning for the eventual closure of mines is a critical component of environmental management for the mining industry), and environmental stewardship, especially concerning energy, carbon and water management. It also reported the challenges the company faces with local communities, as well as its efforts to include them through consultation, education and employment. Gold Fields' 2013 annual report was named the best integrated report in South Africa for that year.

Beyond their impact on the four hundred or so companies listed on the Johannesburg Stock Exchange, what have South Africa's corporate governance codes done for the nation more generally? They have served the needs of financial capital well. South Africa is now considered to be a leading 'emerging economy'. Its GDP has risen 'a credible 3.2 per cent a year since 1995', as the World Bank put it in 2013, business is booming—especially in the areas of telecommunications, banking and retail—and capital keeps rolling in. According to King, investors 'say they invest in South African firms because they regard our listed companies as among the best in the world. And they are.' But the effect of sustainability and now integrated reporting on the country's social needs are harder to gauge. The wealth created by South Africa's exemplary corporate culture and credible economic growth has not been equitably distributed across its population, which seems to confirm Michael Sandel's argument that one of the problems with market rule is that it works in favour of the rich and makes inequality more acute. If South Africa has outsourced its social problems to corporations and capital markets, then it seems they have not yet adequately addressed them. Today there are believed to be more people with HIV/AIDS in South Africa than anywhere else in the world, and in 2012 the World Bank found that South Africa's 2009 income distribution made it one of the most unequal societies on earth (it ranked fourth, below the Seychelles, Comoros and Namibia). The World Bank attributed this largely to the enduring legacy of apartheid. Research by accounting academics Grant Samkin and Stewart Lawrence on the effects of South African business reporting on HIV/AIDS according to the GRI guidelines found that 'although a changing consciousness on the part of individual enterprises in South Africa is taking place, greater rather than less inequality is emerging'. Their 2005 report quotes critics of South Africa's government who accused it of being 'interested not so much in what capital can do for South Africa as what South Africa can do for capital'.

Given the global dominance of corporations and capital markets, and the steady dismantling of the twentieth-century welfare state, the lessons of South Africa are salutary. They suggest that a healthy corporate culture—underpinned by sustainability and integrated reporting and able to attract global capital—does not necessarily lead to a healthy society, despite the new reporting's aim to foster such non-financial benefits.

EVERYWHERE AT ONCE

The intriguing thing about integrated reporting is that while it was evolving in South Africa, it emerged simultaneously in several other places as well, apparently spontaneously and independently. Climate change, water shortages, diminishing resources, unemployment, the knowledge economy, risk, the proper governance of companies on which so many people now depend, and other global phenomena have made it increasingly apparent that long-term corporate value is more important than short-term financial performance. While the King Committee's task force on Integrated Sustainability Reporting was researching non-financial reporting in 2002, Swiss pharmaceutical giant Novartis issued its 2002 annual report, which it called 'Caring and Curing'. The report combined financial and non-financial information and devoted more than half its 160 pages to non-financial reporting. Canadian electric utility BC Hydro subtitled its 2003 annual report 'Reporting on triple bottom line performance' and presented social and environmental performance information with its financial data. At the same time, companies from Scandinavia, Germany, the Netherlands and Brazil similarly issued reports that combined financial and sustainability information. In 2004, the annual report of Danish drug company Novo Nordisk contained a section called 'Competitive Business Results' which included more than sixty pages devoted to 'financial and non-financial performance data'.

In 2005, in an article called 'New Wine, New Bottles: The rise of non-financial reporting', GRI co-founder and non-financial reporting expert Allen White described this phenomenon as a 'quiet renaissance in corporate reporting'. Like King, he also used the term 'integrated reporting' to describe this 'next-generation reporting'. Noting the remarkable rise of non-financial reporting since 2000 ('who would have predicted that an apparel firm like Nike would disclose a complete list of its 750+ contract factories in its *2004 Corporate Responsibility Report*?'), he said that it looked set to become standard business practice in the early twenty-first century. The emergence of non-financial reporting in hundreds of companies worldwide in less than a decade was 'in a historical context, a development whose rapidity has few peers'. And White predicted that the integration of financial and non-financial disclosure, 'a fluid, fast-moving work in progress', would only accelerate.

The 2008 global financial crisis brought the movement to remake accounting to a head with a speed and
unanimity that shocked even its most passionate advocates. In their 2010 book *One Report*, Robert Eccles and
Michael P. Krzus found—as White had predicted—that
the trend towards integrated reporting had only accelerated. It was happening everywhere at once. They saw
this synchronicity as a sign that the time for integrated
reporting had come, analogous to the way paradigm-
shifting breakthroughs are made in science, as described
by Martin Goldstein and Inge F. Goldstein:

> there are times when in a particular field
> there will be a sense of discovery in the air,
> a shared feeling about the best way to solve
> some important problem, and many indi-
> viduals will be working simultaneously in the
> same direction. The result is that very often a
> major breakthrough will be made simultan-
> eously or almost simultaneously by several
> different people, although each may come to
> it by slightly different paths.

In 2009, after the near-collapse of the global economy,
the International Federation of Accountants held a
meeting to discuss growing concerns about the inad-
equacies of corporate reporting. Mervyn King spoke to
the gathering about integrated reporting, which he had
just recommended in King III. His work on corporate

governance and as chair of the GRI has given King strong and much-sought-after views on the role of the corporation in the twenty-first century and the critical importance of corporate reporting and accountants. To gain an insight into his view of corporations themselves— and his resulting belief in the high moral seriousness of the role of directors and managers in steering these giant entities in the twenty-first century—it is worth considering the human analogy he uses to describe them in his many talks and interviews. For King, the company is neither monster nor psychopath. Rather, it is an incapacitated human. Its directors are therefore those people responsible for its care. In King's view:

> Any one of us who became a curator of an incapacitated human being would not dream of acting other than in the best interests of that unfortunate human being. Not one of us would endeavour to filch any of his or her interests for ourself. We would take great care with that person's assets, would use our practised abilities (skills) to try and enhance that person's assets. We would apply ourselves to understanding the issues concerning that person.

And further, in King's analogy, the company directors are not just responsible for the corporation's interests but are its animating intelligence and act on its behalf rather like a regent for an incapacitated monarch. When a company comes into being, he says, 'it is a totally incapacitated person in law. It only functions and earns a reputation through directors and senior managers appointed to act on its behalf'. So, King asks, why is it that the vast majority of people

> would not act wrongly when acting for
> an incapacitated human being but might
> contemplate doing so in acting for an inca-
> pacitated juristic person? Do people not
> realise that in the twenty first century a
> company, which is an employer, a purchaser
> of products, a provider of products or ser-
> vices plays as critical a role in society as the
> family unit?

King's personification of the corporation is echoed in his view of it as needing to be a good citizen and in White's belief that non-financial reporting is a window to a company's character. He might almost have said its soul.

A TEA PARTY AND A MEETING
OF THE WHO'S WHO

If the 2008 crash brought this reporting movement to a head, a phone call in 2009 from the Prince of Wales' Accounting for Sustainability project (A4S) to the Global

Reporting Initiative headquarters in Amsterdam gave it a body—or two bodies—when Sir Michael Peat rang to ask Mervyn King to tea. King said about this call, 'I've been in corporate life long enough to know that when someone of that stature asks me for a cup of tea, it's not for the tea.' So he went to London and met Peat and Paul Druckman, who was then committee chairman of A4S. Over tea, Peat put forward his proposal: given that they were both working with the same end in mind—King III's 'integrated thinking and reporting' and the 'connected reporting' that A4S was developing—they should join forces and unite their efforts. 'Why don't the GRI and A4S become one?' he suggested. In reply, King proposed that they get the who's who of corporate reporting around the table to see what they thought of the idea of a new reporting initiative. Peat agreed. Within half an hour Prince Charles had agreed to convene the meeting at St James's Palace in central London; soon after, invitations to a meeting at the palace in December 2009 to discuss the future of accounting were sent to the world's luminaries of accounting and sustainability.

And, as King put it, everyone came. Prince Charles hosted the meeting, which included the heads of the International Accounting Standards Board, the US Financial Accounting Standards Board, the International Auditing and Assurance Standards Board, the International Organization of Securities Commissions, the World Bank, the United Nations Environment Programme, the World Wildlife Fund, the 'big four' accountancy firms, the International Federation of Accountants, the World Business Council for Sustainable Development, and of course the GRI and A4S.

'An hour later, corporate history was made,' King told me. 'Because we arrived at consensus: that the way forward was integrated thinking and reporting, and we must form a body that we can all belong to, and try to make this the "end game", as we called it.' In other words, they hoped that this new accounting initiative—what would become the International Integrated Reporting Council—would bring together all the fragments and thinking thrown up by the new wave of wealth creation and the environmental and social challenges of the twenty-first century, and create a new way for the most powerful creatures on the planet to think and behave in response to these epochal changes—and a new way to communicate this behaviour. And further, that it would become international practice. At that meeting, the forces that had been gathering since the 1970s coalesced with the broad agreement that a new integrated corporate accounting was required for the twenty-first century. It was required because this world of volatile markets, electronic information, multinational corporations, scarce resources, climate change and ecosystem destruction on a planet bursting with people is so utterly different from the pastoral world in which industrial financial reporting was born that old ideas of value were as defunct as the spinning jenny.

At that meeting a rare unanimity was reached. Despite the fact that the US Financial Accounting Standards Board and the International Accounting Standards Board cannot agree on basic accounting principles such as those concerning 'inventory', 'stock' and 'revenue recognition', on that winter's day in London they both agreed that 'the future is integrated reporting'. King hopes that integrated reporting will make it possible for boards to understand their businesses' financial and non-financial information and explain it 'with graphics and pictures and in clear, concise and understandable language'. So 'then the trustee of your pension fund can make an informed assessment about whether the business of this company, which is going to take your money and invest it in the equity of their company, is going to sustain value long term or not'. King sets so much store by integrated reporting that he even thinks an accounting scandal of the magnitude of Enron might have been averted by the clear thinking and reporting it aims to encourage. He told me:

> If integrated reporting had been around at the time of Enron, Mr Skilling and Mr Lay [Enron's former chief executive officers] would have had to have told a story about the company in clear, concise and understandable language. And if they had, how could they have avoided, in telling the company's story, reference to the off balance sheet financing?

171

The way companies report matters, King argues, because it influences the way they behave.

But can a mere alteration in the way corporations report their activities to the outside world change those companies and that world? For King the answer is such an emphatic yes that he seems to have dedicated all his time and energies to bringing it about. Mervyn King is that rare creature: a man with a mission—possessed by a vision, filled with conviction, powerfully persuasive—and with the means, qualities and opportunities to carry it out. And he believes the future of the planet rests in the hands of accountants. Why? For him it boils down to this: corporations are the most powerful entities on earth and we are all now implicated in their fortunes. And who does the businessperson in the real world turn to first for advice? His or her accountant. 'The advisory role of the accountant has become very, very important for the future of the world.' And if the accountant's 'mindset' has been changed to think in terms of integrated reporting, then he or she will advise that businessperson to consider not just profit, but also the impacts of how the company makes its money and its products on society and the environment.

King then repeated a remark he originally made to the International Federation of Accountants in 2012 when accepting their International Gold Service Award for his work on corporate governance and integrated reporting. He told the gathered accountants that he had seen many movies on lawyers, on doctors, but he had never seen a movie about accountants. He then made a prediction: if accountants adopted integrated thinking when advising businesses, then there will be a blockbuster movie about accountants because they will have enabled 'human society to move as a sustainable society into the twenty-second century'.

But agreement that the future of accounting is integrated reporting is one thing; finding a way to frame this new accounting in broad principles is quite another. The change required and the practical challenges of implementing it are enormous. And given South Africa's experience, surely we must also ask: in the name of what? Of the planet and society? Or of financial capital? It seems the answer to this question is very difficult to reach, not only because of the ethical dilemmas it poses—Juniper's we cannot afford to be ideologically pure versus Monbiot's can you put a price on the beauty of the natural world?— but for more fundamental reasons as well. Simply put, it is becoming increasingly difficult to draw such distinctions. Because in the new model of the world being conceived under the aegis of the International Integrated Reporting Council, everything becomes capital. Or, capital spreads virus-like through everything and recombines it in its name. Or in six names. But while the challenges might be enormous, those leading the new integrated reporting initiative believe they have the Holy Grail of reporting in their grasp.

THE HOLY GRAIL: INTEGRATED REPORTING AND THE SIX CAPITALS

The difference is that integrated reporting, unlike
financial reporting, is not technical. It is the
company telling its story.

PAUL DRUCKMAN, 2013

An integrated report aims to provide insight
about the resources and relationships used and
affected by an organization—these are collectively
referred to as 'the capitals' in this Framework.

THE INTERNATIONAL <IR> FRAMEWORK, 2013

ON 9 DECEMBER 2013, THE INTERNATIONAL Integrated Reporting Council (IIRC) published online the framework of a new way of business thinking and reporting, the *International Integrated Reporting (<IR>) Framework Version 1.0.* Just as in 1494 Luca Pacioli had codified the leading accounting practice of his day—Venetian double-entry bookkeeping—so in 2013 the men and women of the IIRC formulated an already existing practice they considered suited to the demands of the twenty-first century. Calling itself a 'global coalition', the IIRC comprises regulators, shareholders, accounting professionals and others from 25 countries. Together they believe that 'communication about value creation should be the next step in the evolution of corporate reporting', and that integrated reporting and thinking can improve the allocation of financial capital—or investment in business—and in doing so bring greater financial stability and a sustainable future.

So this new way of reporting—and of thinking about—business value purports to address two of the most urgent problems of our times, turbulent stock markets and a turbulent earth, the latter manifested most spectacularly in extreme weather such as Hurricane Sandy, which devastated the eastern United States in 2012, as well as droughts and floods; disappearing plants, animals and polar ice; shortages of food, oil and gas; and proliferating waste and environmental destruction. In the IIRC's view, the strength of integrated reporting lies as much in the holistic thinking it aims to encourage—by directors and managers, about the place of their business in the world and its part in the creation and destruction of value (financial, social and natural)—as in the reporting it seeks to elicit. But what exactly is this integrated reporting that might just allow homo sapiens to make it into the twenty-second century?

The IIRC's chief executive officer Paul Druckman says that integrated reporting is a matter of getting businesses to tell their story (or strategy). And businesses tell this story by addressing six different 'capitals', or stores of value they can use to produce goods or services. As we have seen, these are financial, manufactured, intellectual, human, social and relationship, and natural capital. Information about financial and manufactured capital is currently provided by the financial report, while information about natural and social capital is conveyed by a sustainability report, as promoted by the Global Reporting Initiative; but information about intellectual and human capital is not yet well reported. So an integrated report combines in one report the currently disconnected financial and sustainability data, as well as the (as yet) mostly unreported information about intangible wealth. The six capitals are effectively a conceptual structure to enable businesses (directors, managers, chief financial officers, accountants and employees) to broaden their thinking about value and their business model; in other words, to facilitate the holistic thinking about their organisation's relationship with and impact on the economy, society and nature that the IIRC advocates. So this initiative is as much about encouraging integrated reporting as a process or change of thinking—starting with the board and managers and on through the entire business—as it is about promoting a new sort of corporate report.

The framework's introduction defines an integrated report as 'a concise communication about how an organization's strategy, governance, performance and prospects, in the context of its external environment, lead to the creation of value over the short, medium and long term'. This is vastly different from Pacioli's Venetian merchant making a debit to his cash account and crediting his pepper account for the sale of a sack of pepper; and from Josiah Wedgwood calculating the costs of the various components of vase manufacturing to discover the difference between fixed and variable costs and thus uncover the benefits of mass production. Although the end is the same—maximising financial gain—the conception of the means, the business itself and its place in its environment, is worlds away from the earlier mercantile and industrial models.

It is not difficult to see the need for a new form of business reporting to address the changed world of the twenty-first century—by engaging with the intangible wealth of the information age as well as the wealth of society and nature—and nor is it a stretch to accept that in principle integrated reporting provides such a model. It is difficult, however, to clearly describe just what an integrated report is. As Monash University accounting professor Carol Adams, a proponent of integrated reporting, wrote in March 2014, 'If you are confused about what integrated reporting is, rest assured you are not the only one.' At its simplest, in Druckman's words, it is 'a concise communication of value over time'. This emphasis on concision is aimed at redressing the current complexity and length of annual reports; it must be understandable and clear because its purpose is to communicate not to obfuscate, as current financial reports tend to do; and it must convey the company's whole value as an ongoing concern rather than focusing predominantly on its financial transactions of the previous year.

The key and interrelated concepts of an integrated report as outlined by the framework are 'value creation', 'the capitals' and 'the value creation process'. 'Value creation' is the value a business creates (for itself and others) which is manifested in increases, decreases and transformations of the six capitals. The 'value creation process' describes the dynamic business model through which this occurs and is depicted diagrammatically in the framework as a stylised twelve-legged spider: six streams of the different capitals feed from the 'external environment' into the business model, which transforms them and spits them out the other side in six different streams of capitals that have been increased, decreased or transformed by their processing within the business model. This is complicated by the fact that the business produces not only 'outputs'—such as capitals transformed into mobile phones, t-shirts, software and health care, as well as wastes and other by-products—but also 'outcomes' in terms of effects on the capitals, such as enhancing its employees' skills through training (thus increasing human capital while decreasing financial capital) or emitting carbon dioxide, which diminishes natural capital. This complex and dynamic process and the business's strategy to ensure its viability over time (from the short to long term) make up the story that the integrated report must tell.

As with Pacioli's 27-page treatise on Venetian book-keeping, the IIRC's 35-page framework gives no examples of an integrated report. Nor does it give specific directions about how the four 'new' capitals are to be measured and reported. Its guidance on integrated reporting is skeletal, conceptual and principles-based, as suggested by the spider business model and the framework's four sections: 'Using the framework', 'Fundamental concepts', 'Guiding principles' and 'Content elements'. And yet this framework has created a rare unanimity and excitement in the international accounting community. So what is it all about?

Before looking at the published framework in more detail and at an example of an actual integrated report, it is worth considering the framework's genesis. What happened in the four years between that history-making meeting of December 2009 and Monday 9 December 2013 when the framework was released?

A BRIEF HISTORY OF THE IIRC'S FRAMEWORK

~

For Ian Ball, the then head of the International Federation of Accountants, what was most remarkable about the 2009 meeting at St James's Palace was not the range of players it drew together—'great though that was'—but 'the level of agreement that the need for improved reporting was important, was urgent, and needed immediate action'. Eight months later, on 2 August 2010, the IIRC was launched by the Prince's Accounting for Sustainability Project and the Global Reporting Initiative. 'The world has never faced such challenges,' its press release declared. And the accounting quandary it faces, said Prince Charles, is that we are 'battling 21st century challenges with, at best, 20th century decision making and reporting systems'. In response, the IIRC aimed to create 'a globally accepted framework for accounting for sustainability', one that 'brings together financial, environmental, social and governance information in a clear, concise, consistent and comparable format—put briefly, in an "integrated" format'.

Unlike the GRI, which was designed to create, manage and oversee a sustainability reporting framework and indicators over time through many iterations, the IIRC was formed only to create the framework, which would then be handed to the International Accounting Standards Board to govern. It aimed to do this in three phases: 2010 to 2012 was awareness; 2012 to 2013, education and innovation; and phase three, from 2014, is 'fast followers, face forward, widespread adoption'. The council was originally going to disband at the end of 2014, but it will now continue at least into 2015 because this third phase needs more time.

After the IIRC's launch, the next stage in its 'awareness' phase was the release in September 2011 of its first discussion paper, 'Towards Integrated Reporting:

Communicating value in the 21st century'. The paper set out the reasons integrated reporting was needed and explained the differences between integrated and traditional reporting in eight points. With integrated reporting, it claimed, reporting moves from isolated thinking to integrated thinking; from stewardship of financial capital to stewardship of all forms of capital; from focus on past financial performance to past and future, connected and strategic; from a short-term time-frame to short, medium and long term; from narrow disclosure to greater transparency; from rule-bound to responsive to individual circumstances; from long and complex to concise and material; and from paper based to technology enabled. After its release, the paper received 213 responses from organisations in more than 30 countries; almost unanimously the respondents endorsed the idea of integrated reporting and supported the IIRC.

Mervyn King was appointed IIRC chairman in October 2011, replacing Sir Michael Peat, and Druckman was named its chief executive officer. The IIRC also launched a business pilot program, recruiting 103 companies, including iconic names such as Coca-Cola, Unilever, Volvo, Marks & Spencer and Microsoft, to help develop, test and respond to the framework. Its pilot program for investors was launched in March 2012 to provide the investor point of view on the limitations of current reporting models and to give feedback on the evolving new reporting of the pilot businesses. The

investor network collaborates with the UN Principles
for Responsible Investment and now has more than
thirty-five participants, including AMP Capital Investors,
Deutsche Asset & Wealth Management, Goldman Sachs,
Hermes Equity Ownership Services and Norges Bank
Investment Management.

Druckman has likened this first phase to a 'feasibility
study'. Given that several attempts at such an initiative
had been made since the 1970s, the IIRC needed to
work out whether it was just a good idea, or—as King
believed—a good idea whose time had come. When I
spoke to Druckman in April 2014, he said he had been
'shocked' by the widespread enthusiasm for the project
that he had encountered on his travels to promote it. The
speed (in accounting terms) with which the IIRC and
its framework came into being and the groundswell of
support they continue to receive suggest that it is indeed
an idea whose time has come. Adams also finds its popularity unexpected. As she noted in 2014:

> The extent of support of the professional
> accounting bodies for a form of reporting
> which considers value and the business model
> in anything other than monetary terms is
> perhaps a little surprising, and itself worthy
> of further research.

Druckman himself is a storytelling dynamo who
believes that the new reporting model restores meaning

and purpose to the accounting profession. He says the campaign to promote integrated reporting began as a drive to provide clearer and simpler information to the main users of corporate reports: investors. Unlike financial reporting, integrated reporting is not technical. 'It is the company telling its story,' Druckman says. 'What is its value-creation story? Why is it going to have some value over time?'

In July 2012, the IIRC issued a draft outline of the framework online, and a prototype framework was launched in November. And then in April 2013 a consultation draft of the framework was released for comment over three months, closing on 15 July 2013. Druckman explains that this open, consultative approach to releasing the framework in a series of rough, imperfect versions was designed to raise awareness, encourage broad participation and avoid a 'big bang', as he puts it, or shock revelation at the end. Like many of the advocates of integrated reporting, including King, he believes it should be market led and not enforced by regulation: 'What I want is a regulatory environment that allows companies to tell their story.' For Druckman it is important that integrated reporting is led by the market, because if it cannot make a case for itself so that businesses want to adopt it and investors want to use it, then there is no point to it. He says:

> If this is not relevant to those that are
> providing the information, the businesses,

and those that are using the information,
primarily the providers of financial capital,
well let's not do it. We're wasting our time.
So when I talk about 'market led', it needs to
be relevant. Otherwise let's stop now. There's
plenty of other things that we can all do.

To make sure that as many views as possible were considered in the process of developing the framework, Druckman urged people to respond to the draft version. And respond they did. More than 350 individuals and organisations replied, ranging from big institutional investors to food activists, and from environmental groups to banking associations, reporting councils, corporations, trade unions and industry councils, academics, accounting bodies, and the Ukrainian assurance provider BDO Ukraine. The responses were largely supportive of the framework. Common concerns were how it would fit with existing reporting standards and requirements, how it would relate to the GRI and other established non-financial reporting frameworks, and how it would actually 'integrate' the financial and non-financial information in meaningful ways. But the main focus of the feedback was on the framework's key characteristics, those that distinguish it from financial reporting—the capitals, value creation and the business model. Some respondents asked for sample integrated reports, and others were concerned about how the new capitals would be reported. BDO Ukraine said: 'We agree with the stated capitals but would like the IIRC to provide a fuller description of human, social and relationship capitals and the interaction between them. The concepts are new to most Ukrainian stakeholders so more detailed guidance would be appreciated.'

The concepts are new to most of us. Although the Integrated Reporting Committee of South Africa— established in 2010 after the release of King III—had issued guidance in 2011 on how to do an integrated report, until December 2013 there was no accepted definition of what an integrated report was, and nor was there a generally accepted framework for how to do one. With its framework, the IIRC was boldly attempting to articulate an emerging practice still in flux. It did so fully aware of the evolving nature of the field—the fact that integrated reporting is a 'journey'—but determined to make a start in order to bring about what it called its 'long term vision': a world where mainstream business, both private and public, does integrated thinking, and integrated reporting is the corporate reporting norm.

BDO Ukraine also said: 'We believe the IR Framework should live up to its evolutionary reporting ideal and require companies to be more open about the nega- tive impacts and more importantly about how they are mitigated.' In response, the IIRC's December 2013 *Framework Version 1.0* makes clear that the term 'value creation' refers not only to increases in value but also to its decreases and transformations.

While some respondents had reservations about the word 'capital' for the four new areas of value—for example, objecting that human beings, communities and ecosystems are not 'merely forms of capital provided to companies in order to be drawn down or built up' and that the word is too associated with finance and economics—the term was deliberately chosen *because* it evokes the financial, which is ultimately what business reporting is all about. Others acknowledged the history of the concept of multiple capitals. It has been used by organisations such as the UK sustainability think tanks Forum for the Future and the SIGMA Project, both of which use a five-capital model of wealth (the IIRC added a sixth, intellectual capital), and the World Bank used the idea in the 1990s when expanding its measures of wealth. The International Council on Mining and Metals welcomed the addition of intellectual capital and social and relationship capital but noted they were also perhaps the hardest to quantify and measure. The discussion of the capitals raised questions about their measurement generally, including the distinction between quantitative and qualitative information, and the use of narrative and metrics.

Questions were also raised about the ownership of capitals—who owns the atmosphere? A network of customers?—and the fact that the framework did not suggest placing limits on their use, such as a global limit on carbon emissions or water usage. Several respondents argued that without stated or implied limits to the use of the capitals, the potential of integrated reporting to address the environmental crisis is restricted. As the Climate Disclosure Standards Board pointed out: 'As it currently stands, an integrated report simply requires a company to report THAT it uses, changes and affects capitals.' Having made a similar point, David Korten of the Living Economies Forum (which works to reframe economics to address social and environmental issues) added that one benefit of integrated reporting might be that as corporations attempt to use it, it might become evident that we need 'a comprehensive community-based societal capitals accounting system for the global territorial system' in which they operate. In other words, it is not enough to make each individual corporation sustainable. To be truly effective in addressing the problem of sustainable development, individual corporations must work within a full global accounting of the planet's entire stocks of each capital, including social and natural capital.

Not surprisingly, investors strongly supported the IIRC's focus on financial capital providers as the primary audience of integrated reports. Their main reservation about the model was that it would be unrealistic to expect investors to accept a smaller return on financial capital in exchange for larger returns on the other forms of capital, which the draft framework seemed to suggest. In other words, investors would not be likely to accept lower profits in exchange for employee training or cleaning up local waterways. In response, the published framework makes clear that returns on financial capital have primacy over the other capitals.

INTEGRATED REPORTING
FRAMEWORK VERSION 1.0

~

At the launch of the official framework in December 2013, Druckman said that the *Framework Version 1.0* had given 'technical rigour and cohesion' to an organic process that had evolved because people needed it. He said that those tempted to dismiss it as futile or just one more in a sea of reporting initiatives would be underestimating 'the consensus that has grown and the global movement that has been galvanized over the past four years around the belief that corporate reporting is in urgent need of change'. This is why Druckman calls integrated reporting an 'evolution' and not a revolution.

The framework is based on broad principles so that businesses can interpret it for their own particular circumstances, which is appropriate given its global intent. As we have seen, an integrated report explains how an organisation creates value over time. The value it creates is influenced by the external environment and relationships with stakeholders, and depends on various capitals. This value manifests as increases, decreases and transformations in the capitals caused by the organisation's activities and outputs, and is created for the business itself and for others. The value it creates for itself 'enables financial returns to the providers of financial capital'. And here the real meaning of value creation is evident: it concerns financial returns, or profits. The business must also provide information about externalities, positive or negative, because investors also need this information. This is expressed in terms of the capitals.

According to the framework, an integrated report has seven guiding principles: strategic focus and future orientation; connectivity of information; importance of stakeholder relationships; materiality; conciseness; reliability and completeness; and consistency and comparability. While the framework does not require a specific structure or sequence, the report must have eight 'content elements', which are all inextricably linked: organisational overview and external environment; governance; business model; risks and opportunities; strategy and resource allocation; performance; outlook; and basis of preparation and presentation.

THE BUSINESS MODEL AND THE
VALUE-CREATION PROCESS

The term 'business model' became popular in the 1990s with the rise of online electronic commerce, so it is a quintessentially information-age concept. In the IIRC's version the business model is the stylised spider previously mentioned. The business draws on the various capitals as inputs then converts them into outputs (such as goods or services, by-products and waste), which leads to 'outcomes'. These outcomes affect the capitals, both those internal to the business, such as its employees or its store of financial capital, and external, such as the natural environment or society. So an outcome might be a better-trained workforce, which would positively affect human capital, while its training costs negatively affect financial capital. Or it might be the pollution of a river by a pulp and paper manufacturer which negatively affects natural capital. Despite the fact that this value-creation model of business with its focus on 'outcomes' is a departure from the traditional business model—the earnings model with its focus on profit—positive outcomes in terms of the organisation's financial capital (or profits) are nevertheless also its primary purpose.

SIX CAPITALS

The capitals are part of the conceptual basis for 'value creation', which is seen in terms of its impact on the six values. The IIRC chose the idea of six capitals to encourage organisations to think beyond financial capital to all the capitals they use or affect. As we have seen, this includes those capitals that lie outside the traditional boundary of the financial accounting entity, that is, capitals that the business does not own or control, such as its carbon emissions into the atmosphere, its pollution of a river, or the labour practices of its key suppliers. The framework does not require businesses to address all six capitals or even to use the language of the six capitals, just to consider them and report on those that significantly affect their value creation. As Druckman puts it, 'For too long businesses have expressed themselves only in the narrow form of financial transactions, an exclusive form of communication that hides from view the rich seams of value that can be found in knowledge, intellect, natural resources and relationships.' These rich seams of value are expressed by the additional capitals.

Alluding to the perspective-changing quality of the six capitals model, the IIRC calls it 'a prism through which organizations should assess, and then report, the degree to which they are creating, diminishing, or destroying value over time'. So the capitals are both the lens through which the business looks and the object at which it looks. The use of multiple capitals in reporting is relatively new, and so their measurement is relatively undeveloped. Before looking in more depth at the four new capitals—intellectual, human, social and relationship, and natural—here is the way the framework defines all six of the capitals.

Financial capital

The funds available to an organisation to produce goods or provide services. These funds are sourced through debt, equity or grants, or generated through operations or investments.

Manufactured capital

Manufactured physical objects available to an organisation to produce goods or provide services, including buildings, equipment and infrastructure (such as roads, bridges, and waste and water treatment plants).

Intellectual capital

Knowledge-based intangibles, including intellectual property, such as patents, copyrights, software, rights and licences; and 'organizational capital' such as systems, protocols and 'tacit knowledge' (knowledge of the business held by employees and managers that is difficult to communicate). (According to the IIRC, the 'carrier'—or owner—of intellectual capital is the organisation.)

Human capital

People's skills, abilities, experience, motivation, intelligence, health and productivity. It includes their support for an organisation's governance framework, risk management approach and values; their understanding of an organisation's strategy and the ability to implement it; and their loyalty and ability to lead and collaborate. (The 'carrier' of human capital is the individual person.)

Social and relationship capital

This category includes institutions and relationships within and between communities, stakeholder groups and other networks; shared norms, common values and behaviour; trust the organisation has fostered, brand and reputation; and an organisation's social licence to operate. (The carriers of social and relationship capital are networks of humans.)

192

Natural capital

All renewable and non-renewable environmental resources and processes that provide goods and services that support the organisation's past, present and future prosperity, including air, water, minerals, forests, biodiversity and ecosystem health.

A CLOSER LOOK AT THE LIVING CAPITALS
~

INTELLECTUAL CAPITAL

As discussed, since the 1980s there has been an increasing divergence between businesses' book value (value according to their financial reports) and their market value because of the rise of intangible value courtesy of digital information and the internet. In June 2010, Chicago-based intellectual-assets financial-service provider Ocean Tomo published a study on the rapid increase in intangible assets in US businesses since 1975. Its analysis was based on the market value of the Standard & Poor's 500 (S&P 500) companies, an index of the market capitalisations of 500 large companies on the New York Stock Exchange or NASDAQ. Ocean Tomo's research showed that since the 1980s the market value of these companies has increasingly diverged from their book value. In 1975, a company's balance sheet showed a sound 83 per cent of its value, with only 17 per cent in intangibles, reflecting the fact that its value was deeply rooted in tangible assets (manufacturing and financial assets). In 1985, intangible assets had risen to 32 per cent of book value, and by 1995 this figure had shot up to 68 per cent. These changes correspond to key moments in the introduction of new information technology: in 1985 the first personal computers were invented, and in 1995 the internet was beginning to take off. Knowledge and information were booming, along with the dotcom industry, but as we have seen, none of this value was being recorded in financial accounts. In 2009, intangible value spiked to a huge 81 per cent of the S&P 500 market value. This meant that a company's accounts could then capture only 19 per cent of its value. This rose marginally to 20 per cent in 2010. Ocean Tomo found that patented technology comprised a significant part of this missing value. This becomes visible when it is traded—such as the 2012 sale by AOL of 800 patents for internet applications to Microsoft for US$1.1 billion—but is not shown in financial reports. In 2005, economists Kevin Hassett and Robert Shapiro estimated the intellectual property of the United States to be worth US$5–5.5 trillion, more than the GDP of most countries. This is the vast 'missing' realm of intellectual capital that companies are now being asked to consider in an integrated report.

One promising initiative in intellectual capital measurement is being conducted by the Japanese public–private sector collaboration WICI (World Intellectual Capital Initiative), founded in 2007. WICI is creating a voluntary global framework for measuring and reporting corporate performance, especially intellectual capital, to shareholders and other stakeholders.

HUMAN CAPITAL

Human capital is another area of value reporting that is in its infancy. As management guru Peter Drucker noted in 1999, 'The most valuable assets of a 20th century company were its production equipment. The most valuable asset of a 21st century institution, whether business or non-business, will be its knowledge workers and their productivity.' The IIRC framework asks companies to report on the value of staff, their skills and experience, their enrichment through training and development programs, and so on. In regular financial reports, any expenditure on staff training and development appears as an expense; but in an age when staff are an organisation's most valuable asset, such expenditure should be redefined as an investment and thereby contribute to the wealth of the business. Pioneering accounting professors from New York University, Baruch Lev and Paul Zarowin, have long argued that the obvious solution to this problem—which they define as 'the measurement distortions caused by expensing items that are really assets'—is to treat knowledge workers as capital, or 'capitalise them'. Attempts to value employees—or 'human assets'—date to the 1960s, but only recently have a few companies begun to include such information in their financial statements. Notable among these are

India's global technology company Infosys and corporate giant Tata. In a model co-developed by Baruch Lev, in 2012 Infosys valued its 'human-capital externality' at US$1.4 billion. This value is generated largely through its intensive technical training program, which trains some 15,200 employees a year on its main campus alone. This is a positive externality (or 'outcome' in the framework's terms), where financial capital has been invested (and therefore reduced) to enrich human capital.

But what happens when financial capital is enriched *at the expense of* human capital (in the parlance of the six capitals model)? These trade-offs will occur between the various capitals, as the framework acknowledges (it gives the example of an activity that creates employment but degrades the environment). How will the relevant companies, for example, use integrated reporting to convey the shocking human capital stories that have come from the 'supply chains' that serve some of the world's most powerful multinationals, such as an iPad factory in southern China, or a clothing factory in Bangladesh, where the workers suffer under harsh conditions? When seventeen-year-old Tian Yu threw herself from the fourth floor of her factory dormitory at Foxconn's Longhua facility in March 2010 and survived her fall, a twelve-day coma, and spine and hip fractures, to be left paralysed from the waist down, Foxconn agreed to pay her 180,000 yuan (approximately US$29,000) in compensation so she could return to her rural village, which she had left one month earlier to earn money for her impoverished family.

However, it only did so after public pressure forced its hand. Her father said: 'It was as if they were buying and selling a thing.' Was that a human capital mitigation?

In 2010, eighteen Foxconn workers attempted suicide. Foxconn is Apple's primary supplier: in the same year, the factory where Tian Yu worked churned out some 90 iPhones a minute. The Foxconn workers rarely have the opportunity to speak out, but in 2013 a series of interviews with Tian Yu was published, conducted by Jenny Chan and Hong Kong rights campaigners SACOM (Students and Scholars Against Corporate Misbehaviour). Chan and SACOM described how the multinational electronics companies that generate so much of today's 'intangible value' for the US and other economies rely on 'what is effectively a human battery-farming system: employing young, poor migrants from the Chinese countryside, cramming them into vast workhouses and crowded dorms'. Yu threw herself out of the window after working two seven-day weeks straight, more than twelve hours a day, and finding she hadn't been paid for her month's work because of an administrative bungle. The wages she was owed for two seven-day weeks and two six-day weeks with overtime amounted to a quarter of the cost of a new iPhone 5.

On 24 April 2013, 1129 clothing workers were killed and some 2500 injured in Bangladesh when their factory, Rana Plaza, collapsed around them. The eight-storey building had already been deemed unsafe. This tragedy prompted some changes, including a massive 77 per cent increase in the minimum wage for garment workers in Bangladesh—to US$68 a month. Cambodian garment workers are also calling for better conditions. The fact that the vast wealth of successful multinational corporations depends on cheap labour and resources from countries outside Europe and North America—and on the degradation of those countries' natural environments—is long-standing and well known, and is reflected in financial reports only as low costs which contribute to high profits. On 14 December 2001, independent US Congressman Bernie Sanders said: 'The *Free Press* may think that the Tommy Hilfiger company is producing shirts in Pakistan because they want to help the poor people there. I think they're there because they can pay slave wages and increase their profit margins.' Or as US corporate lawyer John Montgomery pointed out in 2012, 'the reason Apple has 30% plus margins is that they outsource labor'.

These human issues are the hardest to measure and therefore will be the most difficult to address. The other challenge with labour issues more broadly is that they are more contested than, say, environmental issues. As Harvard Kennedy School's James Gifford (formerly of the United Nations Principles for Responsible Investment) put it in 2012, 'People don't contest that pollution is a bad thing, but they do contest the degree of freedom of association, for example, or the right to strike.' He said the fact that there are different conceptions of labour standards around the world, such as the acceptability of children working in family businesses in developing countries, makes these issues harder to quantify and evaluate—and more contentious. Gifford said he believes these social issues will be quantifiable—'with metrics in place'—in five to ten years' time, and we will look back and see that 'it was just an evolutionary process'. As we have seen, the GRI already provides various measures for reporting human value, including employee turnover, labour–management relations, occupational health and safety, training and education, and diversity and equal opportunity.

For the authors of *Natural Capitalism*, workplace safety and other human and social issues are accounting matters. They argue that just as nature needs to be accounted for and safeguarded, so are there stocks of social value which produce various vital goods and services, and society and humans must therefore be nurtured in the same way to prevent their breakdown and exhaustion:

> Just as ecosystems produce both monetized 'natural resources' and far more valuable but unmonetized 'ecosystem services', so social systems have a dual role. They provide not only the monetized 'human resources' of educated minds and skilled hands but also the far more valuable but unmonetized 'social system services'—culture, wisdom, honor, love, and a whole range of values, attributes,

and behaviors that define our humanity and
make our lives worth living.

And just as there are better and worse ways of handling
nature, so are there 'unsound methods of exploiting
human resources' that can 'destroy the social integrity
of a culture so it can no longer support the happiness
and improvement of its members'. In the authors' view,
industrial capitalism is not only liquidating its natural
resources, but it is also liquidating its human and social
capital by not valuing it. It captures 'short-term economic
gains in ways that destroy long-term human prospects
and purpose'. When people are overworked and under-
valued, and when their jobs are insecure, community
and civil society break down. Might this new reporting
model, by introducing the concept of 'human capital'
and requiring the reporting of its diminishment as well
as its enrichment and transformation, improve the way
corporations care for their human resources? For the
moment, it does not seem so, as we shall see later in this
chapter with Coca-Cola Hellenic's first integrated report.

SOCIAL AND RELATIONSHIP CAPITAL

As implied by some of the responses to the draft framework, such as BDO Ukraine's, and acknowledged by
the IIRC itself, the categories of human, and social and
relationship capital are sometimes difficult to distinguish,
their boundaries blurred. So the arguments made above by
the authors of *Natural Capitalism* apply equally to social

and relationship capital: our present accounting system depletes our stocks of social capital, and the breakdown of our social structures and societies is evidence of this.

As one component of the 'people, planet and profit' spectrum of sustainability accounting, social capital reporting is relatively well developed, for example with the GRI's measures for corruption, anti-competitive labour, and customer health, safety and privacy, and human rights including non-discrimination, freedom of association and indigenous rights. The task of integrated reporting is to make it widespread and meaningful by connecting such measures with financial data.

NATURAL CAPITAL

Measuring and reporting natural capital is the most advanced field of new capital reporting, thanks to initiatives we have already seen, such as the Global Reporting Initiative (GRI), Carbon Disclosure Project (CDP) and The Economics of Ecosystems and Biodiversity (TEEB), as well as the London-based organisation Trucost, which helps organisations such as companies and governments to calculate the economic consequences of their use of natural resources. In 2012, Trucost found that if companies had to pay for their environmental bills they would lose 41 cents in every dollar they earn. In 2010, according to its estimates, the costs of nature to the food industry alone would have come to a massive US$200 billion—more than the industry's earnings. Trucost also helped German sporting goods company Puma to develop the world's first ever environmental profit and loss account (E P&L). Released on 16 November 2011 by its then CEO Jochen Zeitz, Puma's E P&L put a monetary value on its environmental impacts and the range of ecosystem services it uses to source, produce, market and distribute its products. As far as it is possible in these early days of natural capital accounting, Puma took account of the entire range of its interactions with the natural world. It found it had used €145 million (approximately US$198 million) worth of nature. This figure included the costs of its land use, air pollution and waste, and a €94 million bill for greenhouse gas emissions and water consumption.

In accounting not just for the environmental impact of its own offices and warehouses, but also for as much as possible of those of its many global suppliers, Puma's E P&L attempted to take the broadest measure possible of the company's effect on the planet. Zeitz said in 2013:

> While at Puma, I conceived and developed
> a new reporting and accounting system that
> visualises the full impact of a company's
> activities across the supply chain—including
> the impact upon the natural environment.
> The E P&L puts a monetary value on the
> environmental costs of doing business.

Although Zeitz and Puma are attempting to assume responsibility for nature by costing it, Puma has not yet subtracted these costs from its financial accounts. Instead, it is using them to direct its business practice as it relates to natural capital. Here is qualitative information—the realisation that business as usual is rapidly destroying the natural world—quantified. Zeitz says: 'Companies need to take full responsibility for nature; that is, they need to account for, and take action to mitigate, the environmental damage they cause.' (Puma's parent company Kering has announced that by 2015 it will extend this environmental accounting across all its brands, which include Gucci and Stella McCartney.)

For a company to voluntarily announce previously uncounted corporate costs of some €145 million—more than two-thirds of its €202 million net profit—is extraordinary, unprecedented. When asked why he published this account, which showed such great environmental losses and at potential risk to the brand, Zeitz replied: 'Intuition and creativity are important when running a business. Ultimately, though, you need to know where the accelerator is and where the brakes are. That means understanding what's ahead and trying to quantify it.' Zeitz felt the responsibility to share this information with the public and face the consequences.

Puma's 2010 E P&L showed that only €8 million worth of environmental damage came from Puma's core operations (such as offices, warehouses and stores). The rest—94 per cent—came from its supply chain, over which Puma has limited control. More than half the company's environmental impacts were associated with the production of raw materials—including leather, cotton and rubber—and include damage such as the chemical pollution of waterways. Given the complexity of a multinational company such as Puma, which uses raw materials grown and processed far from its German headquarters, it is very difficult to keep track of how its global operations are really affecting water supplies, air quality, climate change, plants and animals across the world. Zeitz acknowledges the challenge of reducing the environmental impacts of its supply chain because of Puma's limited control over the other businesses concerned. According to Trucost's CEO Richard Mattison, Puma's E P&L approach 'provides a robust framework to help companies unlock this complex challenge and embed sustainability at the heart of business decision making'. In his pragmatic view, 'Puma has demonstrated that accounting for the environment is no longer a "holy grail" objective, but simply makes good business sense.'

Zeitz's move has not only encouraged other companies to consider such accounts—in 2014 around a dozen companies are said to be publishing environmental profit and loss accounts—but has also inspired Puma to extend its natural accounting to two of its products. In 2012, Puma released an E P&L for two of its more sustainable products (a pair of biodegradable shoes and a biodegradable cotton t-shirt), to compare their impact with two standard products, a pair of suede shoes and a conventional cotton t-shirt. Its first 'product environmental profit and loss statement' found that a staggering

31 waste disposal trucks were needed to clear the waste that 100,000 pairs of conventional sneakers cause during their lifetime, from their origin as raw materials to their eventual discarding by consumers, ending up as landfill or in incinerators.

Puma made the accounts to find out if its efforts to produce more sustainable clothing were really making a positive difference. The statement confirmed the benefits to nature of Puma's efforts: it showed that the two new biodegradable products cause 31 per cent less environmental damage than the traditional leather and cotton products they were designed to replace. The analysis looked at air and water pollution, waste, and the natural resources used, such as water and land, along the entire supply chain, from raw materials to production and right down to the 'customer phase', where we use, wash, dry, iron and finally throw away Puma's products. The accounting found that a pair of suede shoes cost the environment €4.29, while the biodegradable shoes cost only €2.95, saving about a third of the cost to nature. At this stage, as with its overall E P&L, Puma is using this information to direct its strategy and production planning and ideally to encourage its customers to choose more environmentally friendly shoes and shirts, rather than costing it into its accounts. Zeitz said, 'Our job is not only to lessen the impact our products have on the environment, but also to engage our customers and help them make better and more sustainable choices for the benefit of our planet.'

As well as using the results of its first E P&L to change the way it does business—by introducing more sustainable materials into its products—Puma is also calling on governments to support sustainable business. This includes changing outmoded policies, or 'antiquated incentives, such as import duties on synthetic materials that are in principle much higher compared with those placed on leather goods regardless of environmental footprint'. To illustrate the tax implications of Puma's switching from suede to more sustainable synthetic shoes, Zeitz said it would cost the company at least €3.4 million a year. Yet as a result of the company's environmental costings, Zeitz has said that Puma will eventually have to stop using leather in its football boots and trainers. As he said, 'We all know that cattle and beef are among the biggest contributors to carbon emissions.' Zeitz's passion for reducing his company's dependence on beef cattle extends to Puma's office canteens, where he has instituted 'meat-free Mondays'. As he told the *Financial Times* at Rio+20: 'We should eat less meat, all of us, and we should use less leather, I mean that's reality.'

The idea of natural capital accounting on which Puma's E P&L is based was endorsed at the Rio+20 Summit with the signing of the Natural Capital Declaration (NCD) to promote the private sector's use of natural capital accounting and its implementation in decision-making by 2020. The forty signatories to the declaration—including the chief executive officers of China Merchants Bank, Standard Chartered Bank, First Green Bank, Earth

Capital Partners and National Australia Bank—acknowledged the importance of natural capital to a sustainable global economy and said that the ecosystem goods and services natural capital yields provide trillions of dollars worth of food, fibre, water, health, energy, climate security and other essential services to the global economy. The NDC called on governments to encourage organisations, including financial institutions, to value and report on their use of natural capital to internalise the costs of environmental damage. Also at Rio+20, 86 private companies committed to valuing natural assets, including Walmart, Woolworths, Unilever, Standard Chartered Bank and Caisse des Dépôts. The World Bank's Rachel Kyte said at the NCD launch, 'Let's look back in twenty years from now and remember that this was the time when we changed the way we accounted for nature.'

The ascendency of natural capital accounting is helped by the fact that much of it is easier to gauge than the other new capitals. For example, there are now rigorous metrics for carbon and measures for water usage are being developed. As Robert Eccles and George Serafeim found in their May 2014 review of integrated reports to date, natural capital is the most reported of the capitals, along with financial capital. Its language is now spreading into the broader environmental conversation. For example, it makes possible the spectre of 'stranded assets' in relation to the stocks of carbon held by fossil fuel companies. These giants have vast reserves of coal, oil and gas on their books, containing five times the amount of carbon dioxide we can release (565 gigatons) if global warming is to stay below two degrees Celsius, the target set for global warming by the Copenhagen Accord if we are to combat climate change. Environmental activist Bill McKibben, founder of 350.org (named for the safe level of carbon dioxide in the atmosphere, 350 parts per million), is using the concept of stranded assets to call for investors to pull out of fossil fuel corporations in an initiative called 'Do the Math'. Launched in 2012 and inspired by the anti-apartheid divestment campaign, its key message is that most carbon in the world must stay underground.

In its first year, this message went from being one environmental activist's marginal idea to being echoed by the World Bank, the International Energy Agency, the UN's Intergovernmental Panel on Climate Change and many others. The concept of stranded assets is also beginning to shape analysts' assessments of future coal, oil and gas projects and to influence investors' decision-making. Investment bank HSBC has been considering the investment risks of carbon since 2008. Responding to a carbon report—'Unburnable Carbon 2013: Wasted capital and stranded assets'—HSBC oil and gas analyst Paul Spedding said: 'The scale of "listed" unburnable carbon revealed in this report is astonishing. This report makes it clear that "business as usual" is not a viable option for the fossil fuel industry in the long term.' HSBC warned that 40 to 60 per cent of the market capitalisation of oil and gas companies was at risk from the 'carbon bubble', or the falsely inflated share prices which do not account for their companies' potentially stranded carbon assets.

As the IIRC's background paper on the capitals acknowledges, value is subjective and impacts on the capitals will be judged differently by various stakeholders. For example, in the case of South African mining company Exxaro Resources, vulnerable medicinal plants were relocated at risk to their lives to allow the opening of a new mine; natural capital suffered to promote a decision which favoured financial capital. Not all the new capitals can be quantified, yet or perhaps ever—for example, intellectual, human and social capital, much of natural capital—and so integrated reports are not expected to provide quantitative measures of each of the capitals. The framework says that in many cases the use of and effects on the capitals will be reported through narrative rather than metrics. When it is not possible or meaningful to quantify effects on the capitals, qualitative information about their availability, quality or affordability can be used, such as the state of stakeholder relationships and how the organisation has responded to stakeholders' legitimate needs. The IIRC also encourages the development of 'integrated metrics' that combine measures of energy, carbon, water or resource use with a financial metric such as output, sales or revenue, for example, carbon emissions per unit of output or research expenditure as a percentage of sales.

DOING INTEGRATED REPORTING

~

Since 2011, some four hundred South African companies have been doing integrated reports, and there
are now around a thousand companies in the world
experimenting with the concept of integrated reporting.
There is no single way of doing integrated reporting. To
date it has been mandated only in South Africa with
King III and in France with its 2012 Grenelle II Act,
which requires companies to include in their annual
reports information on their environmental and social
performance. It is an evolving practice which will
gain coherence and consistency with the framework's
publication and gradual adoption, initially by pioneering businesses, and eventually by most businesses.
Druckman believes that in ten years it will be the
corporate reporting norm.

So how is integrated reporting being practised now?
In June 2013, PricewaterhouseCoopers assessed fifty
IIRC pilot-company integrated reports issued in April
2013. They found the reports had a long way to go before
the 'reality' of integrated reporting caught up with the
'ambition'. Tellingly, they found that

> as expected, the majority do not yet integrate
> their financial and non-financial perform-
> ance in their reporting, which suggests that
> they are a long way from building under-
> standing within their business about how

organisations create and destroy value—not
just creating returns for their shareholders.

In 2014 Robert Eccles and George Serafeim called
the first integrated report issued by Coca-Cola HBC—or
Coca-Cola Hellenic, a European bottler of Coca-Cola
products—a 'best case example' of integrated reporting.
According to the company, it adopted integrated
reporting to reflect its commitment to becoming 'a
stronger, more sustainable business'. It had issued GRI-
compliant sustainability reports since 2004 and saw
integrated reporting as 'the next natural step'. While it
did not use the language of the six capitals, the company
prepared its report according to the IIRC's framework.
The guide to the report has all the hallmarks of the
IIRC's framework:

> This Integrated Report outlines how
> Coca-Cola Hellenic's strategy, corporate gov-
> ernance, performance and prospects enable
> us to create value over the short, medium
> and long term. It also includes the full 2012
> data related to the bottling, distribution and
> sales activities in all 29 countries where we
> operate. It puts our risks and opportunities
> into a broader economic, social and environ-
> mental context and begins to demonstrate the
> links between our financial and non-financial
> performance.

The chairman's letter begins: 'I am very pleased to welcome you to Coca-Cola Hellenic's first Integrated Report which combines the information previously available in the Annual Report with the data and stories from our journey towards sustainability.' The chairman, George David, acknowledges the challenging economic conditions, resource scarcity and food security (such as the availability of sugar and fruit juice) that represent 'significant socio-economic challenges for the world'. Given this, he says, 'understanding the full impact of our business activities is extremely important'. This is the essence of an integrated report.

As integrated reporting aims to do, this report provides a wealth of information about the company, its activities and external environment, from its strategy and values to its efforts to develop the world's lightest can and encourage its suppliers to be more sustainable, and the way it dealt with the 1356 redundancies it made in response to Europe's continuing economic stresses. It is clear and easy to read. Its first page shows that its net sales revenue has increased, its water footprint and carbon emissions have decreased, the number of 'lost time accidents' per 100 employees declined and its employee engagement has remained constant at 56 per cent, despite 'the challenging external and performance environment'. The company considered employee engagement an important part of its strategy and performance, and measured it by tracking the percentage of employees who answer 'engagement questions positively' in the

company's bi-annual engagement survey. As it acknowledged, 'In times of macro-economic uncertainty and
significant restructuring it is crucial to maintain high
employee engagement to deliver the Group's strategy
and results.'

The company's goals also reflect the ethos of financial
and non-financial reporting: 'to deliver sustainable and
profitable growth ahead of the market, together with
our Partners in growth, The Coca-Cola Company, and
enabled by our people'. Its four-part strategy—'community trust, consumer relevance, customer preference
and cost leadership'—expresses the importance of the
new capitals to Coca-Cola HBC: it aims to care for the
communities in which it operates, develop its brands
and build strong relationships. It discusses the way the
company has worked with its suppliers to encourage sustainable agriculture and water use, and reduced carbon
emissions, and its development of the world's lightest
can to reduce its environmental footprint.

It says the company's 1356 redundancies were part of
its 'cost leadership', which also included savings through
process innovation, reducing water use, cleaner energy
systems and recycling. In managing the redundancies, it
was guided by its 'values' and sought to act 'with sens-
itivity, integrity and transparency' and work with trade
unions and other councils, although it faced 'some labour
disruption' in northern Greece. This illustrates the first
of my two key reservations about integrated reporting's
ability to address the bigger questions of 'sustainability' as

Druckman suggests it might. More particularly, it made me question what sustainability means in this context: the sustainability of humans and nature, or of corporations and financial capital? The running down of 'human capital' by 1356 people over seven countries in favour of financial capital—'cost leadership'—does not seem consonant with sustaining society. In the sort of world envisaged by the authors of *Natural Capitalism*, where human and social capital are as valued as financial capital and a company scrupulously maintains the stocks of all its capitals, surely the running down of human capital (in this instance) in favour of financial capital, would be as unacceptable as the running down of financial capital, scandalous even?

But in practice integrated reporting does not value the other capitals as it does financial capital. It addresses them only insofar as they serve a company's ability to generate profits over the medium and long term. This approach was strongly recommended by investors in response to the draft framework, who were concerned lest integrated reporting ask them to accept a return on the new capitals at the expense of financial capital. For example, Dutch pension fund APG said it believed the draft framework

> should explicitly recognise the primacy
> of financial capital in driving investment
> analysis and decisions . . . We agree that
> other forms of capital—manufactured,

> intellectual, human, social and relationship, and natural—can have a significant effect on the ability of a company to sustain value over time, and this should be reflected in integrated reports. But the draft framework should recognize that investors ultimately look for a satisfactory return on their financial capital. Different forms of capital are not completely fungible . . . It is unrealistic to expect investors to accept unsatisfactory returns on their financial capital in exchange for positive returns on other forms of capitals, as the draft framework seems to suggest.

The published framework makes clear that financial capital prevails. This is despite the fact that an organisation such as the International Federation of Accountants also expressed reservations about the primacy integrated reporting grants to financial capital. As it said, given financial capital is only one of the capitals, 'it remains unclear why the integrated report should be primarily directed to the providers of financial capital and only in the second instance to the providers, or for that matter the receivers, of the other capitals'. This concern has been expressed by many others, including Brad Potter, Associate Professor of Accounting at the University of Melbourne, who is disappointed that investors are the primary audience for an integrated report.

When I first considered the six capitals model, it seemed to offer a way to argue for the value of employees (or the other living capitals) and against their dismissal in times of economic downturn, because they comprised essential company value, a human capital stock. But the more I questioned the advocates of integrated reporting about the benefits it offered the capitals other than financial capital, the more it appeared that financial capital remained the ultimate concern of this integrated way of thinking. Early examples such as Coca-Cola Hellenic's integrated report, with its dismissal of 1356 people in favour of cost reduction, suggests that for the moment integrated reporting does not change the rule of financial capital over the other capitals.

Second, given integrated reporting's purported promise to contribute to sustainable development by encouraging more efficient resource allocation, how might it actually achieve this for natural and social capitals on their own terms? It seems integrated reporting does nothing to address a larger question of resource allocation, which in the case of Coca-Cola Hellenic is this: is allocating the world's scarce supplies of water and stocks of arable land to grow sugarcane and beet to create sugared drinks that may contribute to the rising incidence of obesity and diabetes the best use of these limited resources (water and arable land)? To me the fact that integrated reporting cannot address such questions suggests that as with the example of human capital, its promise to foster efficient resource allocation pertains only to financial capital and not to the other capitals. If we accept that the only way to save our societies and planet is to reconceive them in terms of capital, surely the efficient valuing and allocation of all six capitals must lie at the heart of any economics and accounting for the planet's scarce resources in the twenty-first century.

There is a logical inconsistency here: integrated reporting might be the beginning of a new accounting paradigm, but for the moment it is being practised by an old-paradigm corporation: essentially, one obliged to make a return on financial capital at the cost of the other capitals. This was made clear by investors, who would not accept lower profit in exchange for clearing up local waterways or maintaining staff levels through an economic downturn. Of course, in this era of the universal investor, these institutional investors represent all of us—or those of us with investments in pension funds, superannuation schemes and equity markets generally. So the question then becomes, are *we* prepared to accept a lower return on our money for the sake of the health of our societies and the planet?

Regardless of such questions, integrated reporting does at least serve to introduce sustainability information into annual reports and given that in 2011 an enormous 95 per cent of the world's 250 biggest companies were publishing sustainability information, this is about time. By bringing together these two sets of information, integrated reporting has the potential to change industrial-era hierarchies and allow more networked business structures to emerge. As Carol Adams argues, in order to connect this information, companies must get their financial and sustainability people to work together. This breaks down the old silo structure to allow for exchanges between previously separate departments. She says, 'This is advantageous in that accountants could better understand social and environmental risks and their impact on reputation and the bottom line whilst sustainability teams need to develop skills in making a business case for their work.' Another benefit of integrated reporting is its promise to bring this new data into the mainstream reporting cycle. In Adam's view, its 'attempt to encourage mainstream accountants to think longer term, [to] consider what value means to whom, and to acknowledge the role of staff, broader society and the environment in creating it, is bold and surely worthy.' In these terms, integrated reporting is as Druckman sees it: an evolution and not a revolution.

THE INVESTOR CHALLENGE: SHARPENING UP NON-FINANCIAL INFORMATION WITH METRICS AND STANDARDS

The advent of integrated reporting is welcomed by many investors. This is especially true of 'responsible' investors, such as Aviva Investors' Steve Waygood, who have been demanding more rigorous information on the new capitals because it influences long-term financial value.

There is now evidence that doing sustainable business is positively related to long-term financial performance, reduced share-price volatility and lower costs of capital (if investors believe they have a fuller picture of a company's longer term prospects and therefore of the risks associated with investing their funds, they will do so for a lower return or cost). Waygood, who is also a member of the IIRC, sees integrated reporting as the first move to what he calls 'integrated capitalism', in which the whole supply chain of capital is integrated and fund managers, brokers, investment consultants, trustees and stock exchanges all do integrated thinking, reporting and analysis. In 2013 Waygood said he thought it would take about a decade for capital markets to start considering sustainability when they decide which companies to invest in.

While the measurement and reporting of financial and manufactured capital is well established and the advent of the International Financial Reporting Standards (IFRS) from 1973 has made this information increasingly comparable globally (most countries now use IFRS, with the United States a notable exception), this is not the case for the new capitals. Investors' calls for consistent and comparable metrics for these new areas of wealth have prompted several initiatives to do just that. If the online publication of the framework is like the publication of Pacioli's bookkeeping treatise in 1494, then these stand-ard-setting initiatives are equivalent to the early days of standardising financial reporting, which began with the founding of such bodies as the US Securities and

Exchange Commission in 1934. The SEC was charged with establishing and enforcing accounting policies, which it does today with the Financial Accounting Standards Board (FASB), an independent body founded in 1973. A similarly named initiative, the Sustainability Accounting Standards Board, was recently established to set sustainability standards.

SUSTAINABILITY ACCOUNTING STANDARDS BOARD

In July 2011, the SASB was launched in the United States to create standardised measures for the new capitals. It was inspired by the response to research into what sort of non-financial information was most significant—or 'material' in accounting terms—for six different industries. For example, information about water usage is critical for the paper industry, less so for the banking industry. Founded by environmental engineer and sustainability expert Jean Rogers in San Francisco, SASB is creating a full set of industry-specific standards for sustainability accounting, with the aim of making this information more consistent and comparable, and therefore more useful for investors.

SASB sees itself as part of an 80-year history of corporate reporting and standardisation, which was formally launched in the United States in 1934 with the establishment of the SEC and the requirement of corporate reporting. Rogers chose the name deliberately to mimic FASB and emphasise their similarity. SASB's place in the heartland of finance was cemented in May 2014 when former SEC chair Mary Schapiro became its vice chair. The same month, Michael Bloomberg, former New York mayor and founder of the Bloomberg financial information empire, was appointed chairman of SASB, replacing its founding chair Robert Eccles. Of SASB's relationship with the SEC Eccles said, 'We meet with the SEC in an informal way every quarter. They're not mandating us, we're not asking them to. They're not telling us to stop. Regulation S-K already requires companies to disclose material information in the Form 10-K. SASB helps companies comply with existing regulation.' Rogers says that SASB is 'unabashedly focused on capital markets'. This focus is significant because of the debate about the intended audience for sustainability information. SASB is aiming to make this information useful to the providers of financial capital so they can use it in their investment decisions. In other words, its intention is overtly capitalistic, rather than social or environmental. But in making sustainability information cogent for investors, it is breaking new ground.

SASB's aim is to work out the environmental, social and governance factors that potentially affect a company's long-term value creation. As Eccles said, it hopes to incorporate sustainability information into the United States' existing annual financial report, Form 10-K, which is required by the SEC for publicly traded companies. SASB is developing non-financial standards for 89 industries grouped in ten different sectors and aims to have completed this gruelling task by February 2015. It is releasing each new set of metrics as they are completed. The first set, for the health-care sector, was released in 2013; and in early 2014, provisional standards were released for the financial sector and the technology and communications sector. When I spoke to Eccles he praised the work of Rogers and the SASB, calling it essential, 'like plumbing': 'you're creating social infrastructure. It's not very sexy but these are standards.'

BLOOMBERG

Like SASB, which it helped to fund, Bloomberg is striving to make information about the new capitals accessible to financial markets with the aim of improving capital allocation. And like SASB, the GRI and CDP, it aims to use its metrics to start 'standardising the discourse around sustainability, so we're all talking about the same things in the same way', as Bloomberg's senior sustainability strategist Andrew Park puts it. What companies 'desperately want', he says, is 'a legitimate voice' to tell them: 'This is what you need to do. You exist in this particular sector. Here are the metrics that you need to be reporting out on. So SASB will provide that. And we think that's important, because that will help clean up the metrics that ultimately the finance community will start using.'

Bloomberg wants to price environmental, social and governance (ESG) externalities to legitimise them in the eyes of financial capital. As Park and its global head of sustainability, Curtis Ravenel, argued in 2013, for as long as these ESG externalities are unpriced, they are effectively invisible to financial markets and so cannot inform investment decisions. They wrote:

> To the extent that this failure prevents mainstream financial analysts from effectively assessing such social costs and benefits – and their potential effects on *future* corporate performance and value – the result may well be inefficient allocation of capital. ESG data thus has the potential to provide crucial market transparency and a unique lens through which to assess future company and investment performance.

With more than 310,000 subscribers globally, Bloomberg is one of the world's biggest players in the business and financial information world. As a natural extension of its information service, it now wants to make the sustainability information it supplies to investors as rigorous as possible. Because of its respect within the financial community, Bloomberg's provision of such information could also signal 'the legitimacy of ESG as a core investing concern'. In 2009 it added over 100 sustainability indicators to its information service, such as water usage, toxic discharge and employee fatalities, and in 2011 it launched a dedicated sustainability site. It now has over 750 ESG data fields based on its research on 20,000 of the world's most actively traded public companies, which found that over 5,000 companies across 52 countries disclosed ESG data.

According to Jeff Leinaweaver, head of Seattle-based social venture company Global Zen Sustainability, Bloomberg's new data initiative is something to behold. When he saw it in action in 2013 he said it was 'surprising, and, frankly, awesome to witness how the discipline and power of the financial industry had created what could be one of the most helpful sets of tools available for impacting sustainable change'. He said that recent tragedies such as the collapse of the Rana Plaza clothing factory in Bangladesh have put pressure on companies to provide meaningful data to mitigate risks for shareholders and investors. Leinaweaver welcomed Bloomberg's initiative while remaining ambivalent about sustainability data produced at the centre of financial capitalism. He said that despite the power of such data, there is no guarantee analysts will use it properly or be able to report what is important to investors—nor that 'sustainability activists will give credence to anything laced with Wall Street or money'.

Park explained some of the enormous challenges involved in the pioneering work to make externalities visible, effectively by translating qualitative information into quantitative form. As he and Ravenel argue, 'to the extent that the *lingua franca* of modern finance is essentially quantitative, to gain entry into that realm, one must speak the language of numbers and analytics'.

And that is why—as Juniper has found—accounting has become such an important part of this dialogue: it can do this translating. The reporting of ESG implications has mostly been expressed through 'the vocabulary of sustainability, climate change, social justice, and other *qualitative* modes', as Park and Ravenel put it. It has not yet developed its own quantitative language. In terms of the financial industry, this means ESG information is doubly disadvantaged: because of its newness and because it struggles to find an effective way of communicating. As we have seen, in the quantitative realm of modern finance, business and economics, things only exist when they can be measured.

Bloomberg wants to do more generally what Trucost did for Puma's natural capital inputs: create standardised measures for the new capitals—such as ecosystem services and social impacts—so that this information can be aggregated and used by investors. Park and Ravenel call the failure to value clean air, water, stable coastlines and other environmental goods 'as much a failure to measure as it is a market failure *per se*—one that could be addressed in part by providing these "unpriced" resources with quantitative parameters that would enable their incorporation into market mechanisms. Such mechanisms could then appropriately "regulate" the consumption of those resources.' One of Bloomberg's initiatives to price externalities entails creating a 'stranded assets valuation tool'. This would measure the positive or negative effect of assets whose value might change dramatically if, for example, a reasonable price were given to carbon or water, or labour standards in emerging economies were properly regulated.

The pricing of externalities has the potential to lead to global stocktakes of the world's resources such as carbon or water, along the lines of the planetary accounting proposed by David Korten. This would make possible global prices and budgets for these stocks. In terms of water, such information would be geospatially specific: the cost of water in one location would be radically different from the cost of water in another. Various information organisations are now investigating the possibility of creating open-source databases to provide this sort of global spatially-specific information, to make it possible to see the state of different natural resources—coastlines, soil, aquifers, vegetation—and their local interactions by zooming in on particular areas of the earth. While much of this information already exists, these initiatives would aggregate it and then monitor it via remote sensors or people with mobile phones who would map the latest information directly onto a global database. While such a system would help us to manage the earth's natural resources, would it do so in the name of financial capital or of nature? Would it serve, say, to make water more readily available to an oil company intent on fracking? Or to preserve it for thirsty plants, animals and people? Such are the questions prompted by the drive to price externalities.

WHAT NOW FOR INTEGRATED REPORTING?

~

In this possible future world where the earth is mapped into an open-source global database and global limits are set for carbon and water use, there may be no corporate reporting. Or not as we currently understand it. Many at the forefront of corporate reporting believe that in the future we will not be talking about reporting at all; we will be talking about corporate *communication*. Reporting is an industrial-style, one-way process from a company to give information to the mass of its shareholders (or stakeholders). By contrast, communication is a multidirectional form of relating and can encompass individual exchanges between the company and those with a stake in its activities. Such communication is made possible by electronic information and the internet. Japan's WICI initiative is already developing technology that automates the preparation of corporate reporting and that might one day lead to total transparency for corporations: a world where investors, analysts and other capital providers can access a company's own systems so they can build their own reports without the company needing to prepare them.

More broadly, underpinning all of these initiatives is a crucial question. When I asked Robert Eccles whether he had a view on the ability of corporations to take care of the planet through integrated reporting, he said without missing a beat: 'I do have a view. The short-termism thing is a big deal.' He and other proponents of integrated reporting believe that integrated thinking and reporting can shift the focus of managers and investors to the long term. And because of the power of corporations, the future of the planet depends on it. Eccles cited figures comparing company revenue to GDP, a comparison that speaks volumes. In 1980, the aggregate revenues of the world's 1000 largest companies comprised about 30 per cent of the GDP of the OECD countries. In 2010, a mere 30 years later, this had increased to around 70 per cent. And in 2010, these 1000 corporations employed nearly 67 million people, compared to 21 million in 1980. Said Eccles:

> The point is, corporations are huge. And there's a handful that rule the world. Corporations are now the organising entities on earth and nations aren't, for the most part. Globalisation has concentrated economic power within a group of large companies who are now able to change the world at a scale historically reserved for nations. They virtually control the global economy. This vast concentration of influence should be the starting point for any strategy of institutional change towards a sustainable society.

'And our mission,' he said, referring to his work with George Serafeim, 'is to change them.' They aim to change the resource allocation decisions within companies and markets, and Eccles claims that 'integrated reporting [has] turned out to be a really powerful tool for doing that'.

In the eyes of its advocates, there are now two pressing opportunities—or challenges—for integrated reporting, one pertaining to capital allocation, the other to how we account for nature. Promoters of integrated reporting, such as KPMG's Nick Ridehalgh, believe it has the potential to correct one of the most urgent capital-allocation problems of our time: the increasingly evident running down of basic infrastructure, the transport, power, water, communications and other manufactured capital assets our lives depend upon. According to the World Economic Forum, the Swiss non-profit organisation which hosts the annual global business meeting in Davos, there is a US$1 trillion shortfall in global infrastructure spending: current global spending on basic infrastructure is US$2.7 trillion a year but it should be US$3.7 trillion. Meanwhile, there is US$50 trillion locked up in pension funds, insurance companies and other institutional investors. Why is this supply not meeting the demand? Because pension funds are making low-risk investments, and infrastructure projects are by their nature long term and so can seem like high-risk business. Ridehalgh believes this is a problem that integrated reporting could help to solve. If the companies responsible for the planned developments could demonstrate through integrated reporting their strategy and how they will manage risk and deliver effective returns over the long term—in other words, how they will create and preserve value over time—this would make such investments more attractive to pension funds. At the moment, however, with integrated reporting in its infancy, it is still too early to tell what its capabilities are in this area.

The other opportunity is accounting for nature. Jochen Zeitz, the man responsible for the world's first environmental profit and loss account, and John Elkington, who coined the 'triple bottom line' in 1994, believe that natural capital accounting will drive the adoption of the new integrated accounting paradigm. Certainly this is where the most advances have been made in terms of measurement, reporting and investment in the new capitals; it is also where Bloomberg's sights are set, and where the public's eyes are turned because global warming and climate change have made nature front-page news.

It seems the six capitals model of business is an evolving language which is conceptually useful to the new accounting paradigm because it expresses the extended role of business into spheres previously thought separate (such as nature and society) and makes clear their connection to financial capital and profit. But is this a desirable way of reframing the world? Is it the best way we have of making visible the corporation's connection to the external world and of encouraging it to be responsible towards it? And is natural capital the best way to express our relationship with nature and its worth? As it turns out, emerging concurrently with this new accounting paradigm are other—and I think better—ways of answering these questions.

6

REWRITING THE CODE: A TWENTY-FIRST-CENTURY CORPORATION AND THE RIGHTS OF NATURE

Accounting is probably the toughest nut to crack
because it goes to national company law, and
national company law is about as intimate and
personal a national characteristic as you can get.

FIELDS WICKER-MIURIN, 2000

If societies express their values through the
laws they make, one single legal change would
completely transform our understanding of the
relationship between nature and humankind:
giving nature rights.

BEGONIA FILGUEIRA AND IAN MASON, 2009

IN 1734, A COLONY OF TERMITES WAS SUMMONSED
to appear before an ecclesiastical court in Brazil's
province of Riedade Maranhâo. They had been tor-
menting the Franciscan friars in the local cloister by
eating their food, their furniture and houses. The counsel

231

in their defence praised the diligence and industry of the white ants, which he claimed were superior to those of the monks. To boost their case he further argued that the termites' claims to the territory were stronger than the monks' because they were native to the land, whereas the monks were interlopers. The monks' case collapsed in the face of such rhetorical ingenuity and they were forced to broker a compromise with the creatures. And so they agreed to grant the termites a reservation on which they could live in peace without further interference. The court then ordered the termites to leave the monastery and dwell henceforth in their decreed terrain. As the judge read the court's order, so it is chronicled, the termites left the monastery and marched in strict columns towards their new abode.

Almost one hundred years later, Thomas Jefferson said of a different sort of creature: 'I hope we shall crush in its birth the aristocracy of our moneyed corporations which dare already to challenge our government to a trial of strength, and bid defiance to the laws of our country.' In 1816, when Jefferson made his rebuke, corporate powers were carefully constrained by the state. Most American states required corporations to have a clear purpose, which was to be fulfilled but not exceeded. If a corporation's purpose was exceeded or not fulfilled—or if it misbehaved—the state legislature could revoke its licence to do business. A corporation was granted its charter for a fixed period of time and a stated purpose—such as ten to twenty years to build a canal or a railroad—and then it was dissolved. Management and stockholders were liable for all corporate actions, corporations were forbidden from making political contributions, and all corporate records and documents were open to the scrutiny of the state.

In the twenty-first century, both of these scenarios—the case of summonsable termites and Jefferson's shackled corporation—are ludicrous: termites do not have legal standing, and none of these checks on corporate power survives today. But in the new millennium the concepts that underpin them are back with a vengeance. Ideas of extending legal rights to nature, and of curtailing the rights of corporations—or of rebooting them for broader ends than profit alone—are alive and kicking.

Rebooting the corporation

Turning first to the possibilities of revamping the corporation, not just through the language of its accounts but by recombining its DNA—refiguring its code—we find two key initiatives. The first is a broad reconceiving of what the corporation should be in the twenty-first century. The second is a drive to rewrite its laws of charter.

As we saw in Chapter 3, since the late 1960s a new wave of activists has been working to civilise the corporation. Today, though, they are operating from the inside: they are chief executive officers like Puma's Jochen Zeitz, Unilever's Paul Polman and Virgin's Richard Branson, and bankers like Muhammad Yunus and Pavan Sukhdev. Also focused on corporate design itself are think tanks like Tony Manwaring's Tomorrow's Company, Boston-based Corporation 20/20 (co-founded by Marjorie Kelly and the ubiquitous Allen White), and Sukhdev's Corporation 2020. They all have one thing in common: faith that the corporation can drive the changes required to remake capitalism for a new era of sustainable growth—and a belief that it needs to be radically altered in order to do so.

It is worth looking at their vision of the corporation—driven by profit but recalibrated for the long term—before we turn to a new generation of activists working to rewrite the corporate code itself, and then to a move to refigure nature. This latter is a conceptual leap with the potential to generate a genuine paradigm shift—or even, remembering the catalyst at the apex of Donella Meadows' hierarchy, to produce a glitch in the system so powerful it transcends paradigms and profoundly changes our values.

RETHINKING THE CORPORATION

The first group of corporate activists are those working conceptually to redesign the corporation, including business leaders attempting to steer their own titanic corporations away from the dangers that lie in wait in the new millennium. The Centre for Tomorrow's Company was founded in London in 1996 with the aim of developing a new, more inclusive approach to doing business in a rapidly changing world. It was Tomorrow's

Company that proposed the idea of the corporation's 'triple context'—the dynamic relationship between the economy, society and environment—that has shaped the thinking of many of today's businesses and influenced South Africa's King III code, the UN Principles for Responsible Investment and the UK Companies Act 2006 (this Act requires directors to 'have regard' for six specific items, including the community and environment).

Allen White and Marjorie Kelly co-founded Corporation 20/20 in 2004 to redesign the corporation so it has social purpose and not just profit at its heart. They believe that making a new kind of corporation is *the* design challenge of our time, and that such a redesign is a precondition for transforming the world. Their '20/20' refers to corporations' need for 20/20 vision in the twenty-first century. Currently, the laws of most countries make it difficult for corporations to adopt structures not founded on maximising profits for shareholders. Despite this, various manoeuvres are making possible hybrid business forms, such as the joint venture between Bangladesh's microfinancing pioneer Grameen Bank and multinational yoghurt producer Danone, discussed below. Another innovative hybrid is the foundation-owned Danish pharmaceutical company Novo Nordisk—creator of one of the earliest integrated reports, in 2004—which describes its mission as being 'to defeat diabetes'. According to Kelly, one of the distinguishing features of these cutting-edge organisations is that they view themselves as living, evolving systems, as human communities, which is a radically different view from the one still held by most economists and lawyers, who see companies primarily as pieces of property which are owned through their shares and whose net worth is measured by their stock price.

Inspired by Corporation 20/20, in 2011 Pavan Sukhdev set up Corporation 2020 with the aim of formulating a new corporation, which he believes is urgently required by 2020, hence his '2020'. The missing agent in the case of Planet Earth versus Humanity came into Sukhdev's sights after he started to work with The Economics of Ecosystems and Biodiversity (TEEB) to cost the uncounted damage being done to nature by 'business as usual'. Sukhdev calls today's corporation the 'invisible foot' to Adam Smith's 'invisible hand', a term Smith used in his 1776 book *An Inquiry into the Nature and Causes of the Wealth of Nations* to describe the unseen way in which individuals pursuing their own gain also promote the good of society, which apparently explains the self-regulating behaviour of the marketplace. In Sukhdev's view, the corporation is crushing the world with its enormous unseen foot. He calls it an anachronism, a product of the fervent growth of corporate activity between 1820 and 1920, especially in America, and believes it must be remade with four ideas in mind. First, its goals must be clearly aligned with society's. Second, like the Brazilian cosmetics company Natura— which has created a community of over one million women who sell its products—the new corporation could become a community. Third, it could be an institute, like information technology multinational Infosys, which has built the world's largest corporate university in Mysore; the university trained 100,000 software professionals between its founding in 2002 and 2012. And fourth, the corporation of the future will be a 'capital factory', churning out human, social and natural capital as well as financial and manufactured capital. In Sukhdev's vision of the world inhabited by Corporation 2020, 'trusted corporations' would win contracts to manage common resources and public places such as forests, wetlands or coral reefs 'on behalf of and according to the dictates of their host societies and communities'. Sukhdev has such faith in this future Corporation 2020 that he would entrust the entire planet to its care, or at least place it as the cornerstone of a sustainable, green future. He says a new capitalism would prevail in such a world, one that recognises and rewards the creation of all the capitals. Because of their shared aims, Corporation 20/20 and Corporation 2020 have joined to become 'Corporation 2020 Alliance'.

But how are these visions of the future corporation played out in practice? The triple context of Tomorrow's Company has formulated the mission of Richard Branson and Jochen Zeitz's B Team, founded in 2012 under the banner 'people, planet and profit' to 'catalyse' a better way of doing business for the good of people and the planet. It brings together a small group of innovative leaders from the private and public sectors, including Paul

Polman of Unilever, Nobel Prize-winning microfinance guru Muhammad Yunus, Indian industrialist Ratan Tata, TOMS Shoes founder Blake Mycoskie, and the *Huffington Post*'s Arianna Huffington. Its honorary leaders are former Irish president Mary Robinson and former Norwegian prime minister Gro Harlem Brundtland. At its launch in June 2013, the B Team issued a declaration holding companies responsible for most of the problems afflicting the world in the twenty-first century, including poverty, inequality, unemployment and the depletion of natural resources. These problems are too big to be solved by non-profit organisations alone and governments have failed to act, its declaration continues, so the B Team is stepping into the breach and owning that much of the blame for our problems 'rests with the principles and practices of business as usual'. So business must now be done unusually.

Polman is particularly focused on the long term. When he became chief executive officer of Unilever in January 2009 (eight months after Greenpeace's *Dove Onslaught(er)* campaign), he banned quarterly reporting because he believes it encourages short-term thinking, and he urged the public to hold companies accountable for their actions. Polman does not believe it is his fiduciary duty to put shareholders first. He believes the opposite: that if he focuses Unilever on improving people's lives and finding sustainable ways to do business this will ultimately result in good shareholder returns. 'Why would you invest in a company which is out of sync with the needs of society, that does not take its social compliance in its supply chain seriously, that does not think about the costs of externalities, or of its negative impacts on society?' he asks. Similarly evoking today's blurred boundaries between business and the state, Mycoskie speaks about the chief executive officer's duty to listen to their customers in terms that sound like a national leader's duty to attend to their citizens: 'Because they're voting with their dollars.'

At the World Economic Forum in January 2014, the B Team launched eighteen pledges to improve business practices and advocate human rights (the latter informed by the United Nation's Guiding Principles on Business and Human Rights, endorsed in 2011), including a pledge to end quarterly reporting where legally possible and to publish more reports on how companies are meeting their environmental goals. For the moment, the B Team founders are making commitments in their own business practices—including Zeitz's environmental profit and loss account, which in his new role as director of Puma's parent company Kering and chairman of its board's sustainability committee he is now promoting across all Kering's companies, and Polman's aim to double Unilever's turnover while halving its environmental footprint—and urging other businesses to follow their lead. In Branson's words, these new-wave companies who are working for social and environmental good as well as for profits are 'throwing the rulebook out the window'. While such efforts to consider the environment are laudable, we might ask, as with Coca-Cola HBC's use of water and arable land, if we need twice as much turnover of Unilever's products and ever more of Kering's luxury fashion goods.

One partnership that exemplifies the B Team's spirit of 'Screw it, let's do it' (as Branson puts it) is Grameen Danone. This is a collaboration between multinational yoghurt maker Groupe Danone and Muhammad Yunus's Grameen Bank, a community development organisation founded in Bangladesh to make modest loans to poor people to allow them to start small enterprises. Its loans—especially to women, who it found are better at managing money than their husbands and sons—have improved the material existence of thousands of impoverished families around the world. Its work with Danone is the sort of hybrid business Marjorie Kelly champions. In October 2005, Groupe Danone's chief executive officer Franck Riboud invited Yunus to discuss a joint venture he had in mind, convinced that humanity's future 'relies on our ability to explore and invent new business models and new types of business corporations'. Danone was founded in Paris in 1929 to make yoghurt to treat intestinal complaints, and almost a century later its yoghurt is sold around the world. But in 2005 it was not sold in Bangladesh, and Riboud wanted to find a way to feed his yoghurt to Bangladesh's impoverished people. Yunus proposed a new sort of business venture, a cross between a for-profit and a non-profit organisation. Their hybrid would develop a vitamin-fortified yoghurt that could be sold door to door for a few cents in rural Bangladesh. Riboud seized the idea, committed US$1 million, and by that afternoon Yunus was planning the enterprise with the head of Danone's Asian operations.

As with the awesome capabilities of Bloomberg's databases, the ability of multinational Danone to act on this idea was impressive. Yunus could not believe how fast this groundbreaking move was made. He said of its novelty, 'We were creating something new under the sun: the world's first consciously designed multinational social business.' To suit the local needs, Danone scaled down its regular business style of huge factories and opened one small factory in the northern market town of Bogra. The business needed to be profitable so it could recover its full costs from operations (and pay a nominal 1 per cent annual dividend to investors), but the profits would be returned to it rather than mostly paid in dividends to shareholders. Yunus calls it a 'social business', a pioneering initiative for a more humane form of capitalism. One year later, Grameen Danone was making a yoghurt called Shokti Doi, which means 'strong as a lion' in Bengali.

While this was not a profit-driven venture for Danone, it was not without self-interest: it had a strategic marketing intent, allowing the company to establish a presence in Bangladesh for the first time. Given that around half its business is in the developing world, this was an important market to seize. But all did not go as planned. While the operations supported the rural communities—using milk from small farmers, many previously funded by micro loans from Grameen Bank, and employing local women to distribute the yoghurt in remote rural areas—the venture struggled to find reliable supplies of milk. When fresh milk prices doubled in 2008, pushing up the price of Shokti Doi, the company ran at a loss. In order to recover its sales, Danone began to sell its yoghurt to the more lucrative urban market; by 2010, this had grown to 80 per cent of its sales. It turned out that Bangladesh's rural poor do not normally eat yoghurt and so did not take to the scheme.

This hybrid venture between a multinational food producer and a pioneering community development bank makes an instructive comparison with another venture designed to help impoverished rural dwellers—One Earth Designs' efforts to develop solar cookers in western China, discussed below—and suggests that in order to do good such initiatives must be organic and community driven, starting with the people whose needs are being served, rather than with an idea conceived in a distant corporate head office. Interestingly, One Earth Designs is one of the new-generation corporations that has a mandated social and environmental purpose.

Recoding the corporation

This new generation of corporations has been brought into being by an organisation that has taken the idea of corporate social and environmental responsibility one step further than the B Team—and in doing so, I would argue, made a great leap for humankind and the planet. This organisation, called B Lab, has created a new sort of corporation by rewriting the very fundamentals of corporate being—its code—to extend its brief beyond its current profit-maximising purpose to include society and the environment. Unlike the Ford Motor Company and its successors, these new corporations cannot be sued for working with aims other than profit maximisation in mind. They are legally obliged to make a material positive contribution to society and the environment—and are held accountable for doing so. In April 2014, corporate lawyer John Montgomery—who helped to write California's 2012 legislation to make such companies possible—said that the corporation was 'on its own hero's journey and is evolving to acquire a conscience. Indeed, a global movement is afoot to correct the corporation's fundamental design flaw in order to endow it with the legal architecture that activates an internal social and environmental conscience'.

B Lab was founded in Philadelphia in 2006 by long-time friends Jay Coen Gilbert, Bart Houlahan and Andrew Kassoy. The idea came out of the experience of Gilbert and Houlahan, who had set up a successful basketball clothing and footwear company, AND1, which paid higher wages to its factory workers in China and gave 10 per cent of its profits to local charities. But when the pair decided to sell their business after a battle with Nike, they came up against the profit-maximising strictures of corporate law. Under pressure from private

equity partners and in order to fulfil its legal obligation
to maximise shareholder value, the company was forced
to undo all its social commitments so that it could be
sold. Realising that they were not alone in their experience—that there was a growing number of businesses
trying to address the enormous social and environmental
problems of the world but struggling to do so because
business structures were not legally set up to support their
pursuit of purposes other than profits—they conceived
the idea of a for-profit company with a legal mandate
to act in the interests of all its stakeholders, not just
its shareholders. Believing that business is 'the most
powerful man-made force on the planet', and in order
to harness its potential to work legally unimpeded for a
greater benefit than profit alone, they created B Lab to
support a global movement of entrepreneurs trying to
use business to change the world. They call these new-
paradigm businesses 'B Corporations'. The 'B' stands for
'benefit'—to workers, the community and the planet.

The benefit corporation redefines fiduciary duty to
include non-financial considerations in decision-making
and holds companies accountable to create a material
positive impact on society and the environment. This
impact must be measured by—and publicly reported
using—an independent, transparent third-party standard.
This is a radical departure from current fiduciary duty.
As Montgomery says, 'essentially what that does is
require the directors to exercise the beginnings of a
planetary consciousness'. To be certified, B Corporations

must undergo a rigorous testing process that measures their social and environmental performance standards, transparency and legal accountability. The certification process covers four key areas: governance, treatment of workers, community engagement and environmental responsibility. B Lab offers this rigorous certification process, which has been used by popular new-generation businesses such as outdoor clothing company Patagonia, vintage and handmade e-commerce website Etsy and icecream makers Ben & Jerry's.

Measurement and accounting are critical features of this model. With their new, extended purpose encoded in law, B Corporations also legally require a different sort of accounting. Directors of public B Corporations must meet a 'tripartite balancing requirement' in line with their public-benefit purpose, which includes reporting on overall social and environmental performance. This communicates to investors not only the return on their investments in financial terms, but also the companies' impact on the world around them.

As part of its rethinking of business behaviour, B Lab has issued a 'Declaration of Interdependence' which holds the following truths to be self-evident: "That we must be the change we seek in the world. That all business ought to be conducted as if people and place mattered. That, through their products, practices, and profits, businesses should aspire to do no harm and benefit all.' The declaration concludes: 'To do so requires that we act with the understanding that we are each dependent upon another and thus responsible for each other and future generations.' True to this vision, their mission is to make benefit corporations possible in all 50 states of the United States. In order to do so, B Lab is going across the country asking state legislatures to amend their corporate charters so that companies can be incorporated with explicit social and environmental ends. By mid 2014, 26 US states had passed benefit corporation legislation, and fourteen states were working on it. Montgomery began working on California's legislation in December 2010 and it was eventually passed in January 2012. He says that while he thinks the new generation has no problem with the idea of benefit corporations:

> My generation is squealing like a stuck pig.
> There is a lot of resistance to this. It's a new
> concept. It's very foreign to the prevailing
> paradigm that corporations exist solely to
> maximise profit for shareholders. It breaks
> the no longer tenable assumption in the
> current paradigm which is that the commons
> are infinite, resources are infinite, and that
> a corporation can maximise profit while
> ignoring all of the negative consequences of
> its behaviour . . . This is a profound shift.

The first two states to pass the legislation were Maryland and Vermont, in April and May 2010 respectively. On the day Maryland's benefit corporation legislation passed, B-Lab co-founder Gilbert said: 'Today marks an inflection point in the evolution of capitalism. With public trust in business at an all-time low, this represents the first systemic response to the underlying problems that created the financial crisis.' Maryland state senator Jamie Raskin said that he had sponsored the legislation because the world needs a new way of doing business:

> The corporations we've got are told by
> law that they have to pursue one exclusive
> objective, which is to maximize profit. And
> that singular command is not only incon-
> sistent with the broader yearnings of so many
> people in business, but it also has proven to be
> a deeply troubling public policy that creates
> terrible incentives and results. Think about
> the BP oil spill, the collapsing mines of the
> Massey company in West Virginia [when 29
> miners were killed in a mine explosion in the
> Appalachian coal fields in April 2010] and the
> multi-trillion dollar nightmare on Wall Street.

Raskin said he had hoped that by the end of the law's first year the state would have a dozen businesses incorporated as benefit corporations; in fact, a dozen registered on the very day the legislation was passed.

On 12 February 2012, New York became the seventh US state to pass benefit corporation legislation. The first company to adopt the status of a New York State benefit corporation was Greyston, a pioneering bakery started in the Bronx in 1982 by a Zen Buddhist meditation group under the leadership of Bernard Tetsugen Glassman. An aerospace engineer turned entrepreneur, Glassman created Greyston to employ people who had trouble finding work—including the homeless, ex-cons and former drug users—and to revitalise the impoverished community of southwest Yonkers, New York.

Greyston's first *Benefit Corporation Report 2012* looks like an exemplary integrated report: it clearly tells the company's story, conveys its ethos, its goals and its achievements in social, environmental and economic terms. The report measures its progress according to a rigorous evaluation that B Lab publishes in its B Impact Report. This assesses business practice against measures of social and environmental performance, accountability and transparency. True to Greyston's founding purpose, it excelled in its contribution to the community. However, it needed to improve its environmental performance. With that in mind, its focus for the following year was to bring its environmental performance to the level of its community performance. It set itself some ambitious goals: reducing its greenhouse gas emissions by 15 per cent in 2013 and by 25 per cent by the end of 2014; reducing its use of electricity for lighting by 70 per cent; auditing its supply chain; and reducing its landfill by 75 per cent in 2013 and by 90 per cent by the end of 2014.

B Corporations are now spreading across the world. In mid 2014, there were 1045 B Corporations in 34 countries in 60 different industries. As B Lab says, long before there were B Corporations, entrepreneurs were trying to use their business as a force for doing good, but they lacked the legal means and a collective voice. Now they are part of a global movement. One such company is China's One Earth Designs, which designs solar cookers (a device powered by solar energy which cooks, heats or pasteurises food or drink). Co-founder and environmental scientist Catlin Powers said that in becoming a B Corporation she and co-founder Scot Frank feel they have 'joined forces as part of a movement that we hope will change the way that businesses all around the world think and operate'.

Frank, an electrical engineer and computer scientist, first went to China in 2005 and ended up teaching an engineering course at Qinghai University in western China. There he helped his students with engineering projects in their local villages, such as building wells and greenhouses. Two years later, Powers, then a chemistry student, was studying climate change in the same Himalayan region when a local Qinghai family asked her why scientists were studying outdoor pollution when the pollution indoors was so much worse. Powers discovered that the air inside the family's house was ten times more polluted than the air in Beijing. She then learnt that every year more than half a million people in China died from toxic smoke from their stoves, and that around the world four million people died from similar causes. Powers decided to leave her university program to work with the villagers to find a solution to their problem. She realised that there was one abundant fuel source in the region that was clean and affordable: the sun. As Powers said, 'Every year in western China, enough sunlight falls on the Himalayan plateau to replace 170 billion tons of coal.' But the solar cooker technology at the time was too expensive and unsafe for the families to use in their homes. She then heard about a teacher, Frank, who was helping students to solve engineering problems in their communities— and together she and Frank founded One Earth Designs. They worked with the families to develop an inexpensive domestic solar cooker. After thirteen prototypes and scores of iterations they finally produced a cooker that the people liked to use. Named SolSource, it is more than 90 per cent energy efficient and is portable and durable. And it now brings clean energy to thousands of people in Asia. According to Powers, it generates power equivalent to that produced by cutting down and burning nearly 30,000 trees, the families' previous fuel for cooking. It is also sustainably manufactured and 100 per cent recyclable.

In 2012, One Earth Designs became the first company in China to be certified as a benefit corporation by B Lab for using sustainable practices in every aspect of its business operations. Powers says that their company performs in the near term for its shareholders and in the long term for the planet. They are now selling their products into the barbecue, camping and disaster-preparedness markets in the hope that this will allow the company to reduce prices for their customers in the developing world. Because SolSource harnesses such enormous amounts of energy, it can be used for a wide range of other household needs. One Earth Designs is now collaborating with the US, Hong Kong and Chinese governments to turn SolSource into a household energy plant, a single solar device that can heat, power computers and purify water.

In July 2013, B Lab celebrated a legislative milestone when Delaware became the nineteenth US state to enact benefit corporation legislation. This was massively significant because with its long history of corporation-friendly law Delaware is *the* state for incorporation. It is home to one million businesses, including 64 per cent of the Fortune 500 (an annual list published by *Fortune* magazine of the top 500 US corporations ranked by their gross revenue), and it has now validated this radically different business form. *Esquire* magazine noted the potentially epoch-shifting nature of this move when it said: 'B Corps might turn out to be like civil rights for blacks or voting rights for women—eccentric, unpopular ideas that took hold and changed the world.' When Delaware passed its benefit corporation legislation, the state's governor, Jack Markell, acknowledged that many people were sceptical about B Corporations but said that for him they were an important component of the twenty-first-century business landscape. Markell believes benefit corporations can help to re-create the old ties of businesses to their local communities by returning business's focus to its place in the social and natural world.

Although commentators have questioned the ability of benefit corporations to appeal to investors and access traditional capital markets, at the public ceremony for the passing of Delaware's legislation, Albert Wenger of New York investment firm Union Square Ventures gave them his seal of approval. He said that the legislation was an important foundation 'for both the venture funding process but also ultimately for these companies to be able to go public'. In other words, this legislation will allow them to become publicly listed because they are no longer under the legal obligation solely to maximise profit. Wenger noted that the critical challenge for capitalism today is not how to make more stuff but to work out how we can live in harmony with the environment, and what we can do about disappearing jobs, income inequality, and providing better access to affordable good-quality health care and education. He said that Union Square Ventures was seeing more and more entrepreneurs who are 'as much motivated by wanting to make the world a better place as they are motivated by wanting to make money'. But the firm had found it difficult to invest in such companies because to ensure their business's social or environmental vision, the founders would request board control or super voting shares; according to Wenger, these do not make for good governance, and are ultimately bad for investors and the business itself. The benefit corporation, in his view, 'provides an elegant solution to this':

It lets companies put social objectives right
up front, putting them in their charter, and
putting them right next to shareholder value,
on equal footing. And most importantly, it
empowers investors to hold founders and
management teams accountable for actually
pursuing these objectives.

Montgomery believes that benefit corporations are
doing something radical: they are beginning to impose
a conscience on the old-style corporation. In 2012, after
the Californian benefit corporation legislation had been
passed, he said, 'I fantasize about what . . . the global
economic system [would] look like if every single corporation on the planet had a planetary collective conscience.
It'd be a very different ball game.' If the advent of benefit
corporation legislation has the potential to create a very
different world by wiring a conscience into corporations, then another innovative piece of contemporary
legal engineering is endeavouring to do something very
similar for nature.

Recoding nature

While this rewriting of corporate being is happening
across the United States and spreading around the world,
another rewriting of being is also taking place: that of
nature. The challenge of how to live in harmony with

nature is finding its way into the courts and legislatures of regions and nations. Unlike the move to account for nature reconceived as 'natural capital', this is not about counting nature. It is about making nature count.

In 1972, legal scholar Christopher D. Stone published an article called *Should Trees Have Standing?: Toward legal rights for natural objects*, which challenged the legal precedent that trees—nature—are objects and therefore have no rights in law. Stone argued instead that trees should be given legal rights. In a carefully reasoned, deeply thoughtful and groundbreaking 31 pages, Stone overturns the perceptions enshrined in western legal codes of nature as property to be possessed, governed and used by man, for man. He argues that just as over the centuries we have extended legal rights to an increasing number of human beings—including slaves, women, children and racial minorities—and granted legal person-hood to various inanimate things such as trusts, ships, nation states and the ubiquitous corporation itself, so it is time to extend these rights of legal personhood to nature. Limiting himself to a discussion of 'non-animal' natural objects, Stone first outlines the broad case for why we might entertain such a thought, then clarifies exactly what it would mean to give legal standing to nature, before moving to the pragmatic reasons for doing so—our increasing destruction of the natural world—and finally turning to some powerful ethical and existential speculations on why such a move might turn out to be critical not only for human consciousness and our own future but for the future of the planet itself.

Stone first defines his use of the term 'legal rights' (because there is no accepted legal definition). He says that for something to be a '*holder of legal rights*' requires more than that an authority will review the actions of those who threaten it. Three extra criteria are required for a natural body, such as a river, to have its own rights: any legal proceedings must be made in the object's own name (not a human's); when granting legal relief, the court must take into account the damages to the natural entity (not limited to economic loss to humans); and relief (such as monetary compensation) must be for the benefit of the natural entity.

In an introduction called 'The Unthinkable', Stone draws on Darwin's *The Descent of Man* (1871) to argue that just as in the history of moral development our social instincts and sympathies have extended slowly outward from the family to ever wider circles of humans and other animals, so the history of the law shows a similar movement: over the centuries, legal rights have been extended to include ever wider groups of humans and entities. But as Stone points out, each such extension has initially seemed unthinkable. Early American jurists, for example, had trouble conceiving of the corporation as being a 'person', a 'citizen' with its own rights. And medieval scholars struggled with the same mental barriers regarding the Church and the State: 'How could they exist in law, as entities transcending the living pope and king?' As Stone says, the medieval mind saw—as we have lost the capacity to—'how unthinkable it was, and worked out the most elaborate conceits and fallacies to serve as anthropomorphic flesh for the Universal Church and the Universal Empire'. In the same way, nineteenth-century jurors found it impossible to conceive of a woman as having legal personhood. At the time, the definition of legal 'person' so incontrovertibly signalled masculinity that in 1875 a Wisconsin court could not begin to imagine how it might apply to a woman. It was so unthinkable to the court that a woman could be a legal 'person' that to call her one was the same as calling her a man. So much so that in the court's view it would then follow that she would be subject 'to prosecution for the paternity of a bastard, and . . . prosecution for rape'. As Stone says, these examples show that any extension of rights is at first so astonishing that it sounds 'odd or frightening or laughable'. He asks why people made jokes about the women's liberation movement. 'Is it not on account of—rather than in spite of—the underlying validity of the protests, and the uneasy awareness that recognition of them is inevitable?'

Stone turns this same cool logic to contemplating the rights of nature. 'The reason for this little discourse on the unthinkable, the reader must know by now . . . I am quite seriously proposing that we give legal rights to forests, oceans, rivers, and other so-called "natural objects" in the environment—indeed, to the natural environment as a whole.' Common law (and all but the most recent legislation) sees natural objects as things 'for man to conquer and master and use—in such a way as the law once looked on "man's" relationship to women and African Americans'. But Stone says it is not inevitable or wise that natural objects have no right to seek redress on their own behalf, especially as they are no less voiceless than corporations, states, universities, infants and others who have lawyers to speak for them. Just as legal guardians are provided for children and the mentally unfit, and for unfit (bankrupt) corporations, so they could be provided for nature. The only thing it requires to call an endangered river a person, says Stone, are lawyers as 'bold and imaginative' as those who convinced the Supreme Court that a corporation was a person under the Fourteenth Amendment, which had been enacted to secure the rights of former slaves. If judges could 'unabashedly' refer to the environment's legal rights when deciding cases of environmental damage, such as the pollution of a river or the destruction of a forest, then a new body of law addressing the rights of the environment would develop.

More intriguingly, Stone then considers what he calls the 'psychic and socio-psychic aspects' of giving trees standing. Given that our own health and wellbeing are so inextricably linked to the health of the environment, the aim of ensuring our wellbeing and that of nature 'will often be so mutually supportive' that it will be hard to see whether 'our rationale is to advance "us" or a new "us" that includes the environment'. This new 'us' that embraces a continuum of humans and nature is the mind shift at the heart of Stone's essay—and appreciation of this inextricable interrelationship between humans and the natural world is expressed by several recent legal moves to enshrine the rights of nature to protect it from corporations. Alone among the thinkers in this book, Stone makes a penetrating and 'frank' avowal: 'what I am proposing is going to cost "us", i.e., reduce our standard of living as measured in terms of our present values.' But, he argues, not only do our present values depend on spurious measures such as the GDP, but the crises of the earth actually demand that we change our ways 'radically'. Giving rights to nature is a powerful way of doing this. As Stone then argues, this radical change 'depends in part upon effecting a radical shift in our feelings about "our" place in the rest of Nature'.

Stone then digresses into the territory of ethics and metaphysics, to argue that such a radical reconception of our relationship with nature would not only help to solve the material problems of the planet, it would also make us better humans. He argues that leaving behind the Enlightenment view of nature as a collection of 'useful senseless objects' is 'deeply involved in the development of our abilities to love'. We can only reach a 'heightened awareness' of others, including nature, if we 'give up some psychic investment in our sense of separateness and specialness in the universe'. He says that this is

hard giving indeed, because it involves us in
a flight backwards, into earlier stages of civi-
lization and childhood in which we had to
trust (and perhaps fear) our environment, for
we had not then the power to master it. Yet,
in doing so, we, as persons, gradually free
ourselves of needs for supportive illusions.

Or perhaps this is no 'flight backwards', but a new
way of thinking for those who have lost their native
ties to the earth—still retained by many indigenous
peoples and others throughout the world—courtesy of
the industrial era. Stone concludes by suggesting that if
the US Supreme Court awarded rights in the case of the
environment, the effect on popular consciousness could
be significant: 'It would be a modest move, to be sure,
but one in furtherance of a large goal: the future of the
planet as we know it.'

So what prompted this sober legal scholar to write
such a radical tract? Thirty-five years after he wrote it,
Stone responded to questions about where he got the
idea. He said he knew the exact moment 'when the idea
and I met up'. And at that moment, his thoughts were
not even on the environment. He was teaching a class
on property law and discussing the way changes to the
law have been accompanied by changes in power and
consciousness. He suddenly found himself asking what
a radically different law-driven consciousness would look
like. Say, 'one in which Nature had rights?' He elaborated

this scenario before asking: 'How would such a posture *in law* affect a community's view of *itself*?' The classroom burst into uproar. The students thought the idea preposterous. When the class was over, Stone stepped outside and asked himself: 'What did you just say in there? How could a tree have *rights*?' He had no idea. But his urge to answer his question became *Should Trees Have Standing?*

Initially, Stone was driven by the desire to show that his idea was not incoherent. He set out to find a pending case to test his nature-centred idea of rights. Within half an hour his library had found such a case, involving Mineral King Valley in the Sierra Nevada mountain range of California, at the time entitled *Sierra Club v. Hickel*, which had recently been decided by the Ninth Circuit Court of Appeals. The US Forest Service had granted Walt Disney Enterprises a permit to build a complex of motels, restaurants and recreation areas in the Mineral King Valley and the environmental organisation the Sierra Club was contesting it, alleging that the construction would damage the valley's 'aesthetic and ecological balance'. When Stone came to it, the case had been docketed for review by the US Supreme Court under the name *Sierra Club v. Morton*. In the initial trial, the court had held that the Sierra Club could not bring the case to trial because the damage was not done to the organisation itself but to the valley. But in Stone's new conception, although the injury to the Sierra Club might have been tenuous, the potential damage to Mineral King Valley was real. If the court could be persuaded to think of the valley as a legal person—as corporations are—then the idea of nature having rights would be the difference between the case being heard and not being heard. In other words, if the valley were a legal person it could become the plaintiff 'adversely affected' and the Sierra Club its guardian, and the case could be heard in the valley's own name. This seemed to Stone a more direct way of getting to the real issue of the case, which was not about how the valley's development would affect the club, but about what its clearing for roads and buildings would do to the valley.

Stone wrote his essay in time to get the attention of the only judge on the court likely to respond to his argument: Justice William O. Douglas, the most 'committed civil libertarian ever to sit on the court', in the words of *Time* magazine in 1975. Although the Supreme Court held with the original decision and the case was thrown out, Justice Douglas opened his dissent by endorsing Stone's view. He said:

> The critical question of 'standing' would be simplified and also put neatly in focus if we . . . allowed environmental issues to be litigated . . . in the name of the inanimate object about to be despoiled, defaced, or invaded . . . Inanimate objects are sometimes parties in litigation. A ship has a legal personality, a fiction found useful for maritime purposes . . . The ordinary corporation is a 'person'

for purposes of the adjudicatory process . . .
Contemporary public concern for protecting
nature's ecological equilibrium should lead to
the conferral of standing upon environmental
objects to sue for their own preservation. See
Should Trees Have Standing? . . . This suit
would therefore be more properly labeled as
Mineral King [Valley] v. Morton.

Following Justice Douglas's radical dissent, people
clamoured to read Stone's essay. It was immediately published in book form and then in a mass-market edition
in 1975. Stone's thinking was picked up by the environmental movement, fed into debates about the nature of
legal rights, and influenced courts, legal scholarship and
the wider society.

COMMUNITY ENVIRONMENTAL LEGAL DEFENSE FUND

One group promoting the idea of legal rights for nature
is the Community Environmental Legal Defense Fund
(CELDF), founded in Pennsylvania in 1995 by Thomas
Linzey and Stacey Schmader to provide legal services to
contest the rights of corporations over local communities
and the environment. CELDF now works with groups
in the United States and around the world to organise
and draft legislation to change the legal status of natural
communities (interrelated systems of plants and animals,
their physical environment, and the natural processes

that affect them) and ecoystems from that of property to rights-bearing entities.

Linzey wanted to help people stop developments that might put public health or the environment at risk. But as Jason Mark, editor of *Earth Island Journal*, said of Linzey's early attempts to do this, 'He found that even when he won, he lost. Companies were almost always able to slip through the regulatory system meant to control their activities.' This was made possible by corporations' constitutional rights as natural persons. So CELDF had to find a way to sidestep the laws that make it illegal for people to become stewards of the environment and create sustainable communities. And so it began to work with city councils to pass ordinances that 'simply asserted a community's right to self-governance and declared that within their jurisdictions corporations would no longer enjoy the rights granted to flesh and blood people'.

After passing dozens of such ordinances, CELDF began to consider a new approach which entailed including a legal statement to give communities rights over their local environment. As one of its organisers, Ben Price, put it, 'we are empowering the community to protect their natural environment, even when they don't have a claim of ownership to the land, or to the river, or whatever'. This idea was first tested when Price asked Tamaqua Borough local councillor Cathy Miorelli if she would sponsor an anti-dumping ordinance with a rights of nature provision. She agreed.

And so the first law recognising the rights of natural communities to flourish was included as a provision to an anti-sewage sludge ordinance passed by the city council of Tamaqua Borough in Pennsylvania in 2006. Section 7.6 of the ordinance says:

> It shall be unlawful for any corporation or its directors, officers, owners, or managers to interfere with the existence of natural communities or ecosystems, or to cause damage to those natural communities or ecosystems. The Borough of Tamaqua, along with any resident of the Borough, shall have standing to seek declaratory, injunctive, and compensatory relief for damages caused to natural communities and ecosystems within the Borough . . . ecosystems shall be considered to be 'persons' for purposes of the enforcement.

This meant that not only did nature have inalienable rights, but that any human resident could act as the legal guardian of a threatened ecosystem, 'even if she couldn't demonstrate financial harm from the destruction of that ecosystem'. The old guard on the council wanted to allow the dumping of sludge because of the money it would bring in. The town's solicitor warned that Tamaqua would be sued if the ordinance was passed. The council voted three in favour, three against, with the mayor casting the deciding vote in favour of the ordinance.

When journalist Elisabeth Eaves covered the story for *Forbes* magazine in May 2007 she noted the radical nature of the ordinance. She wrote that the borough of Tamaqua had

> passed an unprecedented law giving ecosystems legal rights of their own. Yes, you read that right. The trees, rivers, mountains and all the little critters that live in them have rights just like people, at least in Tamaqua . . . and at least until the law is struck down . . . The law flies in the face of thousands of years of Western legal precedent that treats nature strictly as property.

The Tamaqua Borough ordinance inspired other communities, in Vermont, Massachusetts and Pennsylvania, to adopt similar local laws that recognise the rights of nature. In 2010, the City of Pittsburgh became the first major municipality in the United States to recognise rights for nature.

ECUADOR GRANTS CONSTITUTIONAL RIGHTS TO NATURE

In September 2008, assisted by CELDF, Ecuador became the first nation in the world to grant rights to nature when two-thirds of its citizens voted to approve a new Constitution that includes such rights. The Constitution states: 'Natural communities and ecosystems possess the unalienable right to exist, flourish and evolve within

Ecuador. Those rights shall be self-executing and it shall be the duty and right of all Ecuadorian governments, communities and individuals to enforce those rights.' The legislation was introduced to protect Ecuador's environment from multinational corporate interests. Belen Paez from the indigenous and nature rights organisation Fundación Pachamama said of the new law: 'As a country devastated by oil exploitation, industrial agriculture and international debt, Ecuador needs a bulwark against the corporate plunder of our natural riches. Recognizing the Rights of Nature in our national laws begins to provide that protection.'

Because of their experience with environmental legislation, members of CELDF worked with Ecuador's constitutional assembly to draft the legally enforceable rights of nature. Mari Margil, associate director of CELDF, said that the new law marked a watershed in the trajectory of environmental law. According to Ecuadorian lawyer Mario Melo, who specialises in environmental law and human rights, 'the new Constitution redefines people's relationship with nature by asserting that nature is not just an object to be appropriated and exploited by people but is a rights-bearing entity that should be treated with parity under the law'. In this sense, he said, 'the new constitution reflects the traditions of indigenous people in Ecuador, who see nature as a mother and call her by a proper name, Pachamama'. At first, however, Ecuador's indigenous community had resisted the idea of including rights for nature in the Constitution. As jounalist Jason

Mark said of their view, 'The whole idea seemed yet another example of industrial society's arrogance. Nature already had rights, some Indigenous people felt; it wasn't for humans to "grant" nature anything.' But eventually they did support it.

The new legislation was tested in 2011 when a suit was brought against the provincial government of Loja on behalf of the Vilcabamba River. Work to widen a road beside the river had tipped rocks and excavation debris into the river and caused severe flooding over the riverside communities. The case was presented before the Provincial Court of Justice of Loja in March 2011, and the court found in favour of nature—the river itself—against the provincial government. The court acknowledged the importance of nature and said that damage to it affects not only the present generation but also future generations. The government was forced to stop the roadwork and rehabilitate the river. It also had to make a quarter-page apology in the local newspaper for starting the road construction without an environmental licence.

However, in December 2013 the Ecuadorian government controversially shut down the environmental activist group Fundación Pachamama, which had been involved in Ecuador's move to grant rights to nature. In July 2014, its centre in Quito which had been operating since 1997 was officially closed. Before it was shut down, the group had been working with local indigenous people to oppose proposed oil drilling in the Yasuni National Park in the Amazon Basin. Six months after the organisation was shut down, in May 2014, Ecuador's environment minister signed the environmental licence permitting oil exploration in Yasuni National Park. The first barrels of oil are expected in 2016.

This turn against the rights of indigenous communities and the Yasuni National Park was said by President Rafael Correa to have been forced on his government by the failure of foreign support for the trust fund set up to leave the park's oil in the ground. Of its goal to raise US$3.6 billion only US$13 million was donated, by individuals such as Al Gore and Leonardo diCaprio, and by Germany, Spain, France, Sweden and Switzerland. There were also suggestions (uncovered by the *Guardian* in February 2014) that since 2009 the Ecuadorian government had been negotiating a secret US$1 billion deal with the China Development Bank to allow oil exploration in the Yasuni National Park and had no intention of preserving it. This signals not only the might of the energy industry and the world's current dependence on petrochemicals. The experience of the rights of nature to date in Ecuador also suggests that as with the enactment of human rights, such laws not only need strong bodies to enforce them, but that their recognition takes time to be accepted by and change the prevailing culture.

Universal Declaration of the Rights of Mother Earth

The idea of rights for nature was one of three key topics addressed by the World People's Conference on

Climate Change and the Rights of Mother Earth held in Cochabamba, Bolivia, in April 2010. As a companion to the United Nations' 1948 Universal Declaration of Human Rights, the conference proposed a People's Agreement containing a Universal Declaration of the Rights of Mother Earth. Supporters of the Declaration include Canadian environmental activist Maude Barlow and South African environmental lawyer Cormac Cullinan, whose work helped to inspire CELDF's Tamaqua ordinance. Its advocates see it as the only way of achieving the global shift in thinking required to deal with climate change and the destruction of the earth, and in terms that will also address the increasing inequality between the nations of the northern hemisphere and those of the south. The Universal Declaration of the Rights of Mother Earth states that the people and nations of the earth are 'all part of Mother Earth, an indivisible, living community of interrelated and interdependent beings with a common destiny'. It defines Mother Earth, outlines her rights and those of each being, and the obligations of human beings to Mother Earth, including promoting economic systems that are in harmony with her.

The document was part of the negotiating text for the United Nations Framework Convention on Climate Change (UNFCCC) at its conference in Mexico at the end of 2010. But when the official conference text was eventually released with no trace of the Declaration, three of the groups responsible for it—the social action organisation the Council of Canadians, the Fundación

Pachamama, and the human-rights organisation Global
Exchange—released a report called *Does Nature Have
Rights?* Calling the continuing failure of international
leaders to agree on solutions to climate change 'predict-
able', the report argued that the UNFCCC 'is based not
on the root causes of environmental exploitation' but on
'"market fixes" to the same corporate-led economic model
and "endless-more" value system that have driven us to
the cliff's edge'. It asserted that solutions will not come
from our current property-based view of human relations
with nature which allows it to be exploited, but from
recognising that nature has rights. The authors called
for the UN General Assembly to adopt the Universal
Declaration of the Rights of Mother Earth as 'a common
standard of achievement for all peoples and all nations
of the world'.

Its fate in terms of its United Nations adoption is
pending. However, Maude Barlow has high hopes for
the potential of the Declaration, claiming that one day
it will stand as 'the companion to the 1948 Universal
Declaration of Human Rights as one of the guiding
covenants of our time'.

Bolivia's Mother Earth Law

On 15 October 2012, Bolivia passed the world's first law
granting all nature equal rights to humans: the Framework
Law on Mother Earth and Integral Development to Live
Well (law no. 300 of 2012). The inclusion of 'Integral
Development to Live Well' refers to Bolivia's indigenous

philosophy of '*vivir bien*', which is central to a new body of legislation passed by the country since 2006. It is defined as 'a civilizational and cultural alternative to capitalism based on the indigenous worldview' that 'signifies living in complementarity, harmony and balance with Mother Nature and societies, in equality and solidarity and eliminating inequalities and forms of domination. It is to Live Well among each other, Live Well with our surroundings and Live Well with ourselves'.

Under the new law, Mother Nature is defined as 'the living and dynamic system formed by the indivisible community of all life systems and living things who are interdependent, interrelated and which complement each other sharing a common destiny', and natural resources—including the country's rich mineral deposits—are called 'blessings'. The law created a Ministry of Mother Nature and an ombudsman to advocate the rights of nature. Among the eleven new rights for nature are the rights to pure water and clean air; the right to maintain the integrity of life and natural processes; the right not to have cellular structures modified or genetically altered; the right to continue vital cycles and processes free from human alteration; and the right not to be affected by mega-infrastructure and development projects that affect the balance of ecosystems and the local inhabitant communities. The law acknowledges Mother Earth as sacred, which is consonant with the views of indigenous Bolivians, who like the Ecuadorians call her 'Pachamama' (she is worshipped in this name by the indigenous people of the Andes). It also contains principles that acknowledge the rights of nature, society and future generations, and affirm the value of harmony, collective good and multiculturalism.

Bolivia's president Evo Morales has been a long-time vocal advocate on the world stage of the earth and its rights. Inspired by Bolivia, in 2009 the UN General Assembly proclaimed 22 April 'International Mother Earth Day', and in October of the same year it named Morales 'World Hero of Mother Earth'. Speaking of the new law, Bolivia's UN ambassador Pablo Solón argued that it was necessary in terms of achieving some kind of balance in the relative power of corporations and the natural world. He said: 'If . . . you think that the only [entities] who have rights are humans or companies, then how can you reach balance? But if you recognise that nature too has rights, and [if you provide] legal forms to protect and preserve those rights, then you can achieve balance.'

In its 2014 report on climate change legislation around the world, the London School of Economics called Bolivia's law 'a sweeping overhaul of the national management of natural resources, climate, and ecosystems'. The report says: 'In a novel approach to climate change, the government also believes the planet is an entity with inherent rights to be protected by states.' But it noted that the legislation lacked 'hard targets' by which to measure its implementation.

So far the changes the law has brought are more conceptual than actual. According to environmental lawyer Begonia Filgueira of UK legal consultancy the Environmental Regulation and Information Centre, the law makes two fundamental changes to the legal status of the earth. First, it grants the earth legal personality, which allows it to bring legal action to defend its rights. And second, it characterises the earth as being of 'public benefit'. This is significant because many western laws give public interest precedence over the environment— and define public interest in terms of economic standards. So to conflate public benefit with the wellbeing of the earth community or the earth itself has the potential to shift the distribution of power from the economy towards the earth. Previously in conflicts over development only corporations, humans and governments were relevant subjects. Now, in Bolivia, nature is as well.

The law makes the conceptual leap that Stone postulated in 1972, by breaking down the distinctions between humans and the natural world and seeing them as part of an interconnected continuum. In terms of the future of the planet and our accountability to the earth, this shift is as significant as—if not more significant than—B Lab's reconception of the corporation as having a legally binding social and environmental mandate. Speaking at the UN General Assembly on 20 April 2011, Solón echoed Stone's argument when he said of the rights of nature:

to think that only humans should enjoy
privileges while other living things are simply
objects is the worst mistake humanity has
ever made. Decades ago, to talk about slaves
as having the same rights as everyone else
seemed like the same heresy that it is now
to talk about glaciers or rivers or trees as
having rights.

THE WHANGANUI RIVER

A different conception of the relation between humans
and place—and the polar opposite of the idea of 'biodiversity offsets' which make nature fungible, one place
exchangeable for another—has been found by a western
legislature to govern a river and its local people in New
Zealand. If it is difficult for most urban westerners to
conceive of themselves as part of a continuum with
nature, it is impossible for many indigenous people to
conceive of themselves as apart from it. In September
2012, a river in the North Island of New Zealand became
a legal person. In one of the longest-running court cases
in the country's history, the Whanganui Iwi (the river's
traditional custodians) were recognised as having an
inextricable relationship with the river, and the river
was recognised as 'Te Awa Tupua'—an integrated, living
whole. In the preliminary agreement signed between
the Whanganui Iwi and the Crown, the river became a
legal person in the same way a company is, which will
give it rights and interests. Two guardians—one from

the iwi and one from the Crown—were given the role of protecting the river.

On 26 March 2014, the Whanganui River Deed of Settlement was initialled; if agreed to by Whanganui Iwi members, it will settle the historical Treaty of Waitangi claims related to the river. (This Treaty was signed in 1840 between the British Crown and some 540 Maori chiefs; among other things, it recognised Maori ownership of their lands and other properties.) The Minister for Treaty of Waitangi Negotiations, Christopher Finlayson, said that this was 'a major step in resolving a dispute with the Crown which the Whanganui Iwi has been pursuing through the Courts since 1873'. According to Finlayson, the Whanganui River Deed of Settlement and Te Awa Tupua Framework do three things: address and settle longstanding historical grievances of Whanganui Iwi in relation to the Whanganui River in a way that will recognise the innate relationship between the iwi and the river for the first time; recognise the river as 'Te Awa Tupua, an integrated living whole from the mountains to the sea and . . . intrinsically connected to the iwi, with its own legal identity'; and bring together the iwi and the wider community based on Te Awa Tupua values to manage the long-term environmental, social, cultural and economic health and wellbeing of the river. The settlement also includes NZ$80 million in compensation and NZ$30 million for those seeking funding for projects related to Te Awa Tupua.

Te Awa Tupua has no literal translation in English but 'embraces the spiritual aspects of the river and the intrinsic interrelationship of people with it'. It recognises that the river system itself has certain interests and values of its own and gives the river legal standing and an independent voice. After the agreement, the Whanganui Iwi will not 'own' the river, because they do not view their relationship with the river in terms of ownership. Rather, the river 'owns' the iwi, which means its people have obligations and responsibilities towards the river. The iwi's priority is to have the status of the river recognised and ensure its health and wellbeing. The agreement does this.

This is significant beyond its vital importance for the Whanganui River and its iwi because it establishes a vastly different legal understanding of human relationships with the environment from that of western law and the prevailing culture, one which overturns western notions of 'ownership' and promotes concepts of human beings as belonging to and custodians of the environment in which they live.

Christopher Stone's spontaneous question during a lecture on property law was pregnant with possibility. What would a radically different law-driven conscious-ness look like, 'one in which Nature had rights?' His startling question has far-reaching consequences. For a start, if nature were given legal personhood, it would create a duty of care towards the environment (as the Te Awa Tupua framework does). It would also form the basis of a more equal engagement between human beings and the natural world of which we are a part. As environmental lawyers Filgueira and Ian Mason point out:

> If the sea had rights, overfishing would not be a matter of quotas set by the government but of balancing the rights of fish and humans. If the atmosphere could be a legal entity, its representative would have a say in carbon trading. A river with a right to flow continually being harmed by damming would require the courts to intervene in deciding whether the human need is greater than that of the river to subsist.

This idea is consistent with an existing United Nations charter: the 1982 World Charter for Nature, which was ratified by more than 150 United Nations members and which sets out 'human duties towards the earth' and creates 'earth rights'. For the moment there is no way of enforcing it. As Filgueira and Mason say, and as Monbiot, Juniper and Sandel imply, language is a powerful tool. What would happen if we stopped thinking of nature as a resource, as so much property to be owned? What if instead of reframing it as natural capital in order to make it yield financial capital, we saw it as it really is: an extension of ourselves? What if we could make nature count?

Epilogue

CORPORATIONS WITH CONSCIENCE AND A PLANET WITH BEING

Whilst accountants might not be willing or
able to 'save the world' . . . if we (or those other
accountants) are part of the problem, how will it
be saved without our (or their) involvement?

CAROL ADAMS, 2014

Very small changes in the corporate code can
change the world.

JOHN MONTGOMERY, 2012

. . . the question is, how do you value the
resource? [By] the profit you can make? Or the
taonga (treasure's) contribution to the survival of
the group?

HONOURABLE DR PITA SHARPLES, NEW ZEALAND
MINISTER OF MAORI AFFAIRS

TWO QUESTIONS DROVE THIS BOOK: CAN ACCOUNT-
ants save the planet, by making us account for
so-called externalities? And is it time for a psychological

279

intervention in the modern corporation? These questions
are, of course, inextricably linked. They are derived
from the logic that drives the modern corporation and
thus the twenty-first-century global economy: profit
maximisation. We have privileged financial capital
over every other value on earth, including the value of
nature and of human beings and our communities. While
Wall Street booms and nations stagger, we continue to
tear apart the earth and effectively enslave ourselves to
financial capital—money—to fuel our fixation with economic growth. The polar ice caps melt, extreme weather
becomes the norm, species become extinct, the financially
rich nations of the earth are plagued by depression and
obesity and the impoverished nations are haunted by
homelessness and hunger. And yet we remain blind to
their interconnectedness and their cause. Can integrated
reporting address this problem? Can accountants save
the planet?

After wrestling with these questions since I first heard
about a nascent accounting revolution which turned out
to be an evolution—of natural capital accounting for
nations, and of integrated reporting with its six capitals
model for corporations (and having been plunged into
the grey and complex moral territory they open up)—it
seems to me that the single greatest benefit of this new
accounting paradigm is that it makes clear what was
previously shrouded. The daily operations of business are
destroying the planet and human societies and they do so
because they are governed by one sole legal obligation: to

maximise profit. And most nation states act to encourage this at every turn, still speaking the language of GDP and in thrall to the false rule of economic growth it measures—as seen in the recent case in Greece of the potentially treasonable offence of getting such figures 'wrong'—despite talk of going 'beyond GDP' to use a broad range of national metrics expressed by the term 'wellbeing'.

At the national level, the elevation of natural capital to the same status as GDP and the publication of the System of Environmental–Economic Accounting in February 2014 are promising signs. But talk of natural capital has not yet made it to the front pages of newspapers—other than in the United Kingdom, where the proposed use of biodiversity offsetting by the developers of Smithy Wood shows its potential as a way of enabling the destruction of a treasured wood with little regard for its intrinsic value. The International Integrated Reporting Council is the first concerted effort on a global scale to systematically address this problem of (short-term) profit maximisation at a business level. It at least acknowledges that the so-called externalities—society and the environment—are not in fact externalities. The six capitals model is a powerful way of asking corporations to consider their impact on their social and natural environments only so recently accepted as being inextricably linked to their commerce after all. So it does give business the option of responding to the problem of externalities, and within this frame the pioneering work of Puma's environmental profit and loss account has made a start on accounting for nature. Integrated reporting is, as its advocates say, an idea whose time has come.

But there is a logical inconsistency at the heart of the six capitals model which will prevent it alone from saving the planet: it seeks to account for non-financial value but can see it only in terms of financial value. This is because the entity it seeks to govern, the corporation as we know it, is legally bound to make decisions in favour of financial capital. The six capitals model is predicated upon a corporation which privileges this single store of value, even though it is in fact the only metaphoric wealth in the array of six 'capitals'. The other five capitals pertain to—or in the case of manufactured capital are derived from—living systems; they are the only literal wealth the planet can yield. Although these cutting-edge accountants have conceived a new-paradigm accounting scheme to measure the new invisible wealth generated by the information age and the sustainability information required for our era of environmental distress, they are nevertheless applying it to an old-paradigm corporation, one rooted in the industrial era, when financial measures captured most of the value that counted and profit ruled supreme. That this is the case is suggested by the efforts to rethink the corporation of Pavan Sukhdev, Allen White and Marjorie Kelly, and more radically by the advent of benefit corporations. In the hands of the industrial-age corporation, the six capitals model becomes a style of thinking and reporting that helps, say, a multinational giant to better manage its sole purpose of extracting the dying reserves of the earth's water to transform it into sugared drinks which very likely contribute to the diabetes epidemic and which are distributed in countless plastic bottles and aluminium cans that litter the planet, with the single end of enhancing its shareholders' financial capital. This is inconsistent, to say the least, with the values of nature and society—these vital ecosystems whose intricate workings are ultimately as mysterious to us as life itself—many of which cannot be translated into numerical or monetary form despite ideas like ecosystem offsetting and attempts by Trucost, Bloomberg and others to price them, not now and not ever.

Nature, humans and societies are living systems. They are not fungible. They cannot be offset. Can we begin to appreciate this, even while using Juniper's language of accounting to argue for their preservation, as the only language that has value in the global conversation of our age? Or will we learn new respect for those means we already have to communicate their intrinsic and infinite value, the poetry Monbiot alludes to when speaking for nightingales, the pregnant histories he conjures when advocating the preservation of Smithy Wood, the Whanganui Iwi's proverb 'Ko au te awa. Ko te awa ko au'—'I am the river. The river is me'?

But there is a new corporation coming into being. The new-paradigm corporation is the benefit corporation, with its legal obligation to act in ways that produce a material positive benefit for society and nature, as well as making a profit. This obligation is embedded in its very DNA. This corporation must report annually about the ways in which it has had a material positive impact on society and the environment, as well as on its financial welfare. It cannot be sued for favouring the interests of society and the environment over those of financial capital. It is not only held legally accountable to nature and society, but it must act in ways that positively benefit them, even if apparently at a cost to financial capital. This corporation is better suited to the new interconnected information age with its multiple crises. And in the hands of a benefit corporation, an integrated report makes genuine sense; it is a logical outcome. The interests of its stakeholders—not only its shareholders—are written into its very code. As John Montgomery says, 'It's the newest evolutionary form of a business firm', a corporation with conscience.

In terms of the history of accounting, the need for something like integrated reporting announces that the exclusive reign of double-entry bookkeeping is over. It can still yield important information, but it can no longer tell us everything we need to know about a firm or a nation, not even in financial terms. The 'new' 'invisible' value—the value of a company's reputation, of human relationships, worker wellbeing, social and environmental care, the quality of our culture—cannot be measured with an industrial-age tool. And while we can devise various numerical measures for these values—such as the number of work accidents a year or the amount of greenhouse gas emitted or water recycled—ultimately the new value is best conveyed in words, in stories. And this, as Paul Druckman says, is what integrated reporting is all about: telling the company's story. It seems the accountants of the future will be as much storytellers as bean counters. And the stories businesses tell are persuasive. Would you rather invest in a petroleum giant that destroyed a vast swathe of the planet in 2010 or a benefit company working with villagers to make cheap, recyclable solar cookers that may one day power all the energy needs of your own house—and as a consequence, usher in the possibility of a world of clean, decentralised energy sourced in the home? Would you rather put your money into a bakery that employs people who would otherwise struggle to find work, or a company that pledges to double turnover while making yet more cosmetics and cleaning products from palm oil plantations regardless of its vow to use only certified sustainable palm oil products by 2020? These are stories, not numbers and money. And they are telling. A world run by benefit corporations would require us to accept lower returns on our financial capital for the sake of investments in human, social and natural capital. And it might herald the advent of the benefit nation as well as the benefit corporation.

But benefit corporations alone are not enough to save the planet. We need wisdom and we need to change our ways. In *What Money Can't Buy*, Michael Sandel says that to arrest the encroachment of markets into every sphere of our lives we need to change our mindsets. Yet

even Sandel, mustering the full force of his philosoph-
ical might in his case-by-case analysis of market creep,
cannot offer a larger moral framework within which
to argue for limiting markets, precisely because in the
twenty-first century all larger, shared moral frames
have broken down—and it is into this breach that the
market has stepped. In a globalised world with little
common moral ground it is difficult to agree on just
which values are worth caring about and why, and so it
seems easier to outsource such complicated deliberations
to the apparently cool hand of money and the market.
And yet as Sandel points out, although markets purport
to be morally neutral—being governed by the rule of
inert financial capital—they are not, because they make
inequality more acute and because giving money values
to things shapes the way we behave towards them, as we
saw with his example of the late-pickup fee at childcare
centres in Israel. It seems the only value system we have
yet found that comes close to being global is begotten of
money and markets. To change our system we need to
do more than changing the mindset or paradigm (profit
maximisation) that generates it. We need to intervene
at the apex of Meadows' hierarchy: we need to change
our values.

As we have seen, along with the benefit corporation,
another idea is emerging with the power to switch our
collective mindset and provide a unifying non-monetary
value to all humans on earth. And that is the value of
the earth itself, on its own terms.

Writing in the early 1970s while contemplating the legal standing of trees, Christopher Stone got to the heart of our current moral bind: we have created a world predicated on endless growth, because financial capital appears capable of endless growth. But we now realise that as it grows apparently endlessly it chews up the planet and the people it purports to serve. We need a limiting factor and that must be the planet itself, despite our history of dreams of inhabiting heaven or Mars or other extraterrestrial earths. As Stone realised in 1972 when speculating about the 'psychic and socio-psychic' implications of a world in which nature has rights, our own health and wellbeing are so inextricably linked to the health of our natural environment, of this single Planet Earth, that the aims of ensuring our wellbeing and that of nature are so mutually supportive that it is hard to see whether the reason for doing so is to advance ourselves or, as he put it, to advance 'a new "us" that includes the environment'.

Stone's new 'us' that embraces a continuum of humans and nature is the mind shift at the heart of his essay and the one we all must make on a global scale. The new 'us' is all of humanity and the planet and its creatures in an interconnected web of life. But while it may be new on a planetary scale, this 'us' is not new at all—rather, it is ancient, as Stone suggests, and it is still understood by many rural and indigenous people on earth, including by indigenous Englishman George Monbiot writing of the nightingales of Kent and the woods of Sheffield, by the indigenous people of Ecuador and Bolivia, and by the Whanganui Iwi. As New Zealand lawyer Brendan Kennedy points out in an essay called 'I Am the River and the River Is Me', the natural resources of Aotearoa (New Zealand) are often seen through two different lenses: Maori and non-Maori. He quotes noted Maori academic and New Zealand politician the Honourable Dr Pita Sharples on the difference:

> Holding a title to property, whether Crown or private, establishes a regime of rights— to capture, to exclude, to develop, to keep. Rangatiratanga (Maori sovereignty or absolute chieftainship) is asserted through the collective exercise of responsibilities—to protect, to conserve, to augment, and to enhance over time for the security of future generations. Both seek to increase value, but the question is, how do you value the resource? [By] the profit you can make? Or the taonga (treasure's) contribution to the survival of the group?

In the case of the Whanganui River, as of mid 2014 it seems that the river will be defined and governed by the latter view, by the collective exercise of responsibilities to protect, conserve, augment and enhance it for future generations. This view of our responsibility to a place is consonant with the Brundtland Report's definition of sustainable development in 1987. As with the advent of integrated reporting and the benefit corporation, it is still too early to tell how this granting of legal personhood to a river will play out in practice. But the value shift has been made in western law to accommodate a different way of understanding nature, one that suggests its care and protection more powerfully than does the concept of natural capital. And interestingly, John Montgomery suggests an equivalent value shift from 'I' to 'we' lurking at the heart of the benefit corporation: it is part of 'a global shift in consciousness which begins to recognize that we are all part of one planet and one human family. The benefit corporation will help businesses shift from an egocentric focus on profits to include consideration of the "we" and the "one"'.

By rewriting our social codes (our laws), together the benefit corporation (with its new form of accounting, integrated reporting) and the rights of nature have the potential to change the world and save the planet. This will 'cost' affluent societies in terms of our current standards of living and according to our present values, as Stone says. But as we have seen, our present values are measured by financial capital, by profits and GDP figures, whose usefulness now seems questionable even to those who work with them, as is indicated by the concerted efforts to rethink the way national wealth is measured, the advent of non-financial reporting and the integrated reporting initiatives of South Africa and the International Integrated Reporting Council—in short, the accounting paradigm shift this book has sought to document. The future depends on a profound change in the way we see our place in the rest of nature. We must see that we are not above and apart from it, with nature serving as a capacious store of resources freely and infinitely available for us to transform into creature comforts, while also acting as a huge garbage tip in the great beyond. There is no free infinite store. There is no great beyond. Both are the finite planet beneath our feet. As Stone puts it, we need to give up 'some of our sense of separateness and specialness in the universe'.

So the real question becomes not 'Can accountants save the planet?' but 'Can *we* save the planet?' Yes, we can. Let us not miss the real story as we steer our planet into the new millennium, the economic story. Here are two economic coordinates to guide us into the twenty-first century: corporations with conscience and a planet with being.

ENDNOTES

Direct quotes have quote marks; my own words drawn from other sources are without quote marks.

p. ix   'Accountants as agents of revolution? Now there's a thought.' Jonathan Watts, 'Are accountants the last hope for the world's ecosystems?', *The Guardian*, 28 October 2010.

p. ix   'How do you get economists and business people to take . . .' Ross Gittins, *Sydney Morning Herald*, 2012

p. ix   'Without a focus on a range of capitals, providers of financial capital . . .' Paul Druckman, 'Integrated reporting: reshaping corporate reporting for the 21st century', *The Guardian*, 5 June 2013.

p. ix   '. . . everything will be fungible . . .' George Monbiot, 'Can you put a price on the beauty of the natural world?', *The Guardian*, 22 April 2014.

Preface

p. xi   Jonathan Watts 'Can accountants save the planet?' Jonathan Watts, 'Are accountants the last hope for the world's ecosystems?', *The Guardian*, 28 October 2010.

p. xii   'So it has come to this. The global . . .' ibid.

p. xiii   Raj Patel's $200 hamburger, Jane Gleeson-White, *Double Entry: How the merchants of Venice shaped the modern world – and how their invention could make or break the planet*, Allen & Unwin, Sydney, 2011, p. 223.

p. xiv   Pavan Sukhdev *Global Biodiversity Outlook*, ibid, p. 247.

p. xv   Joel Bakan et al, p. 222.

p. xxiii   Mervyn King, then accountants will become '*the* profession that enabled . . .' interview with author.

Chapter 1

p. 23   Robert Solow: 'You can see the computer age . . .' Diane Coyle, *GDP: A brief but affectionate history*, Princeton University Press, Princeton, 2014, p. 126.

p. 23   Nigel Thrift 'a moment in human history . . .' Nigel Thrift in Yann Moulier Boutang, *Cognitive Capitalism*, translated by Ed Emery, Polity Press, Cambridge, 2011, p. viii.

p. 26   'is the conversion of the human resource base . . .' Robert K. Elliott, 'The Third Wave Breaks on the Shores of Accounting', *Accounting Horizons*, June 1992, 6, 2, p. 66.

p. 28   'a powerfully conservative force trapping . . .' Elliott, ibid, p. 69.

p. 28   Elliott 'trying to run my organisation . . .' Elliott, ibid, p. 69.

p. 30   'Much of what users want . . .' Elliott p. 74.

p. 30   'things have changed. For better . . .' J. Frank Brown in Robert G. Eccles, Robert H. Herz, E. Mary Keegan and David M. H. Phillips, *The ValueReporting™ Revolution: Moving beyond the earnings game*, John Wiley & Sons Inc., New York, 2001, p. vii.

p. 35   The authors argued that unless managers . . . ibid, p. 5.

p. 37   'At one level sustainability is . . .' Wayne Visser, Dirk Matten, Manfred Pohl and Nick Tolhurst, *The A-Z of Corporate Social Responsibility*, John Wiley & Sons Ltd, Chichester, 2010, p. 384.

p. 38   In accounting terms, according to Eccles and Serafeim . . . Robert Eccles and George Serafeim, 'A Tale of Two Stories: Sustainability and the Quarterly Earnings Call', *Journal of Applied Corporate Finance*, Volume 25, Number 3, Summer 2013, p. 8.

p. 38   'A sustainable society is one that . . .' ibid, p. 66.

p. 39   'simply not going to be . . .' John Elkington in Mervyn King and Teodorina Lessidrenska, *Transient Caretakers*, Penguin, Parktown North, 2006, p. 2.

p. 41   Details of ecological economics taken from International Society for Ecological Economics, The, isecoeco.org.

p. 42   'This was roughly equal to the 1998 . . .' ibid, p. 154.

p. 43   'It liquidates its capital and calls it income', *Natural Capitalism*, p. 5.

p. 43   'As *Natural Capitalism* says, . . .' ibid, p. 321.

p. 44   'What would our . . .' ibid, p. 9.

CHAPTER 2

p. 47 'We cannot face the future with the tools of the past.' 'Summary Notes from the Beyond GDP conference', November 2007.

p. 47 'What we measure affects . . .' Report on the Measurement of Economic Performance and Social Progress, Stiglitz-Sen-Fitoussi Commission, stiglitz-sen-fitoussi.fr/documents/rapport_anglais, 2009.

p. 48 'The national accounts are a macroeconomic . . .' Australian Bureau of Statistics, www.abs.gove.au/ausstats/abs@nsf.

p. 51 'The availability of bailout money from the EU . . . ' Diane Coyle, *GDP: A brief but affectionate history*, Princeton University Press, Princeton, 2014, p. 2.

p. 54 Smith's view of services . . . ibid, p. 105.

p. 54 Today, services account for over . . .' ibid, p. 84.

p. 56 'Taking risks is not . . .' ibid, p. 101.

p. 56 According to Coyle, because of the way . . . ibid, p. 101.

p. 56 Even the sober Coyle, whose view . . .' ibid, p. 104.

p. 58 'Consumers pay with time, not just money . . .' Erik Brynjolfsson, http://digitalcommunity.mit.edu/community/latest_research/blog/2012/09/19/measuring-the-attention-economy.

p. 59 The anomalies created by the advent of digital technology http://www.progressivepolicy.org/wp-content/uploads/2013/09/09.2013-Mandel_Can-the-Internet-of-Everything-Bring-Back-the-High-Growth-Economy-1.pdf.

p. 61 One of the serious problems with GDP measures . . . Rosemary D. Marcuss and Richard E. Kane, 'US National Income and Product Statistics: Born of the Great Depression and World War II', *Survey of Current Business*, February 2007, p. 40.

p. 63 Everett Ehrlich 'Congress made thinking . . .' 'GPI – GDP is killing us', Linda Baker, 31 May 2010, http://tangibleinfor.blogspot.com/2010/05/gpi-gdp-is-killing-us.html.

p. 64 "Shrimp on the dinner plates . . .', 'Living Beyond Our Means'.

p. 66 'So we decided to do a massive . . .' Pavan Sukhdev, 'Put a value on nature!', TED, 16 March 2012.

p. 67 'Economics has become the currency of policy' ibid.

p. 68 lens of public benefit, ibid.

p. 68 'ending poverty and boosting . . .' Rachel Kyte, 'An accounting system worthy of Earth Day: natural capital accounting', *Voices*, 22 April 2013.

p. 69   definition of PES from Ecosystem Marketplace, ecosystemmar-
ketplace.com.

p. 71   'we needed to generate . . .' Tony Juniper, – *What Has Nature
Ever Done for Us? How money really does grow on trees*, Profile
Books, London, 2013, p. 287.

p. 71   'They soon saw that they could estimate . . .' ibid, p. 287.

p. 71   'When [the finance minister] saw . . .' ibid, p. 288.

p. 72   'Its national PSA program receives between . . .' http://
www.ecosystemmarketplace.com/pages/dynamic/web.page.
php?section=water_market&page_name=crwb_market.

p. 72   'In 1985, only half Costa Rica's . . .' Tony Juniper *What Has
Nature Ever Done for Us? How money really does grow on trees*,
Profile Books, London, 2013, p. 288.

p. 72   'there is no long-term economic growth . . .' ibid, p. 289.

p. 73   'While its program has been criticised for favouring . . .' https://
www.american.edu/sis/gep/upload/Johns_Bryan_SRP-The-Big-
Kahuna.pdf

p. 77   'maintain, enhance, and . . .' UN Environment Programme
definition of green economy, Green Economy Portal, unep.org/
greeneconomy.

p. 78   'At Rio+20 we have seen . . .' People's Summit, 'Final
Declaration: People's Summit "at Rio+20" for Social and
Environmental Justice in defence of the commons, against the
commodification of life', 15-22 June 2012.

p. 79   'This dwarfs the entire third-world debt . . .' Raj Patel, *The
Value of Nothing*, p. 50.

p. 80   'Native people . . .' Warantan in Jonathan Watts, 'Rio+20
People's summit gathers pace', *The Guardian*, 19 June 2012.

p. 80   'Humanity finds itself . . .' Pablo Solón, 'It's the time of
the Rights of Mother Earth', pablosolon.wordpress.com,
4 April 2012.

p. 81   'nature is being valued and commodified . . .' George Monbiot,
'Putting a price on the rivers and rain diminishes us all', *The
Guardian*, 7 August 2012.

p. 81   'commodification, economic growth, financial abstractions . . .',
ibid.

p. 81   'economic, health and social benefits . . .' UK National
Ecosystem Assessment, uknea.unep_wcmc.org.

p. 82   'theoretically challenging' ibid.

p. 82   'that the tendency . . .' ibid.

p. 82   'green goods, services, products, investment vehicles . . ' UK
          Ecosystems Markets Task Force, gov.uk.

p. 82   'new ways for business to profit . . ' Ian Cheshire, ibid.

p. 83   'Business currently treats the natural world . . ' Monbiot,
          The Guardian, August 2012.

p. 83   For Monbiot, these phrases are a sure sign . . . ibid.

p. 83   He rejects ecosystem offsetting in principle . . . ibid.

p. 85   'of the right sort, of the right quality . . ' Environment Bank
          Ltd, The, 'Biodiversity Offsetting to compensate for nightingale
          habitat loss at Lodge Hill, Kent', November 2012.

p. 85   'offsetting could work in principle for nightingales . . '
          Environment Bank Ltd, The, 'Biodiversity Offsetting to com-
          pensate for nightingale habitat loss at Lodge Hill, Kent',
          November 2012.

p. 86   'Accept the principle of biodiversity offsetting . . ' George
          Monbiot, 'Biodiversity offsetting will unleash a new spirit of
          destruction in the land', *The Guardian*, 8 December 2012.

p. 88   'For local people, Smithy Wood . . ' George Monbiot, 'Can you
          put a price on the beauty of the natural world?', *The Guardian*,
          22 April 2014.

p. 88   'Costing nature tells us that it . . ' – 'Can you put a price on the
          beauty of the natural world?', *The Guardian*, 22 April 2014.

p. 90   Calling Monbiot's arguments a 'one-sided picture . . ' Tony
          Juniper, Juniper, Tony, 'We must put a price on nature if we are
          going to save it', *The Guardian*, 10 August 2012.

p. 90   'an economically costly distraction . . ' ibid.

p. 90   'I have spent the past 25 years . . ' ibid.

p. 91   'more forests are cleared, oceans polluted . . ' ibid.

p. 91   he argues that the only alternative is to 'open a new dis-
          course . . ' ibid.

p. 92   'Where there is no alternative . . ' Tony Juniper in John Vidal,
          'Conservationists split over "biodiversity offsetting" plans',
          The Guardian, 4 June 2014.

p. 92   'embedded in virtually . . ' Robert Costanza, Simone Quatrini
          and Siv Øystese, 'Response to George Monbiot: The valu-
          ation of nature and ecosystem services is not privatization',
          15 August 2012.

p. 93   'this certainly does not mean . . ' ibid.

p. 93   'Many natural capital assets are, and should remain . . ' ibid.

p. 93   'propertise our common assets . . ' ibid.

p. 94   'by the laws of nature . . .' David Bollier, 'The Vermont Common Assets Trust', bollier.org, 3 October 2011.

p. 95   Everard, Mark, 'Nature is worth a lot more than nothing!', Institute of Environmental Sciences, April 2014.

p. 96   'the current dominant political mantra . . .' ibid.

p. 96   'The most generous thing that can . . .' – 'Can you put a price on the beauty of the natural world?', *The Guardian*, 22 April 2014.

p. 97   'unresponsive to anyone . . .' – 'Can you put a price on the beauty of the natural world?', *The Guardian*, 22 April 2014.

p. 97   'those messy, subjective . . .' ibid.

p. 98   'All systems of government are flawed . . .' George Monbiot, 'The Self-Hating State', The Permaculture Research Institute, permaculturenews.org, 24 April 2013.

p. 98   'markets don't only allocate goods . . .' Michael Sandel, *What Money Can't Buy: The moral limits of markets*, Penguin Books, London, 2012.

p. 99   'To them, the fine . . .' ibid, p. 65.

p. 99   'says in effect . . .' ibid, p. 72.

p. 99   'though not for the . . .' ibid, p. 73.

p. 100   'the spirit of shared sacrifice . . .' ibid, p. 75.

p. 100   'buy their way out of . . .' ibid, p.

p. 100   'may make it harder to . . .', ibid, p.

p. 100   'Global action on climate change . . .' ibid, p. 76.

p. 100   'a painless mechanism . . .' ibid, p. 77.

p. 101   'Markets leave their mark . . .' ibid, p. 9.

Chapter 3

p. 104   'worrying undertones hanging heavy . . .' Pavan Sukhdev, Sukhdev, Pavan, *Corporation 2020: Transforming Business for Tomorrow's World*, Island Press, Washington, 2012.

p. 104   'Was there something pathological . . .' ibid.

p. 105   'I can think of no entity . . .' George Monbiot, 'How have these corporations colonised our public life?', *The Guardian*, 8 April 2014.

p. 108   'Reading Hewes account, I learned that the Boston Tea . . .' Thom Hartmann, *Unequal Protection: The rise of corporate dominance and the theft of human rights*, Mythical Research Inc., and Thom Hartmann, United States of America, 2002, p. 75.

p. 109   'a fair and competitive local marketplace' ibid, p. 83.

p. 109 ' nation was founded . . .' ibid, p. 3.

p. 110 'a corporation is an artificial being . . .' ibid, p. 19.

p. 110 'looming up a new and dark power . . .' ibid, p. 94

p. 111 'British common law dating from . . .' ibid, p. 7.

p. 112 'legally it did not, because the judge's . . .' ibid, p. 11.

p. 112 President Grover Cleveland warned of . . . ibid, p. 25.

p. 112 'of the cases in this court . . .' ibid, p. 54.

p. 113 'an instrument of service . . .' Henry Ford, Gibbons, Chris and Tanya Barman, 'Sustainability in emerging markets: Lessons from South Africa', Chartered Institute of Management Accountants, 2010.

p. 114 'My ambition is to . . .' Henry Ford in *Dodge v. Ford Motor Co.,* 170 N.W. 668 (Mich. 1919), law.illinoir.edu.

p. 115 'providing employment, eliminating . . .' Milton Friedman, 'The Social Responsibility of Business is to Increase its Profits', *The New York Times Magazine*, 13 September 1970.

p. 115 'an accountability deficit in which company stakeholders . . .' Allen White, 'New Wine, New Bottles: The rise of non-financial reporting', *Business for Social Responsibility*, 20 June 2005, p. 2.

p. 116 'This corporation became the main agent . . .' Pavan Sukhdev, *Corporation 2020*, p. 23.

p. 116 A 2013 study . . . Paul Polman in Mahanta, Vinod and Priyanka Sangani, 'Resist the short term decisions that damage the long term: Paul Polman, CEO, Unilever', *The Economic Times*, 8 November 2013.

p. 117 'Humanity has the ability . . .' The Brundtland Report, United Nations, 'Report of the World Commission on Environment and Development: Our Common Future', un_documents.net, 1987.

p. 119 'a whole set of disturbing . . .' Bob Massie in Tracy Fernandez Rysavy, 'Can the Miracle Work Again? Climate divestment interview with Bob Massie', *Green American*, January/February 2013.

p. 121 '[In 1989,] the whole idea of having . . .' Bob Massie, 'History of the Global Reporting Initiative (GRI)', youtube, 12 March 2014.

p. 122 'One of the problems was that every group . . .' ibid.

p. 123 'Don't wait for the US . . .' Ellie Winninghoff, 'Accounting for Sustainability', *Financial Advisor*, 3 August 2011.

p. 123 'Let me get this straight . . .' ibid.

p. 126 'We built GRI . . .' Eccles, Robert G. and Michael P. Krzus, *One Report: Integrated reporting for a sustainable strategy*, John Wiley & Sons, Inc., Hoboken, 2010, p. 102.

p. 126 'expectations that the long-term . . .' G4, Global Reporting Initiative, website.

p. 128 'The GRI was built . . .' Bob Massie, Eccles, Robert G. and Michael P. Krzus, *One Report: Integrated reporting for a sustainable strategy*, John Wiley & Sons, Inc., Hoboken, 2010, p. 102.

p. 134 'I have real confidence . . .' Paul Dickinson in Kaufman, Leslie, 'Emissions Disclosure as a Business Virtue', *New York Times*, 28 December 2009.

p. 136 Nigel Topping, 'Don't Blame the Hammer!', Schumacher College, https://www.youtube.com/watch?v=RR-0AQR9yMA, 2 February 2012.

p. 137 Donella Meadows, 'Leverage Points: Places to Intervene in a System', donellameadows.org, http://www.donellameadows.org/archives/leverage-points-places-to-intervene-in-a-system/.

p. 139 Waygood calls Paragraph 47 'weak' Steve Waygood in Holmes, Lawrie, 'Information Overdrive', *Financial Management*, 22 August 2013.

p. 139 'if the information we rely on from companies . . .' Steve Waygood, ibid.

p. 140 'denotes the quality of being clear and honest' Wayne Visser, Dirk Matten, Manfred Pohl and Nick Tolhurst, *The A-Z of Corporate Social Responsibility*, John Wiley & Sons Ltd, Chichester, 2010, p. 402.

p. 140 'an old force with new power . . .' Don Tapscott in Robert G. Eccles and Michael P. Krzus, *One Report: Integrated reporting for a sustainable strategy*, John Wiley & Sons, Inc., Hoboken, 2010, p. x.

p. 140 'Firms are being held to . . .' Don Tapscott, ibid.

p. 141 'The irresistible force . . .' Don Tapscott, ibid.

p. 143 In King's telling . . . interview with author

p. 143 'It's no good just . . .' Michael Peat in Chris Quick, 'Accounting for Sustainability – Green: by royal assent', *Accountancy Live*, 1 January 2008.

p. 144 Peat calls it a 'revolution' . . . ibid.

p. 144 'We all know that annual reports . . .' Peat, ibid.

Chapter 4

p. 146 'The proper governance of countries . . .' James Wolfensohn, http://www.ecgi.org/codes/documents/cacg_final.pdf, 1999.

p. 146 There is a growing weight of expectation . . .' King II Report, 2002, https://www.saica.co.za/tabid/695/itemid/2344/language/en-ZA/An-integrated-report-is-a-new-requirement-for-list.aspx.

p. 146 'Today, the majority of South Africans . . .' http://www.anc.org.za/show.php?id=4520.

p. 148 According to Patrick Bond, an economic advisor . . . in Naomi Klein, *The Shock Doctrine* Penguin Books, Camberwell, 2007, p. 203.

p. 148 'The very mobility of capital . . .' ibid, p. 207.

p. 148 As South African journalist and former student activist William Gumede . . . ibid, p. 204.

p. 149 But then Nelson Mandela intervened . . . Stewart, Neil, 'An audience with the GRI's Mervyn King', *IR Magazine*, 9 September 2010.

p. 150 'a motivational tool' ibid.

p. 151 'The decisions had not been made . . .' Schulschenk, Jess, 'Richard Wilkinson', EY.com, 23 March 2012.

p. 153 'The 19th century saw . . .' King Committee on Corporate Governance, 'The King Report 2002', Institute of Directors, South Africa, March 2002.

p. 154 'There are always ways of getting around . . .' Mervyn King, http://www.forbes.com/sites/dinamedland/2013/10/21/if-i-had-more-time-i-would-have-written-a-shorter-letter-in-tegrated-reporting/.

p. 155 'a big move away from . . .' Mervyn King and Leigh Roberts, *Integrate: Doing business in the 21st century*, Juta & Company Ltd, Cape Town, 2013, p. 32.

p. 155 'to recognise what the previously . . .' Schulschenk, Jess, 'Richard Wilkinson', EY.com, 23 March 2012.

p. 155 'we couldn't just cookie-cut . . .' Mervyn King in Stewart, Neil, 'An audience with the GRI's Mervyn King', *IR Magazine*, 9 September 2010.

p. 155 'an act of commercial folly . . .' Mervyn King interview with author.

p. 156 'The penny dropped and I suddenly . . ' Mervyn King in Neil Stewart, 'An audience with the GRI's Mervyn King', *IR Magazine*, 9 September 2010.

p. 157 'that these so-called non-financial issues . . ' King Committee on Corporate Governance, 'The King Report 2002', Institute of Directors, South Africa, March 2002.

p. 157 'Failure to do so might . . ' ibid.

p. 157 'Increasingly, South African companies . . ' ibid.

p. 158 'can make countries . . ' ibid.

p. 158 'everyone willingly or not . . ' ibid.

p. 159 'the cornerstone has got to be . . ' Mervyn King in Olin, Dirk, 'King of Transparency', *Corporate Responsibility Magazine*.

p. 159 'a key challenge for leadership . . ' Institute of Directors, Southern Africa, The King Code of Governance for South Africa 2009, c.ymcdn.com, 2009.

p. 159 'a radical shift in thinking . . ' ibid.

p. 160 'engaging with sex workers . . ' Impala Platinum Holdings Integrated Report 2013.

p. 160 'offsetting its carbon emissions . . ' Exxaro Resources Integrated Report 2010.

p. 160 the medicinal flowering plant *Frithia humilis* http://www. nbi.org.za/Lists/Events/Attachments/39/RChangan_Exxaro_ Biodiversity_Managment_presentation.pdf.

p. 161 Sven Lunsche in Laurie Havelock, 'All together now', *IR Magazine*, March 2014, p. 8.

p. 161 'Do you have a social licence . . ' ibid, p. 8.

p. 162 According to King, investors 'say they invest in South African firms . . ' Neil Stewart, 'An audience with GRI's Mervyn King', *IR magazine*, 9 September 2010.

p. 163 World Bank found South Africa's 2009 income distribution . . . http://www.worldbank.org/content/dam/Worldbank/docu- ment/Poverty%20documents/Inequality-in-Focus-April2013.pdf.

p. 163 'interested not so much in what capital can do for South Africa . . ' Grant Samkin and Stewart Lawrence, 'Limits to Corporate Social Responsibility: The Challenge of HIV/Aids to Sustainable Business in South Africa', The University of Waikato Department of Accounting, Working Paper Series, Number 83, Hamilton, November 2005, p. 20.

p. 165 'a quiet renaissance . . ' Allen White, 'New Wine, New Bottles: The rise of non-financial reporting', *Business for Social Responsibility*, 20 June 2005.

p. 165 'in a historical context . . .' ibid.

p. 165 'a fluid, fast-moving . . .' ibid.

p. 166 'there are times when in . . .' Martin Goldstein and Inge F. Goldstein in Robert G. Eccles and Michael P. Krzus, *One Report: Integrated reporting for a sustainable strategy*, John Wiley & Sons, Inc., Hoboken, 2010, p. 26.

p. 167 'Any one of us who became a curator . . .' Mervyn King in Wayne Visser, Dirk Matten, Manfred Pohl and Nick Tolhurst, *The A-Z of Corporate Social Responsibility*, John Wiley & Sons Ltd, Chichester, 2010, p. 97.

p. 168 'it is a totally incapacitated . . .' ibid, p. 97.

p. 168 'would not act wrongly . . .' ibid, p. 98.

p. 170 'An hour later, corporate history . . .' Mervyn King interview with author.

p. 171 'If integrated reporting . . .' ibid.

p. 172 'The advisory role . . .' ibid.

p. 173 'human society to move . . .' ibid.

CHAPTER 5

p. 174 The Framework defines an integrated report . . . The International <IR> Framework, http://www.theiirc.org/wp-content/uploads/2013/12/13-12-08-THE-INTERNA-TIONAL-IR-FRAMEWORK-2-1.pdf.

p. 177 'If you are confused about . . .' Carol Adams, 'What is integrated reporting? And how do you do it?', drcaroladams.net, 3 March 2014.

p. 177 'a concise communication of value . . .' Paul Druckman, ibid.

p. 180 'The world has never . . .' 'Formation of the International Integrated Reporting Committee (later Council)', Press Release, 2 August 2010, http://www.theiirc.org/wp-content/uploads/2011/03/Press-Release1.pdf.

p. 180 'battling 21st century . . .' Prince Charles, ibid.

p. 180 'a globally accepted framework . . .' ibid.

p. 180 'fast followers . . .' Michael Bray, interview with author.

p. 180 'Towards Integrated Reporting: Communicating Value in the 21st century', September 2011, http://theiirc.org/wp-content/uploads/2011/09/IR-Discussion-Paper-2011_spreads.pdf.

p. 182 Druckman likened the first phase to a 'feasibility study' in 'Paul Druckman: a different story', *economia*, 2 December 2013.

p. 182   'The extent of support of the professional accounting . . .' Carol
         Adams 'The International Integrated Reporting Council: A call
         to action', drcaroladams.net, 17 July 2014.

p. 183   'It is the company telling its story . . .' Paul Druckman: a dif-
         ferent story', *economia*, 2 December 2013.

p. 183   Druckman explains that this open, consultative approach
         to . . . ibid.

p. 183   'What I want is a regulatory . . .' ibid.

p. 183   'If this is not relevant . . .' Paul Druckman in Jessica Fries
         interview with Paul Druckman 'What problem is integrated
         reporting trying to fix?', PwC, 15 April 2013.

p. 184   BDO Ukraine said 'we agree with the . . .' http://www.theiirc.
         org/wp-content/uploads/2013/08/344_BDO-Ukraine.pdf.

p. 185   'We believe the IR Framework . . .' ibid.

p. 186   'forms of capital provided . . .' 'Capitals: Background paper for
         <IR>', http://www.theiirc.org/wp-content/uploads/2013/03/
         IR-Background-Paper-Capitals.pdf.

p. 187   'As it currently stands . . .' Climate Disclosure Standards Board,
         http://www.theiirc.org/wp-content/uploads/2013/08/193_
         Climate-Disclosure-Standards-Board.pdf.

p. 187   'a comprehensive community-based . . .' David Korten, http://
         www.theiirc.org/wp-content/uploads/2013/08/096_Living-
         Economies-Forum.pdf.

p. 188   'technical rigour and cohesion . . .' Paul Druckman, Integrated
         Reporting Framework aims to promote lasting sustainable
         change', *The Guardian*, 9 December 2013.

p. 188   'the consensus has grown and the global movement . . .' ibid.

p. 188   'enables financial returns . . .' International Integrated
         Reporting Council, *The International <IR> Framework*, theiirc.
         org, December 2013.

p. 190   'For too long businesses . . .' Mervyn King and Leigh Roberts,
         Integrate: Doing business in the 21st century, Juta & Company
         Ltd, Cape Town, 2013, p. 134.

p. 191   'a prism through which . . .' International Integrated Reporting
         Council, *The International <IR> Framework*, theiirc.org,
         December 2013.

p. 195   'The most valuable assets . . .' Peter Drucker in R. Paul
         Herman, 'Let's Value People as an Asset, and Bring Financial
         Statements into the 21st Century', *Huffington Post*, 28 October
         2011, http://www.huffingtonpost.com/r-paul-herman/lets-
         value-people-as-an-a_b_1063698.html.

p. 195 'the measurement distortions caused by expensing items that are really . . .' Robert G. Eccles, Robert H. Herz, E. Mary Keegan and David M. H. Phillips, *The ValueReporting™ Revolution: Moving beyond the earnings game*, John Wiley & Sons Inc., New York, 2001, p. 57.

p. 196 the value is generated largely through its employee training system . . . Pavan Sukhdev, *Corporation 2020: Transforming Business for Tomorrow's World*, Island Press, Washington, 2012, p. 71.

p. 196 Aditya Chakrabortty, 'The woman who nearly died making your iPad', *The Guardian*, 6 August 2013.

p. 197 'what is effectively a human . . .' ibid.

p. 198 'The Free Press may think that . . .' Thom Hartmann, *Unequal Protection: The rise of corporate dominance and the theft of human rights*, Mythical Research Inc., and Thom Hartmann, United States of America, 2002, p. 139.

p. 198 'the reason Apple . . .' John Montgomery in David M. Carl and Hank Nguyen, 'California Benefit Corporations: Installing a Corporate Conscience', *Business Law Journal*, 23 March 2012.

p. 198 'People don't contest that pollution . . .' James Gifford, http://www.thesustainabilityreport.com.au/qa-with-james-gifford-executive-director-of-the-unpri/.

p. 199 'Just as ecosystems produce . . .' Paul Hawken, Amory Lovins and L. Hunter Lovins, *Natural Capitalism: Creating the next industrial revolution*, Little, Brown and Company, New York, 1999, p. 286.

p. 200 'short-term economic gains . . .' ibid, p. 286.

p. 201 Trucost found that if companies had to pay their environmental bills . . . http://www.environmentalleader.com/2012/02/16/environmental-impacts-cost-41-cents-for-every-1-of-revenue-report-finds/.

p. 202 'While at Puma . . .' Jochen Zeitz in Mervyn King and Leigh Roberts, *Integrate: Doing business in the 21st century*, Juta & Company Ltd, Cape Town, 2013, p. 18.

p. 203 'Intuition and creativity . . .' ibid, p. 19.

p. 204 'provides a robust framework to help . . .' Richard Mattison, http://about.puma.com/puma-completes-first-environmental-profit-and-loss-account-which-values-impacts-at-e-145-million/.

p. 205 'Our job is not only to lessen the impacts . . .' Jochen Zeitz, http://about.puma.com/

new-puma-shoe-and-t-shirt-impact-the-environment-by-a-
third-less-than-conventional-products/.

p. 206 'antiquated incentives, such as . . .' ibid.

p. 206 'We all know that cattle . . .' Jochen Zeitz in Pilita Clark, 'Puma
to kick leather into touch', *Financial Times*, 22 June 2012.

p. 206 Natural Capital Declaration, http://www.naturalcapitaldeclara-
tion.org.

p. 207 'Let's look back . . .' Rachel Kyte, 20 June 2012, http://www.
worldbank.org/en/news/press-release/2012/06/20/massive-
show-support-action-natural-capital-accounting-rio-summit.

p. 208 Jo Confino, 'Bill McKibben: fossil fuel divestment campaign
builds momentum', *The Guardian*, 31 October 2013.

p. 208 'The scale of "listed" unburnable carbon . . .' Damian
Carrington, 'Carbon bubble will plunge the world into another
financial crisis – report', *The Guardian*, 19 April 2013.

p. 210 'as expected, the majority . . .' 'Integrated Reporting Making
Progress, Needs to Catch Up', Environmental Leader, 21 June
2013, http://www.environmentalleader.com/2013/06/21/
integrated-reporting-making-progress-but-needs-to-catch-up/.

p. 211 Robert G. Eccles and George Serafeim, 'Corporate and
Integrated Reporting: A functional perspective', 31 January
2014, updated May 2014, http://papers.ssrn.com/sol3/papers.
cfm?abstract_id=2388716.

p. 211 'best case example' Robert G. Eccles and George Serafeim,
'Corporate and Integrated Reporting: A functional perspective',
31 January 2014, updated May 2014, http://papers.ssrn.com/
sol3/papers.cfm?abstract_id=2388716.

p. 211 'Coca-Cola HBC AG 2012 Integrated Report', http://www.
coca-colahellenic.com/~/media/Files/C/CCHBC/Annual%20
Reports/ar.pdf.

p. 211 'This Integrated Report outlines . . .' ibid.

p. 212 'I am very pleased . . .' Chairman's letter, ibid.

p. 212 'understanding the full . . .' Chairman's letter, ibid.

p. 213 'In times of macro-economic uncertainty . . .' ibid.

p. 214 'We believe the Draft Framework should . . .' APG, http://www.
theiirc.org/wp-content/uploads/2013/08/297_APG-Asset-
Management.pdf.

p. 215 'As financial capital is only . . .' International Federation of
Accountants, http://www.ifac.org/sites/default/files/public-
ations/files/IFAC%20Response%20to%20IIRC%20IR%20
Framework.pdf.

p. 218 'This is advantageous in that accountants . . .' Carol Adams, 'What is integrated reporting? And how do you do it?', drcaroladams.net, 3 March 2014.

p. 218 'attempt to encourage mainstream . . .' Carol Adams, 'The International Integrated Reporting Council: A call to action', drcaroladams.net, 17 July 2014.

p. 219 Waygood sees integrated reporting as the first . . . Waygood in Lawrie Holmes, 'Information Overdrive', *Financial Management*, 22 August 2013, http://www.fm-magazine.com/feature/depth/information-overdrive.

p. 219 in 2013 Waygood said he thought . . . ibid.

p. 221 'We meet with the SEC . . .' Robert Eccles interview with author.

p. 221 'unabashedly focused . . .' Jean Rogers in Marc Gunther, 'Will sustainability reporting standards change the way business does business?', *The Guardian*, 7 August 2013.

p. 222 'like plumbing . . .' Robert Eccles interview with author.

p. 223 'To the extent that this failure . . .' Andrew Park and Curtis Ravenel, Integrating Sustainability into Capital Markets: Bloomberg LP and ESG's Quantitative Legitimacy', *Journal of Applied Corporate Finance*, Volume 25 Number 3, Summer 2013.

p. 224 He said that despite the power of such data . . . Jeff Leinaweaver 'Might new financial tools translate ESG data into real-world loss and profit?', *The Guardian*, 26 November 2013.

p. 224 Andrew Park interview with author.

p. 227 When I asked Eccles . . . Robert Eccles interview with author.

p. 229 According to the World Economic Forum . . . 'The trillion-dollar gap', *The Economist*, 22 March 2014.

CHAPTER 6

p. 231 story of termites in Jan Bondeson, *The Feejee Mermaid and Other Essays in Natural and Unnatural History*, Cornell University Press, Ithaca,1999, p. 149.

p. 232 'I hope we shall crush in its birth . . .' Thom Hartmann, *Unequal Protection: The rise of corporate dominance and the theft of human rights*, Mythical Research Inc., and Thom Hartmann, United States of America, 2002, p. 103.

p. 235 UK Companies Act 2006 http://www.bbklr.org/uploads/1/4/5/4/14547218/187_ashton_p_how__fred_the_

shred_got_away_with_it_loud_calls_for_company_law_reform. pdf.

p. 235   According to Kelly, one of the distinguishing . . . Marjorie Kelly, 'Not Just for Profit: Emerging Alternatives to the Shareholder-Centric Model', 2009 Summit on the Future of the Corporation, p. 40.

p. 236   Sukhdev calls today's corporation . . . Pavan Sukhdev, *Corporation 2020: Transforming Business for Tomorrow's World*, Island Press, Washington, 2012, p. 4.

p. 237   In Sukhdev's vision of the world . . . ibid, p. 13.

p. 238   the B Team issued a declaration . . . Jo Confino, 'Richard Branson and Jochen Zeitz launch the B Team challenge', *The Guardian*, 13 June 2013.

p. 238   'Why would you invest in a company . . .' Paul Polman in Jo Confino, 'Unilever's Paul Polman: changing the corporate status quo', *The Guardian*, 24 April 2012.

p. 239   Mycoskie speaks about the chief executive officer's . . . Bruce Upbin, 'Davos Dispatch: Richard Branson and The B Team Make Business Case for Human Rights', *Forbes*, 22 January 2014.

p. 239   In Branson's words, these new-wave . . . Richard Branson, 'Profit is not all that matters', *Business Day Live*, 8 August 2012.

p. 240   convinced that humanity's future 'relies on our ability to explore and invent . . .' Marjorie Kelly, 'Not Just for Profit: Emerging Alternatives to the Shareholder-Centric Model', 2009 Summit on the Future of the Corporation, p. 34.

p. 240   Yunus proposed a new sort of business venture . . . ibid.

p. 241   He said 'We were creating something new . . .' ibid.

p. 243   'on its own hero's journey . . .' John Montgomery, 'The Benefit Corporation: The unlikely hero of a sustainable economy?', *TheHumanist.com*, 22 April 2014.

p. 243   The idea for B Lab came out of the experience . . . 'B Corporation movement wins rich backers in Australia', Ben Hurley, *Business Review Weekly*, 20 November 2013.

p. 244   believing that business is 'the most powerful man-made . . .' Jay Coen Gilbert in Joan Brunwasser, 'B Lab: Helping Companies Not only Be the Best in the World, But the Best FOR the World', OpEdNews.com, 10 October 2013.

p. 244   As Montgomery says, 'essentially what that does . . .' in David M. Carl and Hank Nguyen, 'California Benefit Corporations:

Installing a Corporate Conscience', *Business Law Journal*, 23 March 2012.

p. 245 'Declaration of Interdependence', 'The B Corp Declaration: Declaration of Interdependence', bcorporation.net.

p. 246 'My generation is squealing like . . .' John Montgomery in David M. Carl and Hank Nguyen, 'California Benefit Corporations: Installing a Corporate Conscience', *Business Law Journal*, 23 March 2012.

p. 247 B Lab co-founder Gilbert said . . . B Lab, 'Maryland First State in Union to Pass Benefit Corporation Legislation', Press Release, CSRWire.com, 14 April 2010.

p. 247 Maryland state Senator Jamie Raskin said . . . *B Corporation 2011 Annual Report*, 'If Not Now, When?', http://www.bcorporation.net/sites/all/themes/adaptivetheme/bcorp/pdfs/B%20Corp_2011-Annual-Report.pdf, p. 18.

p. 249 Catlin Powers said that in becoming a B Corporation . . . youtube 2014 Skoll Award for Social Entrepreneurship, https://www.youtube.com/watch?v=wboYZ_rdRAc, 29 April 2014.

p. 250 'Every year in western China . . .' http://www.actionhub.com/news/2013/08/06/solsource-solar-cooker-reduces-air-pollution-enters-consumer-market/.

p. 251 'B Corps might turn out to be like . . .' *Esquire Magazine* in Why B Corps Matter, https://www.bcorporation.net/what-are-b-corps/why-b-corps-matter.

p. 252 Albert Wenger of New York . . . Albert Wenger, 'What Benefit Corp Legislation Means to Investors', https://www.youtube.com/watch?v=AUCTL_uV0GI, 17 July 2013.

p. 253 'It lets companies put . . .' ibid.

p. 253 Montgomery believes that benefit corporations . . . John Montgomery in David M. Carl and Hank Nguyen, 'California Benefit Corporations: Installing a Corporate Conscience', *Business Law Journal*, 23 March 2012.

p. 255 Stone first defines his use of the term 'legal rights . . .' Christopher Stone, *Should Trees Have Standing? Law, morality and the environment*, Oxford University Press, Oxford, 2010.

p. 255 Early American jurists, for example . . . ibid, p. 2.

p. 256 'to prosecution for the paternity of a bastard . . .' ibid, p. 181.

p. 256 As Stone says, these examples show . . .' ibid, p. 181.

p. 256 'The reason for this little . . .' ibid, p. 3.

p. 257 Stone says it is not inevitable . . . ibid, p. 8.

p. 257 Given that our own health . . . includes the environment.' ibid, p. 23.

p. 258 Alone among thinkers in this book . . . ibid, p. 24.

p. 258 As Stone then argues, this radical shift . . . ibid, p. 27.

p. 258 We can only reach a 'heightened awareness' ibid, p. 28.

p. 259 'hard giving indeed . . .' ibid, p. 268.

p. 259 Stone concludes by suggesting . . . ibid, p. 31.

p. 259 He said he knew the exact . . . ibid, p. xi.

p. 260 'How would such a posture *in law* . . .' ibid, p. xi.

p. 260 because the construction would damage its 'aesthetic and ecological balance' ibid, p. xiii.

p. 261 the most 'committed civil libertarian . . .' *Time*, 'The Law: The court's uncompromising libertarian', 24 November 1975.

p. 261 'The critical question . . .' Christopher Stone, *Should Trees Have Standing? Law, morality and the environment*, Oxford University Press, Oxford, 2010, p.

p. 262 definition of natural community, *The Encyclopedia of Earth*, http://www.eoearth.org/view/article/154786/.

p. 263 as journalist Jason Mark said . . . Jason Mark, 'Natural Law', *Earth Island Journal*, Spring 2012.

p. 263 'simply asserted a community's . . . ibid.

p. 263 'we are empowering . . .' ibid.

p. 264 the Tamaqua Borough ordinance, ibid.

p. 264 'It shall be unlawful . . .' Tamaqua Borough Sewage Sludge Ordinance, http://www.celdf.org/article.php?id=440.

p. 265 She wrote that the borough . . . Elisabeth Eaves, 'Tree Rights', *Forbes*, 24 May 2007.

p. 265 'Natural communities and ecosystems . . .' Clare Kendall, 'A new law of nature', *The Guardian*, 24 September 2008.

p. 266 'As a country devastated by . . .' Global Exchange, 'Does Nature Have Rights?', globalexchange.org, 6 December 2010.

p. 266 Because of their experience with environmental legislation . . . Cyril Mychalejko, 'Ecuador's constitution gives rights to nature', upsidedownworld.org, 25 September 2008.

p. 266 'the new Constitution redefines people's . . .' ibid.

p. 267 'The whole idea seemed yet another example . . .' Jason Mark, 'Natural Law', *Earth Island Journal*, Spring 2012.

p. 267 The new legislation was tested . . . Natalia Greene, 'The first successful case of the Rights of Nature implementation in Ecuador', therightsofnature.org.

p. 268   Universal Declaration of Rights of Mother Earth states
that . . . 'The Universal Declaration of Rights of Mother Nature',
therightsofnature.org, 22 April 2010.

p. 268   Yasuni National Park . . . Associated Press in Quito, 'Yasuni:
Ecuador abandons plan to stave off Amazon drilling', 16
August 2013.

p. 268   David Hill, 'Leaked documents cast doubt on Ecuador's commitment to forest plan', *The Guardian*, 2 July 2014.

p. 270   the report argued that the UNFCCC 'is based not . . .' Global
Exchange, *Does Nature Have Rights?: Transforming Grassroots
Organizing to Protect People and the Planet*, globalexchange.org.

p. 270   Maude Barlow has high hopes . . . Thalif Deen, 'Global
Campaign to Bestow Legal Rights on Mother Earth', *Inter Press
Service*, 24 May 2011.

p. 271   which is central to a new body of legislation . . . 'Law 300
Framework Law of Mother Earth and Holistic Development
for Living Well', http://theredddesk.org/countries/laws/
law-300-framework-law-mother-earth-and-holistic-develop-
ment-living-well, 2012.

p. 271   Under the new law, Mother Nature is defined . . . ibid.

p. 272   Pablo Solón said 'If . . . you think that the only entities . . .'
Steven Edwards, 'UN document would give "Mother Earth"
same rights as humans', canada.com, 13 April 2011.

p. 272   The London School of Economics called Bolivia's
law . . . Michael Nachmany, Sam Fankhauser, Terry Townshend,
Murray Collins, Tucker Landesman, Adam Matthews, Carolina
Pavese, Katharina Rietig, Philip Schleifer and Joana Setzer,
'The GLOBE Climate Legislation Study: A Review of Climate
Change Legislation in 66 Countries', London School of
Economics, Fourth Edition, Globe International, 2014.

p. 273   Begonia Filgueira 'And about time for rights to nature?', ukhu-
manrightsblog.com, 2 June 2011.

p. 274   'to think that only humans . . .' Pablo Solón, '"Green economy"
versus the rights of nature', climateandcapitalism.com, 7 June
2012.

p. 274   In the preliminary agreement . . . Kate Shuttleworth,
'Agreement entitles Whanganui River to legal identity', *The
New Zealand Herald*, 30 August 2012.

p. 275   Christopher Finlayson said that this was 'a major step . . .'
Christopher Finlayson, 'Whanganui River Deed of Settlement
Initialled', National Party website, 26 March 2014.

p. 275 recognise the river as 'Te Awa Tupua, an . . .' ibid.
p. 276 'embraces the spiritual aspects . . .' ibid.
p. 277 'If the sea had rights . . .' Begonia Filgueria and Ian Mason, 'Wild side of the law', *The Guardian*, 4 May 2009.

EPILOGUE

p. 287 or, as he put it, to advance . . . Stone, p. 23
p. 288 'Holding a title to property . . .' Dr Pita Sharples in Brendan Kennedy, 'I am the River and the River is Me: The implications of a river receiving personhood status', Cultural Survival Inc, December 2012.
p. 290 we need to give up 'some of our . . .' Stone, p. 28

BIBLIOGRAPHY

3Degrees Benefit Corporation 2013 Annual Report.

Adams, Carol, *Understanding Integrated Reporting: The concise guide to integrated thinking and the future of corporate reporting*, Dō Sustainability, Oxford, 2013.
—— 'Integrated reporting – what it is – and is not: an interview with Paul Druckman', drcaroladams.net,15 October 2013.
—— 'What is integrated reporting? And how do you do it?', drcaroladams.net, 3 March 2014.
—— 'The International Integrated Reporting Council: A call to action', drcaroladams.net, 17 July 2014.
Alembakis, Rachel, 'Q&A with James Gifford, executive director of UNPRI', *The Sustainability Report*, 16 March 2012.
Armstrong, Murray, 'Leaders challenge "business as usual"', *The Guardian*, 6 November 2006.
Associated Press in Quito, 'Yasuni: Ecuador abandons plan to stave off Amazon drilling', 16 August 2013.

B Corporation, 'If not now, when?: The Case for B Corp' 2011 Annual Report, 2011.
—— 'The B Corp Declaration: Declaration of Interdependence', bcorporation.net.
Balch, Oliver, 'CDP report reveals corporations starting to take water scarcity seriously', *The Guardian*, 31 October 2013.
Ban Ki-Moon, 'Remarks at the launch of the Principles for responsible investment', un.org, New York, 27 April 2006.
Barnes, Peter, *Capitalism 3.0: A Guide to Reclaiming the Commons*, Berrett-Koehler Publishers, Inc., San Francisco, 2006.
Bateman, Ian J., Amii R. Harwood, David J. Abson, Barnaby Andrews, Andrew Crowe, Steve Dugdale, Carlo Fezzi, Jo Foden, David Hadley, Roy Haines-Young, Mark Hulme, Andreas Kontoleon,

Paul Munday, Unai Pascual, James Paterson, Grischa Perino, Antara Sen, Gavin Siriwardena and Mette Termansen, 'Economic Analysis for the UK National Ecosystem Assessment: Synthesis and scenario valuation of changes in ecosystem services', Springer Science+Business Media Dordrecht, 1 April 2013.

Baue, Bill and Marcy Murninghan, 'Integrated reporting in a disintegrating world', *The Guardian*, 25 October 2011.

Blinch, Russ, 'Water as a commodity: can investors boost access to this critical resource?', *The Guardian*, 31 October 2013.

Bissio, Roberto, 'Financial and social sustainability are as vital as environmental sustainability', Social Watch, rio20.net, 13 July 2012.

Bollier, David, 'The Vermont Common Assets Trust', bollier.org, 3 October 2011.

Bondeson, Jan, *The Feejee Mermaid and Other Essays in Natural and Unnatural History*, Cornell University Press, Ithaca,1999.

Borrowmeo, Leah, 'How Adidas supported worker rights in China factory strike', *The Guardian*, 13 June 2014.

Branson, Richard, 'Profit is not all that matters', 8 August 2012.

Brooksbank, Daniel, 'European leaders reach agreement on corporate non-financial information disclosure', 27 February 2014.

Brunwasser, Joan, 'B Lab: Helping Companies Not only Be the Best in the World, But the Best FOR the World', OpEdNews.com, 10 October 2013.

Bureau of Meteorology, 'Joint perspectives in environmental accounting', Australian Government.

—— 'An Australian environmental accounting platform', Australian Government, December 2013.

Burgess, Stephen, 'Measuring financial sector output and its contribution to UK GDP', Bank of England, *Quarterly Bulletin*, Q3, 2011.

Butler, Sarah, 'Ethical shopping growing in popularity, survey suggests', *The Guardian*, 20 August 2013.

Carl, David M. and Hank Nguyen, 'California Benefit Corporations: Installing a Corporate Conscience', *Business Law Journal*, 23 March 2012.

Carrington, Damian, 'Carbon bubble will plunge the world into another financial crisis – report', *The Guardian*, 9 April 2013.

Chakrabortty, Aditya, 'The woman who nearly died making your iPad', *The Guardian*, 6 August 2013.

CityWire, 'Responsible ownership and engagement: interview with James Gifford', youtube, 16 March 2010.

Clark, William H. Jr. and Larry Vranka (Principal Authors), 'White Paper. The need and rationale for the Benefit Corporation: Why it is the legal form that best addresses the needs of social entrepreneurs, investors, and, ultimately, the public', 18 January 2013.

Climate Disclosure Standards Board, 'CDSB Framework, consultation draft: Promoting and advancing disclosure of environmental information', February 2014.

Coca-Cola Hellenic Bottling Company, 'Coca-Cola HBC publishes its first Integrated Report and tenth GRI report', 7 June 2013.

—— 'Building a Stronger Coca-Cola Hellenic',Coca-Cola HBC AB 2012 Integrated Report, 2012.

Confino, Jo, 'Unilever's Paul Polman: changing the corporate status quo', The Guardian, 24 April 2012.

—— 'Richard Branson and Jochen Zeitz launch the B Team challenge', The Guardian, 13 June 2013.

—— 'Changing mindsets is key to preventing social and environmental disaster', The Guardian, 29 October 2013.

—— 'World's stock exchanges fail to hold companies to account on sustainability', The Guardian, 30 October 2013.

—— 'Bill McKibben: Fossil fuel divestment campaign builds momentum', The Guardian, 31 October, 2013.

Cosier, Peter, Wentworth Group of Concerned Scientists, 'Accounting for the Condition of Environmental Assets', UN Committee of Experts on Environmental Accounting, 5-7 December 2011.

Costanza Robert, Ralph d'Arge, Rudolf de Groot, Stephen Farber, Monica Grasso, Bruce Hannon, Karin Limburg, Shahid Naeem, Robert V. O'Neill, Jose Paruelo, Robert G. Raskin, Paul Sutton and Marjan van den Belt, 'The Value of the World's Ecosystem Services and Natural Capital', Nature, 15 May 1987.

Costanza, Robert, Simone Quatrini and Siv Øystese, 'Response to George Monbiot: The valuation of nature and ecosystem services is not privatization', 15 August 2012.

Coyle, Diane, GDP: A brief but affectionate history, Princeton University Press, Princeton, 2014.

Council of Canadians, The, Fundacion Pachamama and Global Exchange, 'Does Nature Have Rights?', 22 April 2010.

Creasy, Stella, 'Who made your clothes? It's time we knew – and cared', The Guardian, 19 April 2014.

Deen, Thalif, 'Global Campaign to Bestow Legal Rights on Mother Earth', Inter Press Service, 24 May 2011.

de Koning, Marloes, 'Andreas Georgiou learns the unwritten rules of Greek statistics', Presseurop, 18 March 2013, accessed 24 March 2014.

DiPiazza Jr., Samuel A., and Robert G. Eccles, *Building Public Trust: The future of corporate reporting*, John Wiley & Sons Inc., New York, 2002.

Dodge v. Ford Motor Co., 170 N.W. 668 (Mich. 1919), law.illinoir.edu.

Druckman, Paul, 'Integrated reporting: reshaping corporate reporting for the 21st century', *The Guardian*, 5 June 2013.

—— 'Integrated Reporting Framework aims to promote lasting sustainable change', *The Guardian*, 9 December 2013.

Drummond, Shaun, 'Integrated reports will be ignored if only skin deep', *The Australian Financial Review*, 4 June 2013.

Duke, G., I. Dickie, T. Juniper, K. ten Kate, M. Pieterse, M. Rafiq, M.Rayment, S. Smith and N. Voulvoulis, 'Opportunities for UK Business that Value and/or Protect Nature's Services', London, Valuing Nature Network, 14 June 2012.

Dunn, Helen, 'Payments for Ecosystem Services', Defra Evidence and Analysis Series, Paper 4, London, October 2011.

Eaves, Elisabeth, 'Tree Rights', *Forbes*, 24 May 2007.

Eccles, Robert G., 'Integrated financial reporting in Brazil', *The Cornerstone Journal of Sustainable Finance and Banking*, December 2013.

—— 'The investor conundrum', *Accounting Futures*, ACCA, edition 8, January 2014.

Eccles, Robert G., Robert H. Herz, E. Mary Keegan and David M. H. Phillips, *The ValueReporting™ Revolution: Moving beyond the earnings game*, John Wiley & Sons Inc., New York, 2001.

Eccles, Robert G. and Michael P. Krzus, *One Report: Integrated reporting for a sustainable strategy*, John Wiley & Sons, Inc., Hoboken, 2010.

Eccles, Robert G., Michael P. Krzus and George Serafeim, 'Market interest in nonfinancial information', Working Paper 12-018, 22 September 2011.

Eccles, Robert G. and George Serafeim, 'Top 1,000 Companies Wield Power Reserved for Nations', Bloomberg, 11 September 2012.

—— 'A Tale of Two Stories: Sustainability and the Quarterly Earnings Call', *Journal of Applied Corporate Finance*, Volume 25, Number 3, Summer 2013.

—— 'Corporate and Integrated Reporting: A functional perspective', Harvard Business School, unpublished, January 2014.

Economist, The, 'Meet Sir William Petty, the man who invented economics', London, 2013.

Economist, The, 'The trillion-dollar gap', 22 March 2014.

ecosystemmarketplace.com

Edwards, Steven, 'UN document would give "Mother Earth" same rights as humans', canada.com, 13 April 2011.

El-Ansary, Yasser, 'Completing the picture', Institute of Chartered Accountants, Australia, 1 August 2013.

Elkington, John, 'Partnerships from *Cannibals with Forkes: The Triple Bottom Line of 21st Century Business*', Environmental Quality Management, Autumn 1998.

—— 'Get ready for the breakthrough decade', csrwire.com, 30 June 2014.

Elkington, John with Nelmara Arbex, Maggie Lee, Amy Birchall, Sam Lakha, Alejandro Litovsky and Charmian Love, 'The Transparent Economy: Six tigers stalk the global recovery – and how to tame them', globalreporting.org, 2010.

Elliott, Robert K., 'The Third Wave Breaks on the Shores of Accounting', *Accounting Horizons,* June 1992, 6, 2.

Encyclopedia of Earth, The, http://www.eoearth.org/view/article/154786/.

English, Denise M. nad Diane K Schooley, 'The evolution of sustainability reporting: Utilizing the GRI's latest guidelines and looking to integrated reporting', *The CPA Journal,* March 2014.

Environment Bank Ltd, The, 'Biodiversity Offsetting to compensate for nightingale habitat loss at Lodge Hill, Kent', November 2012.

Environmental Leader, 'Walmart to Save $150m Sustainability Initiatives in FY13', 12 October 2012.

—— 'Integrated Reporting Making Progress, Needs to Catch Up', 21 June 2013.

European Commission, 'Disclosure of non-financial and diversity information by large companies and groups – Frequently asked questions', Brussels, 15 April 2014.

Everard, Mark, 'Nature is worth a lot more than nothing!', Institute of Environmental Sciences, April 2014.

Exxaro Resources Integrated Report 2010.

Farley, Joshua, 'Natural capital', Berkshire Publishing Group, 2012.

Filgueira, Begonia, 'And about time for rights to nature?', UKhumanrightsblod.com, 2 June 2011.

Filgueria, Begonia and Ian Mason, 'Wild side of the law', *The Guardian*, 4 May 2009.

Finlayson, Christopher, 'Whanganui River Deed of Settlement Initialled', National Party website, 26 March 2014.

Freeland, Chrystia, 'Capitalism, but With a Little Heart', *New York Times*, 18 July 2013.

Friedman, Milton, 'The Social Responsibility of Business is to Increase its Profits', *The New York Times Magazine*, 13 September 1970.

Fries, Jessica, interview with Paul Druckman 'What problem is integrated reporting trying to fix?', PwC, 15 April 2013.

Fry, Elizabeth, 'The inconvenient truth of natural capital accounting', *In the Black*, 10 December 2013.

Furber, Malcolm, 'Integrated reporting requires a considerable shift in attitude', *Financial Management*, CIMA, 19 September 2013.

Gardiner, Stephen, 'The Ethical Dimension of Tackling Climate Change', *Yale Environment 360*, 20 June 2012.

Gibbons, Chris and Tanya Barman, 'Sustainability in emerging markets: Lessons from South Africa', Chartered Institute of Management Accountants, 2010.

Gibbons, Phil, 'The Case for biodiversity offsets', *Decision Point*, Issue 39, May 2010.

Gittens, Ross, 'Environmental accounting is closer to reality', Sydney Morning Herald, 23 June 2012.

Gleeson-White, Jane, *Double Entry: How the merchants of Venice shaped the modern world – and how their invention could make or break the planet*, Allen & Unwin, Sydney, 2011.

Global Exchange, 'Does Nature Have Rights?', globalexchange.org, 6 December 2010.

—— *Does Nature Have Rights?: Transforming Grassroots Organizing to Protect People and the Planet*, globalexchange.org.

Gordon, Kate, 'Risky Business: The economic risks of climate change in the United States, a climate risk assessment for the United States', Risky Business Project, June 2014.

Gosford, Bob, '"Your Honour, I appear for the Whanganui River": A river gets legal standing', Crikey, 13 September 2012.

Gray, Rob, Jan Bebbington and Sue Gray, *Social and Environmental Accounting*, Sage Publications Ltd, London, 2010.

Green Economy Portal, unep.org/greeneconomy.

Greene, Natalia, 'The first successful case of the Rights of Nature implementation in Ecuador', therightsofnature.org.

Greenpeace, 'Beyond Rio+20: A 2012 foreword to the "Beyond UNCED" report Greenpeace published at the Rio Earth Summit in 1992', June 2012.

Greystone's Benefit Corporation Report 2012.

Gunther, Marc, 'Will sustainability reporting standards change the way business does business?', *The Guardian*, 7 August 2013.

—— 'Natural capital: breakthrough or buzzword?', *The Guardian*, 7 March 2014.

Hartmann, Thom, *Unequal Protection: The rise of corporate dominance and the theft of human rights*, Mythical Research Inc., and Thom Hartmann, United States of America, 2002.

Havelock, Laurie, 'All together now', *IR Magazine*, March 2014.

Hawken, Paul, Amory Lovins and L. Hunter Lovins, *Natural Capitalism: Creating the next industrial revolution*, Little, Brown and Company, New York, 1999.

Herman, R. Paul, 'Let's value people as an asset and bring corporate reporting into the 21st century', *Huffington Post*, 28 October 2011.

Hill, David, '448 "Dead Friends of the Earth" in Brazil since 2002', 23 April 2014.

—— 'Leaked documents cast doubt on Ecuador's commitment to forest plan', *The Guardian*, 2 July 2014.

Holmes, Lawrie, 'Information Overdrive', *Financial Management*, 22 August 2013.

Hoskins, Tansy, 'Building trade unions in Bangladesh will help prevent another Rana Plaza, *The Guardian*, 7 May 2014.

Houses of Parliament, Parliamentary Office of Science & Technology, 'Ecosystem Service Valuation', *Postnote*, Number 378, London, May 2011.

Hurley, Ben, *Business Review Weekly*, 20 November 2013.

Impala Platinum Holdings Integrated Report 2013.

Institute of Chartered Accountants in England and Wales, 'Information for Better Markets: New reporting models for business', London, November 2003.

—— 'Information for Better Markets: 'Developments in New Reporting Models', December 2009.

—— 'Paul Druckman: a different story', *economia*, 2 December 2013.

Institute of Directors, Southern Africa, The King Code of Governance for South Africa 2009, c.ymcdn.com, 2009.

International Federation of Accountants, 'Governance is King!', http://www.ifac.org/sites/default/files/downloads/1.3-king-governance-is-king-final.pdf.
International Integrated Reporting Council, 'Capitals: Background paper for <IR>', theiirc.org, March 2013.
—— 'Business Model: Background paper for <IR>', theirrc.org, March 2013.
—— 'Consultation Draft of the International <IR> Framework', theirrc.org, 16 April 2013.
—— 'Submissions to the Consultation Draft of the International <IR> Framework', theirrc.org,16 April-15 July 2013.
—— 'Value Creation: Background paper for <IR>', theirrc.org, July 2013.
—— The International <IR> Framework, theiirc.org, December 2013.
International Society for Ecological Economics, The, isecoeco.org.

Jowit, Juliette, 'Can we really put a price tag on nature?', The Guardian, 22 May 2010.
Juniper, Tony, 'We must put a price on nature if we are going to save it', The Guardian, 10 August 2012.
—— What Has Nature Ever Done for Us? How money really does grow on trees, Profile Books, London, 2013.

Kaufman, Leslie, 'Emissions Disclosure as a Business Virtue', New York Times, 28 December 2009.
Kelly, Marjorie, 'Not Just for Profit: Emerging Alternatives to the Shareholder-Centric Model', 2009 Summit on the Future of the Corporation.
Kendall, Clare, 'A new law of nature', The Guardian, 24 September 2008.
Kennedy, Brendan, 'I am the River and the River is Me: The implications of a river receiving personhood status', Cultural Survival Inc, December 2012.
Kester, Corinna, 'From Brazil to Botswana, nations dig into ecosystem services', GreenBiz.com, 19 March 2014.
Kim, Jim Yong, 'World Bank Group President Jim Yong Kim Remarks at Davos Press Conference', worldbank.org, Davos, 23 January 2014.
King Committee on Corporate Governance, 'Executive Summary of the King Report 2002', Institute of Directors, South Africa, March 2002.

King, Ed, 'IMG chief Lagarde warns of "merciless" climate change', rtcc.org, 5 February 2014.

King, Mervyn, *The Corporate Citizen*, Penguin Book, Parktown North, 2006.

—— 'Speech for ICEAW', ion.icaew.com, 5 March 2014.

King, Mervyn and Leigh Roberts, *Integrate: Doing business in the 21st century*, Juta & Company Ltd, Cape Town, 2013.

King, Mervyn and Teodorina Lessidrenska, *Transient Caretakers*, Penguin, Parktown North, 2006.

Klare, Michael T., *The Race for What's Left: The global scramble for the world's last resources*, Picador, New York, 2012.

Klein, Naomi, *The Shock Doctrine*, Penguin Books, Camberwell, 2007.

—— 'Climate change is the fight of our lives – yet we can hardly bear to look at it', *The Guardian*, 23 April 2014.

Kyte, Rachel, 'An accounting system worthy of Earth Day: natural capital accounting', *Voices*, 22 April 2013.

Labrey, Jonathan, 'Steve Waygood, Aviva Investors, discusses Integrated Reporting', youtube, 7 May 2013.

Lee, Ada, 'A different kind of protest', *South Sydney Herald*, April 2014.

Leinaweaver, Jeff, 'Might new financial tools translate ESG data into real-world loss and profit?', *The Guardian*, 26 November 2013.

Loten, Angus, 'With New Law, Profits Take a Back Seat', *Down Jones & Company, Inc.*, 19 January 2012.

Lynch, Nicholas C., Michael F. Lynch and David B. Casten, 'The expanding use of sustainability reporting: Standards setting and assurance opportunities for CPAs', *The CPA Journal*, March 2014.

Mac Cormac, Susan H., with Jonathan Glass and Julie Cooke, 'The Emergence of New Corporate Forms', 2007 Summit on the Future of the Corporation, Paper No. 9, Boston, 13 November 2007.

Mahanta, Vinod and Priyanka Sangani, 'Resist the short term decisions that damage the long term: Paul Polman, CEO, Unilever', *The Economic Times*, 8 November 2013.

Makovsky, Ken, 'An opportunity to lead on intangibles', *Forbes*, 26 April 2012.

Marcuss, Rosemary D. and Richard E. Kane, 'US National Income and Product Statistics: Born of the Great Depression and World War II', *Survey of Current Business*, February 2007.

Mark, Jason, 'Natural Law', *Earth Island Journal*, Spring 2012.

Massie, Bob, 'History of the Global Reporting Initiative (GRI)', youtube, 12 March 2014.

McCullough, D.G., 'Deforestation for fashion: unsustainable fabrics come out of the closet', *The Guardian*, 25 April 2014.

McGinn, Jack, '"Green" bookkeeping shows hidden cost of business as usual', *Financial Times*, 23 June 2013.

McKibben, Bill, 'False Profits: Doing the maths on Australia's coal exports', *The Monthly*, June 2013.

Meadows, Donella, 'Leverage Points: Places to Intervene in a System', donellameadows.org, http://www.donellameadows.org/archives/leverage-points-places-to-intervene-in-a-system/.

Media Tenor, 'Corporate's DNA Report 2012: Annual reports, elite business media, and analyst sentiment', USA, 2012.

Medland, Dina, 'Lawyer draws up rules for global change', *Financial Times*, 7 November 2013.

Moher, Brian, 'Profile: Paul Druckman, ICAEW president', *Accountancy Age*, 12 August 2004.

Monbiot, George, 'This is bigger than climate change. It is a battle to redefine humanity', *The Guardian*, 14 December 2009.

—— 'We've been conned. The deal to save the natural world never happened', *The Guardian*, 1 November 2010.

—— 'Putting a price on the rivers and rain diminishes us all', *The Guardian*, 7 August 2012.

—— 'Biodiversity offsetting will unleash a new spirit of destruction in the land', *The Guardian*, 8 December 2012.

—— 'This faith in the markets is misplaced: only governments can save our living planet', *The Guardian*, 23 April 2013.

—— 'The Self-Hating State', The Permaculture Research Institute, permaculturenews.org, 24 April 2013.

—— 'The downside of valuing nature', *Corporate Knights*, 15 July 2013.

—— 'How have these corporations colonised our public life?', *The Guardian*, 8 April 2014.

—— 'Can you put a price on the beauty of the natural world?', *The Guardian*, 22 April 2014.

Montgomery, John, 'The Benefit Corporation: The unlikely hero of a sustainable economy?', *TheHumanist.com*, 22 April 2014.

Moulier Boutang, Yann, *Cognitive Capitalism*, translated by Ed Emery, Polity Press, Cambridge, 2011.

Mychalejko, Cyril, 'Ecuador's constitution gives rights to nature', upsidedownworld.org, 25 September 2008.

Nachmany, Michael, Sam Fankhauser, Terry Townshend, Murray
    Collins, Tucker Landesman, Adam Matthews, Carolina Pavese,
    Katharina Rietig, Philip Schleifer and Joana Setzer, 'The GLOBE
    Climate Legislation Study: A Review of Climate Change
    Legislation in 66 Countries', London School of Economics, Fourth
    Edition, Globe International, 2014.
Nallu, Preethi, 'Alternative voices from Rio+20', Aljazeera, 23 June
    2012.
'Natural Capital Declaration', naturalcapitaldeclaration.org
Norris, Ken (Chair), 'Where next for the UK National Ecosystem
    Assessment and IPBES?', Report of a joint session between the
    British Ecological Society (BES) and the UK Biodiversity Research
    Advisory Group (UK BRAG), Sheffield, 13 September 2011.
Novo Nordisk Annual Report 2011
Novo Nordisk Annual Report 2013

Ocean Tomo, June 2010, Report on intangible value.
Office for National Statistics, 'The History of National Accounting and
    its economic relevance', website.
O'Gorman, S. and Bann, C. 'A Valuation of England's Terrestrial
    Ecosystem Services, a report to Defra', Jacobs, 2008.
Olin, Dirk, 'King of Transparency', Corporate Responsibility Magazine.
Osborn, Jeremy, 'It's time to start taking natural capital into account',
    The Guardian, 25 June 2014.

Park, Andrew and Curtis Ravenel, 'Integrating Sustainability
    into Capital Markets: Bloomberg LP and ESG's Quantitative
    Legitimacy', Journal of Applied Corporate Finance, Volume 25
    Number 3, Summer 2013.
Parkinson, Giles, 'Could bankers save the Great Barrier Reef?' The
    Guardian, 3 February 2014.
Patel, Raj, The Value of Nothing: How to reshape market society and
    redefine democracy, Black Inc., Melbourne, 2009.
People's Summit, 'Final Declaration: People's Summit "at Rio+20" for
    Social and Environmental Justice in defence of the commons,
    against the commodification of life', 15-22 June 2012.
Porritt, Jonathan, Capitalism as if the World Matters, Earthscan,
    London, 2007.
Potter, Brad, 'Integrated reporting and social investment: current
    developments, challenges and opportunities', University of
    Melbourne, unpublished, 2011.

Prince's Accounting for Sustainability Project, The and the Global Reporting Initiative, 'Press Release: Formation of the International Integrated Reporting Initiative (IIRC)', 2 August 2010.

Project Delphi, 'ESG "Superfactors", Metrics, KPIs and Validation with Investors', 13 January 2014, http://www.slideshare.net/DVFA/project-delphi-esg-super-factors-metrics-kpis-and-validation-with-investors.

Puma.com

Quick, Chris, 'Accounting for Sustainability – Green: by royal assent', *Accountancy Live*,1 January 2008.

Ranganathan, Janet, 'New integrated reporting framework aims to tackle profit and planet', *The Guardian*, 16 April 2013.

Rapacioli, Sandra, Steve Lang, Jeremy Osborn and Stathis Gould, 'Accounting for natural capitals: the elephant in the boardroom', CIMA, May 2014.

Revkin, Andrew C. 'Ecuador Constitution Grants Rights to Nature', *New York Times*, 29 September 2008.

Rodolico, Jack, 'Benefit corporations look beyond the profit motive', NPR, 18 June 2014.

Rysavy, Tracy Fernandez, 'Can the Miracle Work Again? Climate divestment interview with Bob Massie', *Green American*, January/February 2013.

Sadler, Philip, 'Tomorrow's Company: Systems thinking and the triple context', tomorrowscompany.com, http://tomorrowscompany.com/systems-thinking-and-the-triple-context-by-philip-sadler.

Samkin, Grant and Stewart Lawrence, 'Limits to Corporate Social Responsibility: The Challenge of HIV/Aids to Sustainable Business in South Africa', The University of Waikato Department of Accounting, Working Paper Series, Number 83, Hamilton, November 2005.

Sandel, Michael J., *What Money Can't Buy: The moral limits of markets*, Penguin Books, London, 2012.

Saunders, Andrew, 'The MT Interview: Paul Polman', *Management Today*, 1 March 2011.

Sauven, John, 'Arctic oil: it is madness to celebrate a new source of fossil fuels', *The Guardian*, 19 April 2014.

Schulschenk, Jess, 'Richard Wilkinson', EY.com, 23 March 2012.

Securities and Exchange Commission, 'Commission Guidance Regarding Disclosure Related to Climate Change', Washington, 8 February 2010.

Sharp, Kathleen, 'Millennials' bold new business plan: Corporations with a conscience', *Salon*, 10 February 2014.

Shuttleworth, Kate, 'Agreement entitles Whanganui River to legal identity', *The New Zealand Herald*, 30 August 2012.

Singer, Thomas, 'Sustainability Matters 2013: How companies communicate and engage on sustainability', The Conference Board, USA, 2013.

Skidelsky, Robert, *John Maynard Keynes, 1883-1946: Economist, philosopher, statesman*, Pan Books, London, 2003.

Solnit, Rebecca, 'Jurassic Ballot: When corporations Ruled the Earth', CommonDreams.org, 25 October 2010.

Solomon, Jill and Warren Maroun, 'Integrated reporting: the new face of social, ethical and environmental reporting in South Africa?', The Association of Chartered Certified Accountants, London, 2012.

Solón, Pablo, 'It's the time of the Rights of Mother Earth', pablosolon. wordpress.com, 4 April 2012.

—— '"Green economy" versus the rights of nature', climateandcapitalism.com, 7 June 2012.

Stewart, Neil, 'An audience with the GRI's Mervyn King', *IR Magazine*, 9 September 2010.

Stiglitz, Joseph, Amartya Sen and Jean-Paul Fitoussi, Report of the Commission on the Measurement of Economic Performance and Social Process, Stiglitz-Sen-Fitoussi Commission, stiglitz-sen-fitoussi.fr/documents/rapport_anglais, 2009.

Stone, Christopher, *Should Trees Have Standing? Law, morality and the environment*, Oxford University Press, Oxford, 2010.

Sukhdev, Pavan, *Corporation 2020: Transforming Business for Tomorrow's World*, Island Press, Washington, 2012.

—— 'Put a value on nature!', TED, 16 March 2012.

—— 'What's the world worth?': Putting nature on the balance sheet', Centre for Policy, 16 March 2012.

'Summary Notes from the Beyond GDP conference', November 2007.

Tamaqua Borough Sewage Sludge Ordinance, http://www.celdf.org/ article.php?id=440.

'The Universal Declaration of Rights of Mother Nature', therightsofnature.org, 22 April 2010.

Time, 'The Law: The court's uncompromising libertarian', 24
    November 1975.
Toffler, Alvin, *The Third Wave*, Bantam Books, New York, 1980.
Topping, Nigel, 'Don't Blame the Hammer!', Schumacher College,
    https://www.youtube.com/watch?v=RR-0AQR9yMA,
    2 February 2012.
Tullis, Paul, 'Bloomberg's push for corporate sustainability: Why
    Bloomberg broke into the business of measuring other companies'
    good deeds', Paul Tullis, *Fast Company*, April 2011.

UK Ecosystems Markets Task Force, gov.uk.
UK National Ecosystem Assessment, uknea.unep_wcmc.org.
United Nations, 'Report of the World Commission on Environment and
    Development: Our Common Future', un_documents.net, 1987.
—— 'United Nations Secretary-General launches "Principles for
    Responsible Investment" Backed by World's Largest Investors',
    http://www.unpri.org/press/united-nations-secretary-general-
    launches-principles-for-responsible-investment-backed-by-
    worlds-largest-investors-2/, 27 April 2006.
—— 'The System of Environmental-Economic Accounts' (SEEA):
    Measurement Framework in Support of Sustainable Development
    and Green Economy Policy', seea@un.org.
—— 'The Future We Want', 10 January 2012.
—— 'Report of the United Nations Conference on Sustainable
    Development, Rio de Janeiro, Brazil, 20-22 June 2012', New York,
    2012.
—— 'UN Climate Chief: IPCC science underlines urgency to act
    towards a carbon neutral world', Press Release, Bonn, 13 April
    2014.
—— 'UN Coalition of Leading Investors Outlines a New Corporate
    Governance Paradigm for Sustainability', 16 June 2014.
'Universal Declaration of the Rights of Mother Earth', World People's
    Conference on Climate Change and the Rights of Mother Earth',
    Cochabamba, Bolivia, 22 April 2010.
Upbin, Bruce, 'Davos Dispatch: Richard Branson and The B Team
    Make Business Case for Human Rights', *Forbes*, 22 January 2014.

Vidal, John, 'Bolivia enshrines natural world's rights with equal status
    for Mother Earth', *The Guardian*, 11 April 2011.
—— 'UK mulls biodiversity offsetting despite practice "disappointing"
    in Australia', *The Guardian*, 11 March 2014.

—— 'Conservationists split over "biodiversity offsetting" plans', *The Guardian*, 4 June 2014.

Visser, Wayne, Dirk Matten, Manfred Pohl and Nick Tolhurst, *The A-Z of Corporate Social Responsibility*, John Wiley & Sons Ltd, Chichester, 2010.

Volans Ventures Ltd, 'Breakthrough: Business Leaders, Market Revolutions', Volans Ventures Ltd, London, 2013.

Waage, Sissel, 'Natural capital helps businesses put environmental metrics into context', *The Guardian*, 8 July 2014.

Watts, Jonathan, 'Are accountants the last hope for the world's ecosystems?', *The Guardian*, 28 October 2010.

—— 'Rio+20 People's summit gathers pace', *The Guardian*, 19 June 2012.

WAVES, 'Costa Rica introduces law to mandate valuation of natural capital'.

Waygood, Steve, 'UN must pick up the pace on sustainable finance', *The Guardian*, 5 July 2014.

White, Allen L., 'New Wine, New Bottles: The rise of non-financial reporting', *Business for Social Responsibility*, 20 June 2005.

—— 'Beyond corporate reporting: are integrated ratings next?', *The Guardian*, 5 November 2013.

White, Louis, 'Beyond the bottom line', *Charter*, July 2012.

Williams, Zoe, 'George Lakoff: "Conservatives don't follow the polls, they want to change them . . . Liberals do everything wrong', *The Guardian*, 1 February 2014.

Winninghoff, Ellie, 'Accounting for Sustainability', *Financial Advisor*, 3 August 2011.

—— 'Seeking Assurance', *Financial Advisor*, 2 September 2011.

—— 'Connecting the dots', *Financial Advisor*, 5 October 2011.

Zeitz, Jochen and John Elkington, 'Earth Day 2015 Should Focus on Tomorrow's Bottom Line', *huffingtonpost.com*, 22 April 2014.

Zaremba, Wiktor, Alicia Jimenez, Marina Bakhnova and Mirian Vilela, 'The Earth Charter and the Green Economy', Earth Charter International, March 2011.

INDEX

ACKNOWLEDGEMENTS

MY ENORMOUS THANKS GO TO THE FOLLOWING people:

Jane Palfreyman, as ever, for all her continuing enthusiasm and support for my ideas. She is the best publisher and friend a writer could hope for.

Clara Finlay, whose probing, painstaking, patient, generous editing reminds me that writing is always a collaboration. She is the best editor a writer could hope for.

Michael Hill, as ever, who let me write this book and was there every step of the way.

Jackson and Scarlet Hill, who entertain and challenge me and warm my heart every day.

Laura Mitchell, my generous and attentive in-house editor, and Sarah Baker who stepped in when Laura was away. And Julia Cain for her proofreading and all at Allen & Unwin.

Mark Thacker, for his beautiful cover design.

All those who spared their extremely busy time to talk to me about the new accounting paradigm, especially Michael Bray, Stanley Goldstein, Nick Ridehalgh, Mervyn King, Robert J. Eccles, Andrew Park, Sarah Bostwick,

Daniele Chesebrough, Jeremy Osborn, Paul Druckman, James Gifford, Tony Juniper, Brad Potter.

The wonderful Rachel Skinner and Anna Funder, who listened to my talk about accounting over a long lunch in Brooklyn and said it sounded like a book.

The friends whose conversations stimulated me while I worked, especially Paul Dawson, Jaimee Edwards, Joe Cummins and Adrian Franklin.

My parents and sisters, especially for putting up with my long absences over this difficult past year.

And my special thanks to two libraries, without which I could not have written this book: Fisher Library at the University of Sydney where I wrote most of it and the Waverley Library whose Nib Award for excellence in literary research helped to fund it. I especially note them because in this information age real-space libraries filled with analogue books are an endangered species and like many libraries today the libraries of the University of Sydney are currently under threat of decimation by financial capital.